An Introduction to Geoffrey Chaucer

New Perspectives on Medieval Literature: Authors and Traditions

UNIVERSITY PRESS OF FLORIDA

Florida A&M University, Tallahassee
Florida Atlantic University, Boca Raton
Florida Gulf Coast University, Ft. Myers
Florida International University, Miami
Florida State University, Tallahassee
New College of Florida, Sarasota
University of Central Florida, Orlando
University of Florida, Gainesville
University of North Florida, Jacksonville
University of South Florida, Tampa
University of West Florida, Pensacola

AN INTRODUCTION TO

Geoffrey Chaucer

Tison Pugh

University Press of Florida

Gainesville/Tallahassee/Tampa/Boca Raton
Pensacola/Orlando/Miami/Jacksonville/Ft. Myers/Sarasota

The publication of this book is made possible in part by a grant from
the College of Arts and Humanities, University of Central Florida.

This book may be available in an electronic edition.

18 17 16 15 14 13   6 5 4 3 2 1

Library of Congress Cataloging-in-Publication Data
Pugh, Tison.
An introduction to Geoffrey Chaucer / Tison Pugh.
p. cm.
Includes bibliographical references and index.
ISBN 978-0-8130-4424-8 (alk. paper)
1. Chaucer, Geoffrey, d. 1400—Criticism and interpretation. I. Title.
PR1924.P84 2013
821.1—dc23   2012046695

The University Press of Florida is the scholarly publishing agency for the State
University System of Florida, comprising Florida A&M University, Florida Atlantic
University, Florida Gulf Coast University, Florida International University, Florida State
University, New College of Florida, University of Central Florida, University
of Florida, University of North Florida, University of South Florida,
and University of West Florida.

University Press of Florida
15 Northwest 15th Street
Gainesville, FL 32611-2079
http://www.upf.com

To Augustus McCurdy Pugh, Satcher Sprague Pugh,
Francis Sprague Pugh III, Mary Frances Pugh,
and Francis Sprague Pugh II

Contents

List of Abbreviations viii

Preface: Chaucer and Genre Theory ix

Chronology of Chaucer's Life and Literary Connections xv

1. CHAUCER'S LIFE AND TIMES 1

2. CHAUCER'S LITERATURE 9

Dream Visions: *Book of the Duchess, House of Fame,
Parliament of Fowls,* and *Legend of Good Women* 9

Troilus and Criseyde 34

Canterbury Tales 51

Miscellaneous Verse and a Treatise 125

3. CHAUCER'S SOURCES AND INFLUENCES 141

Glossary of Literary Terms and Chaucerian Themes 191

Pronouncing Chaucer's Middle English 199

Word List of Chaucer's Middle English 203

Plot Outlines of *Troilus and Criseyde* and the *Canterbury Tales*
by Line Number 209

Notes 233

Selected Readings 239

Index 247

Abbreviations

All citations of Chaucer's works refer to *The Riverside Chaucer*, ed. Larry D. Benson, 3rd ed. (Boston: Houghton Mifflin, 1987). Abbreviations for Chaucer's titles are

BD	*Book of the Duchess*
CT	*Canterbury Tales*
HF	*House of Fame*
LGW	*Legend of Good Women*
PF	*Parliament of Fowls*
RR	*Romaunt of the Rose*
T&C	*Troilus and Criseyde*

Also abbreviated is the source for biographical information

CLR   *Chaucer Life-Records*
compiled by Martin M. Crow and Clair C. Olson
(Austin: University of Texas Press, 1966).

Other abbreviations used are

BCE	Before the Common/Christian Era
c.	century
ca.	*circa*, about, approximately
CE	Common/Christian Era (assumed unless BCE is specified)
cf.	*confer*, compare, see by way of comparison
fl.	*floruit*, flourished
passim	here and there, in various places throughout

Preface

Chaucer and Genre Theory

The Father of English Literature: Geoffrey Chaucer holds this title with universal accord. Proving English literature as rich, sophisticated, and entertaining as the French and Italian masterpieces of the Middle Ages, Chaucer availed himself of the English language's inherent poetry at a time when it was derided as an inelegant vernacular. This book introduces readers to Chaucer and his writings to spark an appreciation of the literary accomplishments that make him such an inspiring, provocative, and alluring figure in Western culture, with the explicit purpose of helping novice readers to navigate Chaucer's work in its original Middle English.

Following the structure of the New Perspectives in Medieval Literature series, the first chapter of *An Introduction to Geoffrey Chaucer* provides an overview of Chaucer's life in fourteenth-century England, a time marked by great dangers (including the Black Death), social unrest (including the Peasants' Revolt of 1381), and complex court maneuverings (including the overthrow of King Richard II). The second chapter, which constitutes the bulk of the book, introduces Chaucer's works, including his surreal dream visions *Book of the Duchess*, *House of Fame*, *Parliament of Fowls*, and *Legend of Good Women*; his masterpiece of love won and love lost during the Trojan War, *Troilus and Criseyde*; his incomplete masterpiece of sacred and profane voices clashing boisterously on a holy pilgrimage, the *Canterbury Tales*; and his miscellaneous verse addressing a variety of courtly, religious, and classical themes. Chaucer's role in literary history provides the focus of the third chapter: previous writers and texts—including Greek and Roman authors of the classical past, the Hebrew and Christian Bibles, and the literatures of France and Italy—influenced him, and he likewise influenced many writers who followed. This volume also offers reference materials including a chronology of important dates in Chaucer's literary history, a bibliography for further research, a glossary of literary terms, and three sections designed to assist novice readers and speakers of Chaucer's writing: a guideline for pronouncing Middle English; a list of high-frequency words in Chaucer's literature to expand readers' Middle English vocabulary; and outlines of the *Canterbury Tales* and *Troilus and Criseyde* by line number to help readers negotiate these complex and rich works. Using the three aids in tandem, novice readers of Middle English will be better able to appreciate Chaucer's distinctive voice without relying on arid and simplistic summaries. To read a plot summary of a Chaucerian text is like eating a hearty stew that has been strained down to its broth: much of the good stuff is irrevocably lost. Immersing oneself in the supplementary sections will provide a strong foundation for the pleasures of reading Chaucer's literature without the assistance of an interpreter.

This book is intended for readers new to Chaucer, those who will benefit from broad discussions of Chaucer's themes and the contexts of his literature, and my goal throughout is to demonstrate the allure and intellectual depth of his world. As a tool for this task, I rely on genre theory to structure the introductions to Chaucer's diverse writings. In a sense, genres establish the rules of any given body of literature, and if readers understand the expected parameters of that body, they will also be able to discern when authors reinforce, play with, or subvert these structures to create their unique fictions. Genre gives readers a tool both for understanding Chaucer as an author who represents a specific cultural moment and for deciphering texts foreign to their experience; by learning to recognize the conventions and codes of a certain genre, readers are better able to recognize the parameters and expectations of a specific piece of literature, and thus to understand its place in the literary tradition. As Alistair Fowler suggests, genre provides a necessary point of departure for both writers and readers: writers need to know "which rules are worth breaking," as readers need to know what rules are in effect in a given literary game.[1]

Chaucer uses genres common to the Middle Ages, such as romance, fabliau, epic, dream vision, exemplum, tragedy, ballade, lyric, allegory, and saint's life, but never in a slavish fashion. When readers perceive how Chaucer reimagines genres to his own purpose, they will also be able to generate their own interpretations of his texts by hypothesizing for what purpose Chaucer plays with literary form. (To this end, it may be advisable for some readers to begin this book with the Glossary of Literary Terms and Chaucerian Themes, to become better acquainted with Chaucer's genres.) A brief example of Chaucer's play with genre from the *Canterbury Tales* illustrates his daring use of literary form to engage his readers in unexpected ways. When the Miller announces in his Prologue, "For I wol telle a legende and a lyf / Bothe of a carpenter and of his wyf" (1.3141–42), he hints that he will tell a saint's life ("legende") concerning Jesus's parents Joseph ("a carpenter") and Mary ("his wyf"), not a fabliau, an obscene comic tale of unrestrained sexual desire. The Miller's purposes could not be further divorced from piety, but the ways in which holy language is subverted through profane antics greatly builds the tale's riotous humor. In a similar manner throughout his *Canterbury Tales* and other works, Chaucer and his characters frequently establish expectations for their narratives through claims of genre and then upend them with the infusion of unexpected themes.

Studying Chaucer through his genres also introduces new readers of medieval literature to genres that have largely fallen out of favor with modern writers, or that have metamorphosed greatly from their medieval incarnations. Today's romances, for example, need no longer feature knights and their ladies in a courtly milieu, nor monsters slain during quests; likewise, many modern epics bear little resemblance to their literary forebears, and the term in popular parlance refers mainly to long movies with large casts. Saints' lives, exempla, and other medieval genres have virtually vanished as literary forms. Thus an introduction to Chaucer that simultaneously pays attention to his genres affords readers new to the Middle Ages a better understanding both of Chaucer's literary milieu and of his innovative play with longstanding traditions. As numerous scholars have discussed (including Susan Crane in *Gender and Romance in Chaucer's "Canterbury Tales,"* Angela Jane Weisl in *Conquering the Reign of Femeny: Gender and Genre in Chaucer's Romance,* and Holly Crocker in *Chaucer's Visions of Manhood*), Chaucer's treatment of genre is intimately connected with his treatment of gender, and I also explore throughout this book the ways in which Chaucer deploys genre to tackle questions related to medieval gender roles.

Unlike many other introductions to Chaucer's literature, which typically address a subset of his canon such as the *Canterbury Tales* or his dream visions, *An Introduction to Geoffrey Chaucer* covers his complete literary corpus. It is beyond the scope of most courses on Chaucer, whether undergraduate or graduate-level, to address all of his works, and so this text is designed to facilitate readers' individual explorations of texts that may not be covered in syllabi. Also, instructors may assign students in-class presentations on Chaucer's writings not read by the class as a whole, and here this book should prove helpful in orienting a diverse group of readers to Chaucer's varied corpus. The survey of Chaucer's sources and of his influence on subsequent writers likewise provides a brief look at materials of vast complexity, particularly in regard to Chaucer's translations of Boethius's *Consolation of Philosophy* and the medieval French masterpiece *Roman de la Rose*. Whether read alone or within classrooms or reading groups, this material should ground the reader in the knowledge necessary to pursue further research.

But to appreciate the meaning of Chaucer's literature, one must first be able to read it, and the primary goal of this text is to help readers become familiar with Chaucer's Middle English. Learning to read Chaucer's English is challenging but manageable, and readers find their efforts well rewarded when enjoying his literature without assistance. Students at times find themselves frustrated with Middle English, as I did when I first encountered Chaucer in high school and then again in college. Often my students confess that they missed pivotal plot points, or that they read a passage correctly but assumed they must be mistaken because the sense seemed so senseless. To assist with this problem, the following chapters quote extensively from Chaucer's poetry, and these quotations are augmented with translations of difficult words and phrases so that readers new to Middle English will become adept in this archaic and yet enchanting language. Mastering the words in the glossary will pay ample dividends in reading fluency, and hence in reading pleasure; likewise, learning to pronounce Middle English will amply recompense readers' efforts, for then they can hear Chaucer's artistry come alive, as they can also "hear" modern English words emerging from their Middle English ancestors.

Reading Chaucer's Middle English and comprehending his tales is not simple, but it brings enduring aesthetic and intellectual satisfaction. I invite readers to approach Chaucer's literature in a spirit cognizant of its challenges but anticipatory of its sheer joy. An old adage of poetic pleasure states simply that no one can read a poem for you, and the goal of this book is to help readers experience Chaucer firsthand, either alone or with friends. The rewards of reading Chaucer's poetry in—rather than in spite of—his Middle English are immense, as it is impossible to forget many of the finest moments of his literature. Indeed, some of his most famous images—such as a swarm of friars flying out of Satan's anus in the Summoner's Prologue, or Troilus laughing at his own funeral at the close of *Troilus and Criseyde*—virtually etch themselves in readers' minds. Chaucer's many devoted fans delight in spending time with this man who has been dead for more than six hundred years but whose literature continues to exhilarate readers with its daring mixture of matters sacred and profane, spiritual and earthly, heartbreaking and hilarious.

Chronology of Chaucer's Life
and Literary Connections

ca. 1000–800 BCE: Book of Job is written

9th c. BCE: Homer writes the *Iliad* and the *Odyssey*

ca. 29–19 BCE: Virgil (70–19 BCE) writes the *Aeneid*

2 CE: Ovid (43 BCE–17 CE) writes *Ars Amatoria*

8 CE: Ovid completes *Metamorphoses*

ca. 50–ca. 60 CE: Apostle Paul (ca. 10–67 CE) writes many New Testament epistles

61–65 CE: Lucan (39–65 CE) writes the *Pharsalia*

ca. 65–95 CE: Gospels of Matthew, Mark, Luke, and John are written

ca. 80–92 CE: Statius (45–96 CE) writes the *Thebaid*

524 CE: Boethius (ca. 480–524) writes the *Consolation of Philosophy*

1066: William the Conqueror invades England and establishes Norman rule

1170: Assassination of St. Thomas à Becket

ca. 1230: Guillaume de Lorris begins the *Roman de la Rose*

ca. 1280: Jean de Meun finishes Guillaume de Lorris's *Roman de la Rose*

ca. 1310–21: Dante (1265–1321) writes the *Divine Comedy*

ca. 1327–1368: Petrarch (1304–1374) writes vernacular Italian sonnets in *Rime sparse*

1 February 1327: Coronation of fourteen-year-old Edward of Windsor as Edward III of England

29 May 1328: Coronation of Philip of Valois (1293–1350) as Philip VI of France

1337: Edward III claims French crown; Hundred Years War begins

ca. 1338: Giovanni Boccaccio (1313–1375) writes *Il Filostrato*, basis of Chaucer's *Troilus and Criseyde*

1339–41: Boccaccio writes *Teseida*, basis of Chaucer's Knight's Tale

early 1340s: Birth of Geoffrey Chaucer

1348–49: Outbreak of plague (Black Death) in England

ca. 1349–53: Boccaccio writes the *Decameron*

1357: Chaucer serves as page to Elizabeth, Countess of Ulster and wife of Edward III's son Lionel

1359: Chaucer, armed as a squire, campaigns in France, is captured and held to ransom

ca. 1360–80: William Langland writes *Piers Plowman*

1361: Guillaume de Machaut (ca. 1300–1377) writes *Dit de la fontaine amoureuse*, of particular influence on Chaucer

1361–69: Poet and chronicler Jean Froissart (ca. 1337–ca. 1404) is at English court

ca. 1366: Chaucer marries Philippa de Roet

1367: Chaucer reenters royal service

1367: Birth of Chaucer's first son, Thomas

1368: Death of Blanche, Duchess of Lancaster, first wife of John of Gaunt and presumptive inspiration of Chaucer's *Book of the Duchess*

ca. 1370: Chaucer translates *Roman de la Rose*, writes *Book of the Duchess*

1372–73: Chaucer's diplomatic mission to Genoa and Florence

1374: Chaucer becomes controller of customs in Port of London

21 June 1377: Death of Edward III

16 July 1377: Coronation of Edward's ten-year-old grandson as Richard II

1378: Chaucer's diplomatic mission to Lombardy

early 1380s: Chaucer translates Boethius's *Consolation of Philosophy*, writes dream visions *House of Fame, Parliament of Fowls*

May 1380: Cecily Chaumpaigne releases Chaucer from legal repercussions for her "raptus"

June 1381: Peasants' Revolt

ca. 1382–85: Chaucer writes *Troilus and Criseyde*

ca. 1385: Eustache Deschamps (ca. 1346–ca. 1406) praises Chaucer as "Grant translateur, noble Geffroy Chaucier"

1385–86: Chaucer establishes residence in Kent, becomes justice of the peace, member of next parliament

ca. 1386: Chaucer begins *Legend of Good Women*

ca. 1387: Thomas Usk (d. 1388) praises Chaucer in his *Testament of Love*

ca. 1387: Chaucer writes General Prologue to *Canterbury Tales*, already in progress

ca. 1387: Death of Philippa Chaucer

1389–91: Chaucer serves as Clerk of the King's Works

ca. 1390: John Gower (1330–1408) praises Chaucer in his *Confessio amantis*

1391: Chaucer is named deputy forester at Petherton, Somerset, but maintains residence in Kent

1391–92: Chaucer writes *A Treatise on the Astrolabe*

1393: Oton de Graunson (ca. 1340–1397), whose poetry inspires Chaucer's "Complaint of Venus," receives a grant from Richard II

September 1399: Richard II is deposed; John of Gaunt's son Henry Bolingbroke takes throne as Henry IV

14 February 1400: Richard II dies in detention

25 October 1400: Death of Chaucer; burial in Westminster Abbey

1412: Thomas Hoccleve (ca. 1369–1426) praises Chaucer in his *Regiment of Princes*

ca. 1421: John Lydgate (ca. 1369–ca. 1451) praises Chaucer in his *Siege of Thebes*

1429: Joan of Arc (b. ca. 1412) leads Dauphin's forces to victory over English at Orléans

30 May 1431: Joan of Arc executed in Rouen

1453: End of Hundred Years War

1476: William Caxton's first edition of Chaucer's *Canterbury Tales*

late 1400s: Robert Henryson (ca. 1440–ca. 1505) writes *Testament of Cresseid*

1498: Wynkyn de Worde's edition of Chaucer's *Canterbury Tales*

1532: William Thynne's edition of Chaucer's works

1542: Henry Howard, Earl of Surrey (1517–1547), extols Sir Thomas Wyatt (1503–1542), innovator of sonnet tradition in England, by comparing him to Chaucer in "Wyatt resteth here, that quick could never rest"

1562: John Stow's edition, *The Workes of Geffrey Chaucer, newlie printed with diuers addicions, whiche were neuer in print before*

1579: Edmund Spenser (1552–1599) praises Chaucer in his *Shepheardes Calendar*

ca. 1582: Sir Philip Sidney (1554–1586) praises Chaucer in his *Defense of Poesie*

1598: Thomas Speght's edition, *The Workes of our Antient and Learned English Poet, Geffrey Chaucer*

early 1600s: William Shakespeare and John Fletcher write *The Two Noble Kinsmen*, a dramatization of Chaucer's Knight's Tale

1700: John Dryden (1631–1700) publishes translations of Chaucer in his *Fables, Ancient and Modern*

ca. 1705: Alexander Pope (1688–1744) emulates Chaucer and translates Chaucerian texts

1721: John Urry's edition of Chaucer's works

1775–78: Thomas Tyrwhitt's five-volume edition of the *Canterbury Tales*

1801–2: William Wordsworth (1770–1850) translates several *Canterbury Tales*, having praised Chaucer as one of four great English writers (with Spenser, Shakespeare, and Milton)

1809: William Blake (1757–1827) in *A Descriptive Catalog of Pictures* discusses the Canterbury pilgrims he illustrates

ca. 1850: American philosophers Henry David Thoreau (1817–1862) and Ralph Waldo Emerson (1803–1882) applaud Chaucer for his role in literary history

1894–97: W. W. Skeat's edition of *The Complete Works of Geoffrey Chaucer*

1896: William Morris publishes his *Kelmscott Chaucer*

1925: Virginia Woolf publishes her *Common Reader*, in which she praises Chaucer's narratology

1933: F. N. Robinson's edition of *The Works of Geoffrey Chaucer*

1944: Michael Powell and Emeric Pressburger's film *A Canterbury Tale*

1957: F. N. Robinson's second edition of *The Works of Geoffrey Chaucer*

1972: Pier Paolo Pasolini's film *I racconti di Canterbury*

1987: Larry Benson's edition of *The Riverside Chaucer*

2001: Brian Helgeland's film *A Knight's Tale* depicts a naked Chaucer

1

Chaucer's Life and Times

Had his surname been translated, the Father of English Literature would be known as Geoffrey Shoemaker. The more elegant surname Chaucer, from the Old French *chaucier*, to shoe, derived from the Latin *calceus*, shoe, suggests that Geoffrey Chaucer's forebears labored in the shoe and leather trade.[1] The extant records of Chaucer's life primarily address his administrative duties in royal households and public offices, and so it is difficult to discern a clear picture of his personal life beyond a fairly skeletal outline; nonetheless, it is clear that at some point the family switched their vocational interests from shoes to wine, for Chaucer's father John was a successful wine merchant in London. In a document dated June 19, 1381, Chaucer refers to himself as "son of John Chaucer, Vintner of London," and other such records illuminate the business interests and inheritances of his parents and grandparents.[2] In an incident proving that medieval lives could be as melodramatic as modern soap operas, one of John Chaucer's aunts kidnapped him at the tender age of twelve to marry him to her daughter, with the purpose of retaining assets within the family. It is fortunate for the history of English literature that John Chaucer did not marry this cousin but rather Agnes Copton, and their child Geoffrey was born in the early 1340s.

Chaucer's birth year has not been definitively ascertained, but in the Scrope-Grosvenor trial of 1386, in which two families contested ownership of a coat of arms, Chaucer testified that he was more than forty years old: "Geffray Chaucere esquier del age de xl ans et plus armeez par xxvii ans" [Geoffrey Chaucer, esquire, of the age of forty years and more, armed for twenty-seven years] (*CLR* 370). If Chaucer was older than forty in 1386, his birth year could be as late as 1345; most scholars agree on an earlier date of sometime between 1340 and 1342. No surviving records detail Chaucer's early childhood and education, but it is apparent from his court positions and literary endeavors that he was well educated. Learning in the Middle Ages focused on the Seven Liberal Arts, composed of the trivium (grammar, rhetoric, and logic) and the quadrivium (astronomy, geometry, music, and arithmetic), and Chaucer's literature reveals his extensive knowledge of these fields. In regard to languages, Chaucer was certainly a polyglot, who throughout his life was exposed to Latin, French, Italian, and English.

Early records of Chaucer's professional career include a document noting his position in the household of Prince Lionel and his wife Elizabeth de Burgh, Countess of Ulster. This receipt records the purchase of some articles of clothing for Chaucer in April 1357, as well as a small Christmas bonus (*CLR* 14–15). From these records, it appears that Chaucer served in a lowly position in the household, most likely as a page. Two years later he fought as a squire in Edward III's invasion of France during early campaigns of the Hundred Years War; he was captured during the siege of Reims, and for his release the king paid a hefty ransom of sixteen pounds (*CLR* 23), which was the equivalent of almost 800 days of labor for a craftsman in the building trade.[3]

Chaucer disappears from court records during the period between 1360 and 1366, but he is recorded as a member of Edward III's royal household in a document dated June 20, 1367, in which he receives an annuity (*CLR* 123). There is a general assumption that Chaucer studied law during this period, based on an intriguing incident documented in Thomas Speght's 1598 edition of his literature: "not many yeeres since, Master *Buckley* did see a Record in the same house [the Inns of Court], where *Geoffrey Chaucer* was fined two shillings for beating a Franciscane fryer [friar] in Fleetstreet."[4] This scene places Chaucer within a juridical environment, and the oblique reference to a legal education tangentially coincides with several points in Chaucer's fictions, including his descriptions of the Sergeant of the Lawe (1.309–30) and the Manciple (1.568–86) in the General Prologue to the *Canterbury Tales*. Readers will likely never know why (or whether) Chaucer attacked this friar, but his satirical treatments of the Friar in the General Prologue (1.208–69) and in the Summoner's Prologue and Tale could likewise be traced to this incident.

By 1366 Chaucer was married to Philippa de Roet, who served as lady-in-waiting to important women of the English royal house, including Elizabeth de Burgh (Edward III's daughter-in-law, wife of his second son

Lionel), Queen Philippa (Edward's wife), and Constance of Castile (second wife of Edward's third son John of Gaunt and thus another of the king's daughters-in-law). Philippa's sister Katherine Swynford was the mistress of John of Gaunt, Duke of Lancaster, for more than twenty years until they married in 1396. Some surmise that Philippa had been—and perhaps continued to be—one of John of Gaunt's mistresses as well. This is pure conjecture, and the "evidence" adduced to support the theory includes Chaucer's frequent depiction of himself and his narrators as failed lovers. Chaucer's predilection for satirizing himself in his literature, however, does not presuppose that romantic disappointments crushed his real-life amatory aspirations. Assuming the voice of an unsuccessful lover is a common trope in medieval courtly literature, and readers need no more conclude that Chaucer faced endless losses in love because his narrators suffered in this manner than that writers of murder mysteries practice homicide before writing of it.

The surviving records provide scant documentation of Chaucer's family life, yet it is clear that Geoffrey and Philippa raised several children. Elizabeth Chaucer joined the Priory of St. Helen in 1377 and then Barking Abbey in 1381, and if one assumes that she joined the abbey as a teenager, it is likely that she was born sometime in the mid-to-late 1360s (*CLR* 545–46). Chaucer's son Thomas was born in 1367, and Chaucer dedicated his *A Treatise on the Astrolabe* to his second son Lewis, who is of the "tendir age of ten yeer" at the time of the work's composition in 1391–92, which places the boy's birth in the early 1380s. A list of men bearing arms dated to 1403 mentions Thomas and Lewis together, which supports suppositions that they were indeed brothers (*CLR* 544). Thomas later served as speaker of the House of Commons. Agnes Chaucer appears in court records detailing the coronation of Henry IV; she appears to be Geoffrey and Philippa's fourth child. It is mostly idle speculation to envision what kind of father Chaucer was, but the dedication of *A Treatise on the Astrolabe* bespeaks a man who attempted intellectual camaraderie with his son in a kindly and affectionate manner. Also, it should be noted that Chaucer may have fathered more children who did not survive long enough to enter court records. No mention of Chaucer's wife Philippa is found after 1387, and it is generally assumed that she died around this time.

While beginning his family with Philippa in the late 1360s, Chaucer began a series of court positions in 1367. As a diplomat, Chaucer traveled extensively in Europe, and his journeys to France and Italy greatly influenced his literary style. Records document his excursions to Genoa and Florence in 1372–73, to Lombardy in 1378, and to Calais in 1387, among numerous other voyages in service to the monarchy, and the records also document the many warrants, letters of protection, and passages of safe-conduct necessary to travel during the Middle Ages (*CLR* 19–66). Beginning in 1374 with his appointment by King Edward III and continuing until 1386, Chaucer worked as controller of customs in the Port of London, a job that focused on export taxes for wool and leather. As one of England's chief exports, wool generated tax income that financed many governmental functions, and in his customs position Chaucer oversaw approximately £24,000 of revenue annually. To reward his service, Edward III granted Chaucer a daily pitcher of wine, and records show that Chaucer last received this gift from Edward in 1377, when the king died. Upon ascending the throne, Richard II continued the gift, but he converted it to an annual cash dispensation. On April 20, 1382, Geoffrey was given the additional responsibilities of the import and export fees associated with wine (*CLR* 148–270).

The most vexing episode of Chaucer's life culminated in 1380, when one Cecily Chaumpaigne released him from an accusation of *raptus*. The document resolving this incident frees Chaucer from further prosecution in regard to "omnimodas acciones tam de raptu meo tam de aliqua alia re vel causa" [all types of actions either regarding my rape or regarding any other matter] (*CLR* 343).[5] It is difficult to parse the exact meaning of *raptus* because in medieval conceptions of crime the word could refer either to rape, as the term is understood today, or to kidnapping. The matter becomes more confusing with the involvement of John Grove, who also released Chaucer from legal charges; complicating matters still further is that Chaumpaigne similarly released Grove from criminal accusations. On July 2, 1380, Grove paid Chaumpaigne ten pounds in a settlement of sorts, and some scholars propose that Grove negotiated the settlement between Chaucer and Chaumpaigne; others propose that Grove was the chief perpetrator of the *raptus*. The legal wrangling over this *raptus* was undoubtedly a serious affair, and many important men—including the king's chamberlain Sir William Beauchamp, Admiral Sir William Neville, the respected poet Sir John Clanvowe, a merchant and tax collector named John Philipot, and Richard Morel, a wealthy member of Parliament—served as witnesses to the release (*CLR* 343).

Numerous other posts followed in Chaucer's courtly career. He was appointed justice of the peace in Kent and represented Kent in the House of Commons for one session in 1385 (*CLR* 348, 364). These positions suggest that Chaucer moved from London and established his residence in Kent, possibly in Greenwich. Chaucer's last recorded journey to the Continent was to Calais in 1387, in the company of Sir William Beauchamp (*CLR* 61). Chaucer appears to have been short of funds during this period: in 1388–89 John Churchman and Henry Atwood separately sued him for debts, and other such small lawsuits followed (*CLR* 384–401). Still, his connections to the royal court were never fully severed, and he was named clerk of the king's works in May 1389, an appointment that charged him with oversight of the royal residences of Richard II. Highwaymen robbed Chaucer in September 1390, but the court records of this event are murky: it is unclear whether ten or approximately twenty pounds were stolen (*CLR* 477–89). In 1390 Richard II hosted a tournament for knights, and Chaucer was trusted to coordinate the necessary preparations, including construction management. Chaucer's tenure in this clerkship ended on June 17, 1391, and he then served as deputy forester of the king's forest at Petherton in Somerset (*CLR* 494). Royal forests provided significant income streams, especially from pasturing fees and toll roads, and this sinecure provides further evidence of Chaucer's esteem within the royal household.

After a reign filled with court intrigues, Richard II was deposed in 1399 and died in 1400, and Henry Bolingbroke, son of John of Gaunt, took the throne as Henry IV. (Shakespeare imaginatively recounts this chapter of English history in his plays *Richard II*, *Henry IV Parts 1 and 2*, and *Henry V*.) Chaucer appears to have had amiable dealings with the new king, and in "The Complaint of Chaucer to His Purse" he gently petitions Henry IV for money—

O conquerour of Brutes Albyon [Britain],
Which that by lyne [lineage] and free eleccion
Been verray [true] kyng, this song to yow I sende,
And ye, that mowen [may] alle oure harmes amende,
Have mynde upon my supplicacion (22–26)

—suggesting that Chaucer saw their relationship as sufficiently strong that he could remind Henry of his financial obligations. It is also possible that Chaucer found himself, as a longtime associate of Richard's court, in a politically awkward situation with Henry IV's ascension. Certainly, in this short poem Chaucer stresses that Henry is Britain's rightful ruler, emphasizing that he holds the throne "by lyne and free eleccion"; these lines highlight the poet's shrewd consideration of his position in a changing court.

Against the backdrop of his busy personal and professional life, Chaucer found the time to write his masterpieces. Most of their dates are uncertain, but it appears that he began his translation of the French allegorical poem *Roman de la Rose* in the late 1360s; the *Book of the Duchess* likely appeared in the early 1370s; and the *House of Fame, Troilus and Criseyde*, the *Parliament of Fowls*, and his translation of Boethius's *Consolation of Philosophy* were tackled during the early 1380s. The *Canterbury Tales* and the *Legend of Good Women*, both unfinished at the time of his death, were begun in the mid-1380s, although several of their constituent tales were written earlier and then added to the composite narratives.

Throughout the fourteenth century, cataclysmic events and social change—the Black Death, the Hundred Years War, the Peasants' Revolt of 1381—altered England in profound ways. Somewhat surprisingly, Chaucer mostly overlooks these events in his writing. This is not to say that readers cannot glean insights into medieval English culture by reading Chaucer's literature, but that he concentrates on creating fictional worlds for Canterbury pilgrims and Trojan lovers rather than directly addressing the leading social and political issues of his day.

And truly, Chaucer lived through tumultuous times. With the Black Death decimating the English population at midcentury and then recurring every decade or so, Chaucer was fortunate to have survived. The plague swept through Continental Europe and then, during the summer of 1348, jumped the English Channel and killed approximately one-third of the population. Combine this devastating epidemic with already high rates of infant mortality, and the Father of English Literature escaped mortal pitfalls that threatened his literary career well before it began. The plague struck its victims with gruesome deaths, and Colin Platt's study of death records in various English communities finds mortality rates ranging widely, with some towns losing approximately 25 percent of their population while others lost up to 75 percent.[6]

As the Black Death seemed capable of destroying civilization through disease, the Peasants' Revolt of 1381 threatened to topple England's longstanding social structures. Many of Chaucer's contemporaries viewed the Peasants' Revolt as apocalyptic. This rebellion of workers sought to upend the prevailing social order, in which the aristocracy ruled over the serfs and received the fruits of their labor. Many medieval thinkers, such as the preacher John Mirk (fl. ca. 1382–1414), deemed this caste system to be divinely sanctioned. Mirk outlines how the three primary estates of English society—the aristocrats, the clergy, and the commoners—should work together:

> So mot [must] vch [each] seruand [servant] of God enforson hym to laberon yn thys gre [degree, position] that God hath set hym in: men of Holy Chyrche schuld laberen bysyly in praying and studying for to techen Goddes pepul; lordus schuld laberen . . . to kepe Holy Chyrche in pesse [peace] and in rest, and al othur comyn [common] pepul; the comyn pepul schuld labore bysyly to geton [get, earn] lyflode [livelihood] to hemself [themselves] and for al othur.[7]

The hierarchical nature of England, it was widely believed, respected God's plan for humanity, and to overturn or tamper with it would be to flout God's will. Thus when Jack Straw, John Ball, and Wat Tyler led a mob of peasants in revolt against the authorities—burning John of Gaunt's palace and executing Simon Sudbury, the archbishop of Canterbury—it appeared that the commoners were radically subverting the foundations of English society. Chaucer's reference to the Peasants' Revolt in the Nun Priest's Tale—"Certes, he Jakke Straw and his meynee [company] / Ne made nevere shoutes half so shrille" (7.3394–95)—casts this earth-shattering event within the mock-epic environs of a story of a prideful rooster menaced by a hungry fox. It is undoubtedly a sign of Chaucer's sense of humor that he can transform such a revolutionary event into a joke, but the Peasants' Revolt nonetheless exposed great discontent with the political and ideological foundations of English society.

The fourteenth century was also a time of international political intrigue, particularly as the Hundred Years War (1337–1453) was waged, with both Philip of Valois and Edward III claiming the French throne. Three primary conflicts defined this struggle: the Edwardian War (1337–1360), the Caroline War (1369–1389), and the Lancastrian War (1415–1429). The English won sufficient battles in the earlier campaigns to establish strongholds in France, especially with the victories of Henry V in the early fifteenth century; however, under the leadership of Joan of

Arc in 1429 the French eventually triumphed. Joan was executed in 1431, but her victories ensured that the Dauphin, now crowned as Charles VII, would maintain his throne. The campaigns of the Lancastrian War and its aftermath occurred years after Chaucer's death, but as a prisoner of war during the Edwardian campaigns, he likely took a keen interest in the conflict's progress throughout his lifetime.

Although medieval people might expect turbulent social times due to plague, rebellion, and international conflict, they would also likely find some sense of stability through their shared religious traditions. England in the Middle Ages was a Christian nation, and the overarching uniformity of religious belief in medieval England brooked few challenges to its spiritual and secular authority. However, even the unifying force of religion confronted the possibility of fragmentation when the preacher John Wycliffe (ca. 1335–1384) laid the foundations for the Protestant Reformation long before Martin Luther nailed his 95 Theses to Wittenberg's Castle Church in 1517. Wycliffe believed that the Bible should be translated into the vernacular languages; he attacked the hierarchy inherent in the Church's administrative structures and monastic orders; and he also rejected the doctrine of transubstantiation, which holds that Eucharistic wafers used in Communion metamorphose into Christ's flesh.[8] Wycliffe's followers, known pejoratively as Lollards, were often oppressed for their beliefs, and belonging to their sect invited political and religious persecution. In the *Canterbury Tales*, Harry Bailly accuses the Parson of Lollardy—"This Lollere heer wil prechen us somwhat" (2.1177)—and his words carry with them a sharp antagonism, given the ways in which the medieval Church harshly responded to dissent.

According to his tomb in Westminster Abbey, Chaucer died on October 25, 1400, in London. His death was likely unexpected, for on December 24, 1399, he signed a fifty-three-year lease for a house in Westminster (*CLR* 535). Chaucer would have been irrationally optimistic to foresee living for fifty-three more years when he was already approximately sixty, and he doubtless saw the lease as an asset to pass on to his progeny. Still, such a long-term commitment does not indicate any foreboding sense of one's imminent demise. Had the Father of English Literature lived even a modest fraction of those fifty-three years, he might have found his way to finishing the *Canterbury Tales* and the *Legend of Good Women*, and so it is to every reader's regret that Chaucer's residence here was so short-lived.

2

Chaucer's Literature

Dream Visions: *Book of the Duchess, House of Fame, Parliament of Fowls,* and *Legend of Good Women*

Dreams have often been linked to religious prophecies, as in the stories of Joseph and Daniel in the Hebrew Bible, but Chaucer's dream visions concern more secular issues, tackling questions of love, loss, literary reputation, life, and death. Much as he does in the *Canterbury Tales*, Chaucer interjects himself as a character in his four major dream visions—*Book of the Duchess, House of Fame, Parliament of Fowls,* and *Legend of Good Women*—and his persona as narrator of these works is often excessively naive. This is in part due to the didactic thrust of most dream visions: because the narrators play the role of students in need of an education, they must commence the dream as ignorant of an important truth.

BOOK OF THE DUCHESS

Within the typical structure of a dream vision, the narrator must fall asleep so that he may begin his dream and thus learn a valuable lesson through his surreal experiences, and, adhering to this formula, the *Book of the Duchess* begins with Chaucer lamenting his insomnia. He is so overcome with sleeplessness and melancholy that he fears his imminent death: "And I ne may, ne nyght ne morwe, / Slepe; and thus melancolye / And drede I have for to dye" (22–24). In a poem that concentrates so keenly on the pains of love and, more, on the pains of losing a beloved to the finality of death, it is appropriate that Chaucer's emotional torpor arises from his beloved's refusal to assuage his pains:

I holde hit be [it is] a sicknesse
That I have suffred this eight yeer;
And yet my boote [cure] is never the ner [nearer],
For there is phisicien but oon
That may me hele [heal]; but that is don. (36–40)

Chaucer, in suggesting that only his lost beloved can cure his malady, deploys the standard tropes of lovesickness. By bewailing his heartbreak, he creates a parallel suffering between himself as narrator and the enigmatic Man in Black, whom he soon meets in his dream.

The *Book of the Duchess* explores the meaning of love and loss in multiple and interweaving ways, and Chaucer (as writer) employs classical mythology to prepare the reader for the presentation of these themes in the ensuing dream vision. Attempting to relieve his sleeplessness, Chaucer reaches for his copy of the story of Ceyx and his wife Alcione (60–230), a tale told by such authors as Ovid, Statius, and Machaut. In brief, the story relates Ceyx's death in a shipwreck, and, when he fails to return, Alcione's endless agony because she does not know whether he is dead or alive. She prays to Juno, and the goddess instructs Morpheus to bring Ceyx's dead body to Alcione so that she will learn the truth of his fate. Ceyx appears before her, and Alcione dies three days later. This story lays the foundation for Chaucer's dream experience, in which the Man in Black mourns his lost love. But before the dream begins, Chaucer captures the desperation to which insomnia drives the restless, as he promises a luxurious feather bed to anyone who can help him to fall asleep (231–69). This brief moment of humor lightens the mood of a poem that continually turns to the question of why loved ones must die and how survivors should confront their loss.

In an abrupt but effective switch of tone, the initial lines of Chaucer's dream crackle with energy and éclat: chirping birds celebrate a beautiful May morning (291–320), and Chaucer sees a riotous roar of color through stained glass windows depicting scenes from classical mythology, including the stories of Achilles, Medea, and others (321–31). The chamber's walls are illustrated with "bothe text and glose [gloss, interpretive commentary], / Of al the Romaunce of the Rose" (333–34), and a hunt begins with Octavian (Augustus Caesar) at the lead. The dream takes on a frenetic pace at this point, as Chaucer proclaims as he joins the chase, "A Goddes half, in good tyme . . . / Go we faste!" (370–71).

Dreams often feature abrupt changes of tempo, and the excitement of this hunt unexpectedly fades to the background when Chaucer encounters a puppy that distracts his attention:

And as I wente, ther cam by mee
A whelp [puppy], that fauned [fawned on] me as I stood,
That hadde yfolowed and koude no good [was confused].
Hyt [It] com and crepte to me as lowe
Ryght as hyt hadde me yknowe,
Helde doun hys hed and joyned hys eres [ears],
And leyde al smothe doun hys heres [hair, fur]. (388–94)

The dog leads Chaucer away from the hunt, and the dream transitions yet again as Chaucer comes upon the "man in blak" (445), a "wonder wel-farynge knyght" (452), who embodies sorrow and sings a tuneless song:

"I have of sorwe so gret won
That joye gete I never non,
Now that I see my lady bryght,
Which I have loved with al my myght,
Is fro me ded and ys agoon." (475–79)

Indeed, this complaint exacts a physical toll upon its singer, as his body appears drained of blood (487–513). The Man in Black's melancholy, as contrasted with the beautiful springtime glories Chaucer witnessed earlier, illustrates the profound disjunctions possible in life and love. Also, love affairs are often metaphorically described as hunts, and so this knight's amatory pursuits, which were ended in an untimely fashion by human mortality, contrast painfully with the pleasures of Octavian's chase.

This dream vision's attention to love and loss allows Chaucer to consider deep questions about the human condition, and the Man in Black's lament also focuses on one of Chaucer's dominant themes throughout his corpus—the mutability of Fortune. In a particularly acerbic passage, the Man in Black compares Fortune to a scorpion:

"I lykne [liken] hyr [Fortune] to the scorpioun,
That ys a fals, flaterynge beste,
For with his hed he maketh feste [pays compliments],
But al amydde hys flaterynge

With hys tayle he wol stynge
And envenyme; and so wol she." (636–41)

Expressing his contempt for Fortune's fickleness, the Man in Black complains bitterly while simultaneously acknowledging his inability to change his destiny. In an extended metaphor, he compares his relationship with Fortune to a game of chess in which she captured his queen (652–69). In chess, a king without a queen to defend him is vulnerable to defeat, and likewise the Man in Black sees no hope for his future happiness without his beloved.

Chaucer borrows extensively from other genres in this dream vision, and his use of the blazon, a standard feature of love poetry in which the lover praises his beloved's unsurpassable attractiveness, interrupts the flow of the narrative to allow the reader to revel in this lost lady's loveliness. Certainly, much of the Man in Black's speech addresses the beauty and magnificence of his beloved, and his words invite the reader and Chaucer as narrator to contemplate her exceptional loveliness and, by extension, the Man in Black's heartache for her loss. She outshined others in her beauty as the summer sun outshines the other planets (817–32). Her hair, her eyes, her pleasure in living, the beauty of her face, her voice and speech, and her neck and throat receive detailed attention for their beauty (855–947). Her outer qualities are matched by her inner graces, such that the Man in Black praises her upright morals and her concern for her reputation:

"Therwith she loved so wel ryght
She wrong do wolde [would do] to no wyght [person].
No wyght myghte do hir noo shame,
She loved so wel hir owne name." (1015–18)

The Man in Black's beloved represents the epitome of female constancy and virtue, and he honors her memory by remaining faithful to her despite her death. He gladly accepts his position as a slave to love, for it provides pleasure for him, as it formerly provided pleasure to his beloved (758–74).

At several points in this dream's dialogue, Chaucer attempts to lure the Man in Black from his mourning. Because the poem focuses on this knight's exemplary suffering, Chaucer's efforts must fail, but they nonetheless maintain the momentum of the discussion and preserve this dream vision from becoming a static portrait of sorrow. In his counterargument, Chaucer cites numerous examples of mythological figures who kill themselves or others for the sake of love, including Medea, Phyllis, and Dido (721–39), and he urges the Man in Black, "But ther is no man alyve her / Wolde for a fers [queen] make this woo!" (740–41). He insufficiently compliments the Man in Black's beloved when he suggests the barest possibility that his interlocutor could find a more exceptional beloved: "Hardely, your love was wel beset; / I not how ye myghte have do bet [done better]" (1043–44), to which the Man in Black responds testily, "Bet? [Better?] Ne no wyght so wel" (1045). Here readers see the implausible naiveté of dream-vision narrators, who must be repeatedly corrected in their erroneous assumptions. In this case, Chaucer learns that he misunderstands love through the Man in Black's instructive suffering, but it is odd that Chaucer confronts this lesson in his dream because the initial descriptions of his lovesickness indicate his personal experience with and understanding of such pains. Dream visions often focus on narrators who appear to be recalcitrantly obtuse so that authors can stress their morals, and Chaucer (as author) characterizes himself (as narrator) with striking ignorance to stress the themes of his poem. Such a narrative stance also allows a gentle humor into a mournful poem, in which Chaucer's naiveté—how could he even momentarily confuse a queen in a game of chess with a human beloved?—leavens an otherwise somber meditation on lost love.

In detailing his courtship of his beloved, the Man in Black shares with Chaucer the song he sang for her, and in this lyric interlude, readers obtain a deeper insight into the Man in Black's suffering. This ode contrasts painfully with the tuneless song that the Man in Black was singing when Chaucer found him:

"Lord, hyt maketh myn herte lyght
Whan I thenke on that swete wyght [person, lady]
That is so semely on to see;
And wisshe to God hit myghte so bee
That she wolde holde me for hir knyght,
My lady, that is so fair and bryght!" (1175–80)

The knight finishes recounting their courtship, detailing his initial failure when she refused his affections and his subsequent success a year later when she realized the sincerity of his devotion (1236–86). Their subsequent union was one of joyful accord: "Oure hertes wern so evene a payre / That never nas that oon contrayre / To that other for no woo" (1289–91). In this abbreviated tale of courtly romance, the lovers unite after the man has proved his worthiness, and the fair beloved finally cedes to his desire for her.

The Man in Black's colloquy with Chaucer reaches its climax when he again reveals that his beloved has died:

"Bethenke how I seyde here-beforn,
'Thow wost [knowest] ful lytel what thow menest;
I have lost more than thow wenest [think].'
God wot [knows], allas! Ryght that was she!"
   "Allas, sir, how? What may that be?"
   "She ys ded!" "Nay!" "Yis, be my trouthe!"
   "Is that youre los? Be God, hyt ys routhe [a pity]!" (1304–10)

The Man in Black told Chaucer this his beloved was dead when they first met (475–79), and so his surprise at this revelation rings narratively hollow and yet emotionally true. The keen pains of loss resonate throughout the *Book of the Duchess*, but Chaucer does not attempt to imbue his poem with an anodyne moral. His heartfelt response of pity offers comfort without any real hope of lessening the Man in Black's emotional torment.

The *Book of the Duchess* concludes abruptly, with the hunt ending, the knight departing, and the narrator waking, and then determining to write down his dream: "Thys ys so queynt a sweven [dream] / That I wol, be processe of tyme, / Fonde [devise] to put this sweven in ryme" (1330–32). Although many dream visions contain a clear moral for readers to glean from the dreamer's experiences, such a lesson is not expressed at the conclusion of this narrative. The lack of a pat ending gives the *Book of the Duchess* much of its power, as death must remain a great mystery, and its cruel ability to leave those who survive their beloveds bereft of any foreseeable joy cannot always be ameliorated by a few words of consolation. If the Man in Black's suffering cannot be salved, however, Chaucer's own sense of malaise has been lifted. In the beginning of the poem, he described himself as emotionally empty—"Al is ylyche [alike] good to me—/ Joye or sorowe, wherso hyt be—/ For I have felynge in nothyng" (9–11)—but he is now inspired to write again. This slight glimmer of hope illuminates a work of insistent mourning with the possibility of one person's suffering helping another to gain insight into life's sometimes painful beauty.

It appears likely that Chaucer wrote the *Book of the Duchess* to elegize the death of John of Gaunt's wife, Blanche, Duchess of Lancaster. She died in 1368, and the poem is typically dated between 1369 and 1372. Numerous textual clues support this interpretation, such as when the Man in Black departs from Chaucer to retire to his home, which is described as "A long castel with walles white, / Be Seynt Johan, on a ryche hil" (1318–19). These lines embed four allusions to the couple: "long castel" plays on the Latin roots of Lancaster; "walles white" features a pun between the English "white" and the French *blanche*; "Seynt Johan" echoes John of Gaunt's given name; and "ryche hil" translates the geographical location Richmond from its French roots, possibly reminding readers that John of Gaunt bore the title Earl of Richmond from infancy until 1372. Also, the mourning knight declares that his beloved's name was White—"And goode faire White she het [was named]; / That was my lady name ryght. / She was bothe fair and bryght" (948–50); these lines give further credence to the connection of the *Book of the Duchess* with John of Gaunt's loss of his wife Blanche. Chaucer emphasizes her exceptional beauty in these lines and throughout the poem, but even the beautiful must die, as the *Book of the Duchess* reminds its readers. Thus this multigeneric dream vision, with its incorporation of the tropes of blazon, lyric, and romance, takes on yet another register as a loose allegory of John of Gaunt's bereavement, which enables readers to see the ways in which Chaucer negotiates the tenuous boundaries between his professional life in court and his artistic desires as a writer.

HOUSE OF FAME

In the *House of Fame*, Chaucer recounts his journey through a literary dream world, and, in so doing, ponders his role in the poetic tradition. The poem's three books depict Chaucer as narrator retelling Virgil's *Aeneid*, his surprising abduction by an eagle, and his travels throughout the realm of Fame. In Fame's dominion, he observes the great authors of the past and the strange companies of petitioners who either curry Fame's attentions or seek to avoid her ministrations. As is often the case with dream visions, Chaucer's *House of Fame* is infused with surreal moments, which in this instance offer the author license to explore his role in literary history.

Book 1 of the *House of Fame* begins with a proem (1–65) in which Chaucer muses on the meaning and nature of dreams. "God turne us every drem to goode!" (1), he proclaims, and he then addresses the nature and meaning of various types of dreams. Within the dream-vision genre, proems often allow the narrator to preview the didactic lesson learned through the dreamer's experiences, but here Chaucer is more concerned with exploring the nature of dreams themselves. He employs a sophisticated lexicon for dreams, distinguishing among *avision*, *revelacion*, *drem*, *sweven*, *fantome*, and *oracle* (7–11) while simultaneously confessing his ignorance about the exact differences among them (12–20). The proem concludes with Chaucer promising to tell the story of his vision:

> Ne no man elles me beforn,
> Mette [dreamt], I trowe [believe] stedfastly,
> So wonderful a drem as I
> The tenthe day now of Decembre,
> The which, as I kan now remembre,
> I wol yow tellen everydel [every part]. (60–65)

Moving to his invocation (66–110), Chaucer requests the assistance of Morpheus, the god of sleep, to assist him with his story. It is ironically unclear how Morpheus would accomplish this goal since he is, somewhat expectedly, sleeping: "There slepeth ay [always] this god unmerie [gloomy] / With his slepy thousand sones, / That alwey for to slepe hir wone [custom] is" (74–76). Chaucer also prays to Jesus in his invocation (94–106), thus melding classical and Christian themes in his work.

After Chaucer falls asleep, his dream commences with a recounting of one of the most famous classical epics, Virgil's *Aeneid*. Discovering himself in Venus's temple, Chaucer finds the epic "written on a table of bras [brass]" (142) and then recalls its many momentous scenes: the fall of Troy and Aeneas's subsequent escape from his doomed homeland (151–211); Venus's intercession to Jove on her son Aeneas's behalf (212–38); Aeneas and Dido's love affair, which ends tragically with her suicide after his departure to Italy (239–432); and Aeneas's arrival in Italy, his victorious battles, and his marriage to Lavinia (433–67). In this condensed retelling of Aeneas's epic journey, Chaucer interweaves a domestic theme in which he advises women to avoid duplicitous men by cataloging stories of steadfast female lovers and fickle men (383–432) in a fashion similar to—but much briefer than—his *Legend of Good Women*. Chaucer is awed by the images he sees—"Yet sawgh I never such noblesse / Of ymages, ne such richesse, / As I saugh graven [engraved] in this chirche" (471–73)—but book 1 of the *House of Fame* ends with an equally wondrous appearance: that of a golden eagle alighting from the heavens, heading directly toward Chaucer (496–508). From this scene, it appears that Chaucer uses the hallucinatory freedoms of the dream vision to address the nature of epic and his relationship to it. (Chaucer did not write an epic, but epic elements characterize several of his fictions, particularly the Knight's Tale and *Troilus and Criseyde*, as well as, in mock-epic fashion, the Nun's Priest's Tale.)

In the proem of book 2 (509–28), Chaucer invokes the assistance of Venus to recount his continuing adventures (518–22), and the narrative then returns to the unfolding dream. The swooping eagle, approaching with the awesome fury of a thunderbolt and then snatching up a terrified Chaucer (529–53), takes a pert if sincere tone with its passenger. It chides Chaucer for his immoderate girth—"Seynte Marye, / Thou art noyous [troublesome, tedious] for to carye!" (573–74)—while nonetheless promising his friendship: "Be ful assured, boldely, / I am thy frend" (581–82). The bewildered poet remains mystified and wonders if he has been summoned to the heavens to serve either the Judeo-Christian God (in the manner of Enoch and Elijah in early Jewish literature) or Jupiter (in the manner of Ganymede and Romulus in Greek and Roman mythology). The eagle reports that he serves Jupiter, who has decided to reward Chaucer for patiently suffering in love while nonetheless praising romance in his writings:

> "Certeyn, he hath of the [you] routhe [pity]
> That thou so longe trewely
> Hast served so ententyfly [attentively]
> Hys blynde nevew [nephew] Cupido,
> And faire Venus also,
> Withoute guerdon [reward] ever yit." (614–19)

The eagle is transporting Chaucer to the House of Fame to reward him for his labor and devotion to love (641–99); there the poet will learn even more about the ways of romance. With this introduction of romance themes into the dream vision, Chaucer shifts the poem from its epic material to a new interest in romance and thus underscores his need to succeed in multiple artistic venues if he is to secure his position among the great authors throughout history.

The very concept of the House of Fame confuses Chaucer, and he asks how Fame could gather all the information she possesses (701–6). The eagle answers his questions patiently, explaining that the House of Fame stands midway between heaven and earth and that all sounds ever spoken retire there (711–24); moreover, the sounds now residing in the House of Fame assume the appearance of the persons who spoke them on earth (1074–77). This learned eagle continues his scientific exegesis, detailing how everything in nature is connected to its natural location (729–64). Since speech is sound, and sound is broken air, all speech therefore ascends to the House of Fame, according to the eagle:

"That every speche of every man,
As y the telle first began,
Moveth up on high to pace
Kyndely to Fames place." (849–52)

Chaucer's strange voyage continues, as he gazes down on the earth and up to the heavens, with the eagle commenting on the journey (887–978). This experience becomes spiritual, and Chaucer marvels at God's power: "'O God,' quod y, 'that made Adam, / Moche ys thy myght and thy no-blesse!'" (970–71). Book 2 concludes with Chaucer's arrival at the House of Fame, with the eagle departing and wishing him to benefit from his experiences there: "And God of heven sende the [you] grace / Some good to lernen in this place" (1087–88).

As book 3 commences, Chaucer continues his pattern of establishing a new theme to his *House of Fame* in his invocation, and he now requests the assistance of Apollo (1091–1109). The god "of science and of lyght" (1091), Apollo is connected to divine revelation, and this aspect of the deity relates to Chaucer's quest for knowledge about the universe and his position in it so that he can cement his status as a great poet. In this poem that foregrounds his place in the Western literary tradition, Chaucer humbly notes his artistic defects in his plea for Apollo's assistance: "Yit make hyt sumwhat agreable, / Though som vers [verse, meter] fayle in a sillable" (1097–98). Particularly he requests Apollo's aid in describing the House of Fame itself, where Chaucer observes tributes to the achievements of his poetic forebears (1101–5).

Following this final invocation, Chaucer returns to the plotline of his dream concerning poetic reputation and literary traditions: the golden eagle departs, and Chaucer finds the House of Fame on a rock of ice (1110–35). There the names of "famous folkes" are carved (1137), but, given Fame's fickle nature, half of the names have melted away, while the other half remain preserved (1136–80). Chaucer proceeds into Fame's residence, where he finds musicians and magicians (1201–81), and he then discovers a group of people crying for a gift: "A larges, larges [largesse], hold up wel! / God save the lady of thys pel [castle], / Our oune gentil lady Fame" (1309–11). Chaucer then espies Lady Fame in all of her protean and monstrous mutability: she shrinks and stretches in size, and she has as many eyes as a bird has feathers, as well as numerous ears and tongues (1356–92). Her shifting appearance captures her capricious nature.

In Lady Fame's hall, numerous pillars bear up images of the great authors of the past for Chaucer to admire, and here Chaucer most directly addresses his interest in the poetic tradition. He first sees Josephus, the Hebrew historian, who bears "on hys shuldres hye / The fame up of the Jewerye" (1435–36), and the subsequent authors whom Chaucer observes are likewise praised for their work in preserving the great narratives of the past: Statius, for the stories of Thebes and Achilles (1451–63); Homer, Dares Phrygius, Dictys Cretensis, Lollius, Guido delle Colonne, and Geoffrey of Monmouth, for the story of Troy (1464–80); Virgil, for the story of Aeneas (1481–85); Ovid, for his stories of love (1486–96); Lucan, for the story of Julius Caesar and Pompey (1497–1506); and Claudian, for the story of Pluto and Proserpina (1507–12). Concentrating on the authors of the classical tradition and their descendants, Chaucer praises the glories of past literature while tacitly acknowledging his debts to these authors who profoundly influenced his writing. As Chaucer establishes throughout this dream vision, his ambition to join these other great artists hinges upon his appreciation of their works, for they imbue his writings with the proper pedigree of aesthetic merit.

Swarms of petitioners then come before Lady Fame, beseeching her to bestow her gifts upon them, and she does so, but in a mercurial fashion. Like Lady Fortune, who callously spins her wheel to determine a person's destiny, Lady Fame does not respond to any inherent sense of justice but merely follows her whims, as Chaucer reports:

But thus I seye yow, trewely,
What her cause was, y nyste [did not know].
For of this folk ful wel y wiste [knew]
They hadde good fame ech deserved,
Although they were dyversly served;
Ryght as her suster, dame Fortune,
Ys wont [accustomed] to serven in comune. (1542–48)

The first group of petitioners requests "good fame" for "good werkes," but Fame dismisses this request. She dispatches her messenger to Eolus, "the god of wynde" (1571), who brings with him his trumpets Clere Laude (Clear Praise) and Sklaundre (Slander), with which the petitioners will be celebrated or defamed (1572–82). The second group of petitioners, similar to the first group in requesting "good fame" to reward good works, is punished with Sklaundre, who will disparage its members such that "every wight / Speke of hem harm and shrewednesse / In stede of good and worthynesse" (1626–28). Seven more groups offer their petitions, and Lady Fame's responses highlight her arbitrary dispensation of justice: the third group requests fame that is truly deserved, and Fame grants it (1657–88); the fourth group requests anonymity for good works, and Fame agrees to let these deeds die with the petitioners (1689–1701); the members of the fifth group, similar to the fourth, request anonymity for their virtuous acts, but Fame promises instead to let the world know of their goodness (1702–26); the sixth group requests a good reputation despite being idle in life and accomplishing little, and Fame accedes to this request (1727–70); the seventh group puts forth the same request as the previous group of idlers, but Fame rejects this petition (1771–1810); the eighth group requests a good reputation despite treacherous acts, and Fame rejects this plea (1811–22); and the final group seeks a reputation congruent with its members' vicious and wicked acts, a request that Fame grants (1823–68).

The *House of Fame* then returns to its thematic focus on Chaucer's position in the poetic community. Authors must incessantly seek new materials to address in their fictions, and Chaucer confesses that his education is incomplete in this regard. An unnamed stranger approaches, wondering if Chaucer has entered Lady Fame's chamber to win her blessings. Chaucer denies this, stating that he has come to learn:

"Somme newe tydynges for to lere [learn],
Somme newe thinges, y not what,
Tydynges, other this or that,
Of love or suche thynges glade." (1886–89)

If he is to join the company of Statius, Homer, Virgil, and the other writers whose reputations have withstood the test of time, Chaucer needs appropriate and novel subject matter for his writings. Authors must continually confront the long shadow of their illustrious forebears, and in his search for new tidings about which to write, Chaucer as narrator and dreamer seeks relief from this aesthetic burden.

In accordance with the inherent instability of dreams and dream visions, Chaucer soon finds himself in an unexpected and bizarre setting: a house built of twigs stretching sixty miles long. This enormous edifice spins endlessly around and is filled with gossip (1916–85); unable to enter, Chaucer requires the assistance of the golden eagle, who returns to deposit him in this strange residence where diverse tidings flow. Dropped into this mysterious abode, Chaucer witnesses truth and falsehood circulating and uniting: "Thus saugh [saw] I fals and soth [truth] compouned [unite] / Togeder fle for oo [one] tydynge" (2108–9).

The *House of Fame* then abruptly ends. Typically dream visions conclude with the narrator explaining what he has learned from his experiences, but this poem is unfinished. In its final lines a mysterious man appears:

Atte laste y saugh a man,
Which that y nevene [name] nat ne kan;
But he semed for to be
A man of gret auctorite . . . (2155–58)

It is difficult to envision how Chaucer intended to complete his poem, or how this "man of gret auctorite" would contribute to the discussion of Chaucer's place in the literary tradition, or even who this powerful but unnamed man might be. Yet in this quirky but strangely compelling dream vision—successful as the most outlandish of Chaucer's endeavors in this genre because it is the one most true to the hallucinatory quality of actual dreams—Chaucer succeeds in praising his fellow poets and positioning himself among their number, even if the dream never ends because the dreamer never awakens.

PARLIAMENT OF FOWLS

Birds and Valentine's Day: the two might appear to have little in common, but Chaucer repeatedly links them in his literature. In his short poem "The Complaint of Mars," the narrator invokes St. Valentine in recounting the story of Mars's disappointing journey in love: "Seynt Valentyne, a foul [bird] thus herde I synge / Upon thy day er sonne [before the sun] gan up-sprynge" (13–14). In the *Legend of Good Women*, birds sing, "Blessed be Seynt Valentyn, / For on his day I chees yow to be myn, / Withouten repentyng, myn herte swete!" (F.145–47), and in "Complaynt D'Amours," the narrator notes the occasion that sparks his love lament:

> This compleynte on Seint Valentynes day,
> Whan every foughel [fowl] chesen shal his make [mate],
> To hir, whos I am hool [wholly] and shal alwey,
> This woful song and this compleynte I make. (85–88)

In the *Parliament of Fowls* Chaucer similarly observes, "For this was on Seynt Valentynes day, / Whan every foul cometh there to chese his make [mate]" (309–10), and he presents in this poem his most lighthearted and sustained excursus on avian amorousness. The *Parliament of Fowls* delights readers with its charming sense of humor, but it is also impressive in its masterful poetics. In a display of onomatopoeic virtuosity, Chaucer captures both the tonal quality of birds and their propensity to give him a headache: "The goos, the cokkow [cuckoo], and the doke [duck] also / So cryede, 'Kek kek! kokkow! quek quek!' hye, / That thourgh myne eres [ears] the noyse wente tho" (498–500).

As might be expected, these cacophonous birds appear in the chimerical dream episode of this dream vision, and before Chaucer as narrator meets these many flirtatious fowls, he must fall asleep. Appropriately enough for a poem concerning the quest for love, Chaucer adopts the persona of a passionate but unfulfilled lover:

> The lyf so short, the craft so long to lerne,
> Th'assay [attempt] so hard, so sharp the conquerynge,
> The dredful joye alwey that slit [passes, slides away] so yerne
>   [quickly]:
> Al this mene I by Love, that my felynge
> Astonyeth with his wonderful werkynge
> So sore, iwis [certainly], that whan I on hym thynke
> Nat wot [know] I wel wher that I flete [float] or synke. (1–7)

Love confuses Chaucer: it instills in him a sense of awe but also leaves him paralyzed into passivity. He admits that his knowledge of love is more intellectual than experiential:

> For al be that [although] I knowe nat Love in dede [deed],
> Ne wot [know] how that he quiteth [repays] folk here hyre [their efforts],
> Yit happeth me ful ofte in bokes reede
> Of his myrakles and his crewel yre. (8–11)

The poem establishes a tension between love and learning, in which the bookish Chaucer realizes that his amatory failings arise in large part because he studies love, rather than pursuing it.

True to his avocation as a bookworm, Chaucer reads Cicero's "Dream of Scipio" and summarizes it for his readers before slumbering (29–84). This book ponders the meaning of heaven, earth, and the afterlife, such as when Scipio's grandfather Affrican advises him how to achieve heavenly bliss:

> "Know thyself first immortal,
> And loke ay besyly [busily] thow werche and wysse [instruct yourself]
> To commune profit, and thow shalt not mysse
> To comen swiftly to that place deere
> That ful of blysse is and of soules cleere." (73–77)

Chaucer then falls asleep, and he establishes a foundation of irony for the ensuing vision by describing how people dream about what preoccupies them in their daily lives: the hunter dreams of the woods, the judge dreams of court proceedings, and lovers dream of winning their beloveds (99–105). Because he is an unsuccessful suitor, Chaucer dreams of love, yet it is certainly amusing that his vision features birds rather than his beautiful beloved. Here the *Parliament of Fowls* comments on the disorienting effects that love generates, and Chaucer as narrator must therefore embark on a pedagogical mission to resolve love's quandaries. In this dream Affrican guides him to a garden of love, and over the garden's entrance a sign proclaims both the pleasures and the woes always potential in love. Since these contradictory inscriptions adorn the same gate, it appears that this garden can be the site of love's joys or its torments, depending on a lover's actions. Proving himself an ineffective lover, Chaucer is flummoxed by the choice before him: "No wit hadde I, for errour, for to chese / To entre or flen, or me to save or lese" (146–47). Affrican, impatient with Chaucer's indecisiveness, shoves him through the gates (154) while calling him a dullard (162). With its blossoming beauty, the lush garden amply repays Chaucer for entering it (172–210). Allegorical figures frequently populate medieval dream visions, and numerous such personas greet Chaucer in this garden. He first meets Cupid, the God of Love, and then many of his allegorical and mythological companions: Wille; Pleasaunce; Aray (Clothing), Lust, and Curteysie; Craft; Delyt and Gentilesse; Beute; Youthe; Foolhardynesse, Flaterye, and Desyr; Messagerye (Note-Passing) and Meede; Dame Pees; Dame Pacience; Byheste and Art; Jelosye; Priapus (a phallic deity whose exploits are commemorated today in the adjective "priapic"); Venus and Richesse; Bacchus; and Ceres (214–76). Diana, the goddess of chastity, is mentioned (281), yet her influence is mainly ignored in this garden of earthly delights. The final allegorical figure whom Chaucer encounters is "this noble goddesse Nature" (303), who plays a pivotal role in the ensuing assignment of avian lovers. Cupid and Nature, serving as bookends of this panoply of allegorical figures and classical deities, represent opposing sides of romance in a manner similar to the conflicting significations of the gate that leads in and out of the garden: Love is a part of the natural world, and Nature embraces love, but their relationship is often fractious.

Chaucer's entrance into the garden is merely the prelude to the true focus of this dream vision, which less concerns his own love than it does those of the birds who select their partners on Valentine's Day. Like medieval English society, Chaucer's avian community is highly stratified, with birds of prey at the top of the social caste structure, followed by worm eaters, and then waterfowl (323–29). A catalog of birds follows, in which each species is quickly characterized (330–64), until Chaucer tires of the list and breaks it off with a dismissive "What shulde I seyn? Of foules every kynde" (365). Through Chaucer's quick shift in tone, *Parliament of Fowls* plays with the likelihood of dream visions slipping into tendentiousness, and Chaucer segues immediately into the unfolding narrative action. Three male eagles are courting an attractive female eagle, and this scenario parodies courtly love, with avian amorousness deflating the rarefied emotions associated with romance. For instance, the first male eagle, while speaking to Nature, deports himself like the knightly hero of a romance in manner and bearing:

With hed enclyned and with humble cheere [facial expression]
This royal tersel [eagle] spak, and tariede [delayed] noght:
"Unto my soverayn lady, and not my fere [equal, peer],
I chese, and chese with wil, and herte, and thought,
The formel [female eagle] on youre hond, so wel iwrought [formed],
Whos I am al, and evere wol hire serve,
Do what hire lest, to do me lyve or sterve [die]." (414–20)

With his subservient demeanor, eloquent speech, and devotion to his beloved, this eagle incarnates the very best of the knightly tradition, albeit
in avian form. He puts his fate as a lover fully at the mercy of his beloved,
establishes her as his sovereign lady and thus the adjudicator of his fate,
and welcomes death if she should will it (423).

This competition among the three eagles for their mutual beloved
throws the parliament of fowls into an uproar. The second and third
eagles proclaim their superior merit as lovers, with the second declaring
that he loves her best (449–62) and the third promising that he is the
truest in his affections (463–83). Obviously, a decision must be made, but
for which of these three worthy lovers? Different birds express differing
points of view, with the birds of lower caste tiring of their social superiors' amatory tussle and requesting dismissal from the congregation,
as the goose exclaims: "Al this nys not worth a flye!" (501). These comic
voices of the lower orders wrangle with one another, until a young falcon recognizes the necessity of an appropriately courtly solution to their
dilemma: "I can not se that argumentes avayle: / Thanne semeth it there
moste be batayle" (538–39). Here the plot appears to be moving in the direction of Chaucer's Knight's Tale, in which the two knights Palamon and
Arcite clash over Emily's affections and Duke Theseus declares a combat
to resolve the conflict; Chaucer, however, elides the combative themes of
romance when this falcon proposes that the female eagle should choose
the best knight:

"Me wolde thynke how that the worthieste
Of knyghthod, and lengest had used it,
Most of estat, of blod [blood, ancestry] the gentilleste,
Were sittyngest [most appropriate] for hire, if that hir leste;
And of these thre she wot [knows] hireself, I trowe,
Which that he be, for it is light to knowe." (548–53)

Nature allows the female eagle to decide for herself which of her suitors will become her beloved, and here readers see a parallel to Chaucer's Wife of Bath's Prologue and Tale in their shared conclusion that women should be granted mastery over their amatory decisions. The female eagle requests of Nature a respite of one year, and she promises to make her decision on the following Valentine's Day: "Almyghty queen, unto this yer be don, / I axe [ask] respit for to avise me, / And after that to have my choys al fre" (647–49). The remaining birds proceed with the selection of their partners, and they celebrate their love with a song to Nature, one that optimistically welcomes summer as an antidote to winter's chill (673–92).

As narrator of the *Parliament of Fowls*, Chaucer begins his dream vision unlucky in love yet lucky in books, and he ends the narrative in much the same state. The chatter of the birds' song in his dream wakes him up, and he contemplates how little his situation has changed:

> And with the shoutyng, whan the song was do [done]
> That foules maden at here flyght awey,
> I wok, and othere bokes tok me to,
> To reede upon, and yit I rede alwey.
> I hope, ywis, to rede so som day
> That I shal mete [encounter] som thyng for to fare
> The bet [better], and thus to rede I nyl nat spare. (693–99)

This poem, ostensibly an homage to love, parodies the courtly love traditions of romance through its avian enactment, yet the narrator's passion for books rings true. A bookworm rather than a lover, Chaucer offers his closing paean to reading and the adventures of the mind that it inevitably inspires. Unlike many dream visions that conclude with a pat moral, Chaucer ends *Parliament of Fowls* simply by celebrating the pleasures of the text, proving that the didactic thrust of many dream visions can be beneficially sacrificed in favor of the joys of reading.

LEGEND OF GOOD WOMEN

Can books compete with springtime flowers? Such is the question Chaucer faces in the prologue to the *Legend of Good Women*, his dream vision limning the qualities that constitute a virtuous woman.[1] He enjoys his books immensely—"On bokes for to rede I me delyte" (F.30)—except when the heady delights of spring drive him outside:

Save, certeynly, whan that the month of May
Is comen, and that I here the foules [birds] synge,
And that the floures gynnen [begin] for to sprynge,
Farewel my bok and my devocioun! (F.36-39)

In particular, Chaucer delights in the springtime blossoming of daisies, the flower that he calls the "emperice [empress] and flour of floures alle" (F.185). He rushes home to sleep so that he can wake up early the next morning to bask in this flower's beauty (F.197-207), and then his dream vision begins. Within the Prologue, Chaucer includes a ballade, one of his preferred metrical forms, in which he praises various virtuous women, yet ends each stanza declaring, "My lady cometh, that al this may disteyne [sully, lessen]" (F.249-69); this repeated line allows Chaucer to perform the role of the courtly lover praising the unparalleled beauty of his beloved, as it also sets the stage for the approach of the God of Love and his queen.

Chaucer's dream assumes a forbidding tone when the God of Love and Alceste, a woman from Greek mythology known for her sacrifices for her husband, chide him for the misogynist tone of some of his literature. According to Cupid, translating the French allegory *Roman de la Rose* was a "heresye ayeins my lawe" (F.330), and Chaucer's masterpiece *Troilus and Criseyde* is found to be equally slanderous to women: "And of Creseyde thou hast seyd as the lyste, / That maketh men to wommen lasse triste [less trusting], / That ben as trewe as ever was any steel" (F.332-34). Alceste speaks up to defend Chaucer, proclaiming that he might have written his poems without misogynistic intentions: "He myghte doon yt, gessyng no malice, / But for he useth thynges for to make [create, write poetry]; / Hym rekketh noght of what matere he take" (F.363-65). She also points out that Chaucer wrote such other poems as the *House of Fame, Book of the Duchess, Parliament of Fowls*, and the Knight's Tale, which present women in a more favorable light (F.417-21). Chaucer defends himself as well: "Ne a trewe lover oght me not to blame / Thogh that I speke a fals lovere som shame" (F.466-67). Assigning Chaucer penance for his narratives maligning women, Alceste orders him to write a compendium celebrating women's virtue, and the God of Love agrees with her decision (F.475-504). Readers also learn that Alceste is symbolized by the daisy (F.517-34), and thus the flower that inspired Chaucer to leave his study for the glories of springtime now sends him back to work so that he can sing the praises of good women.

Chaucer eagerly begins this project (F.578–79), and, following the God of Love's command, selects Cleopatra as the subject of his first legend. With this story, and with many of the other legends, Chaucer reinterprets past narratives to focus his attention on women's virtues, even when the woman under consideration is not traditionally revered for any such ennobling qualities. In Cleopatra's brief story of 125 lines, Chaucer omits the background story of Julius Caesar and the first triumvirate, concentrating instead on the conflict between Antony and Octavius. Antony abandoned his wife Octavia (Octavius's sister) for Cleopatra, and after a sea battle between the two men, Antony kills himself in despair (657–61). Cleopatra proves her devotion to Antony by casting herself into a pit of snakes: "Anon the nadderes [adders] gonne hire for to stynge, / And she hire deth receyveth with good cheere / For love of Antony that was hire so dere" (699–701). Embodying the standard gender dynamics of the *Legend of Good Women*, Cleopatra showcases women's willingness to suffer for love, and Chaucer both celebrates her devotion to Antony and condemns men's inability to match women in the depth of their affections: "Now, or [before] I fynde a man thus trewe and stable, / And wol for love his deth so frely take, / I preye God let oure hedes nevere ake!" (703–5). In these lines Chaucer establishes the dominant theme of a woman's greater capacity to suffer for love than a man's. Love stimulates suffering throughout the *Legend of Good Women*, but these female protagonists embrace the powerful passivity sparked by love's pains.

Chaucer builds his theme of women's constancy in love in the following narrative, the Legend of Thisbe. Like the protagonists of Shakespeare's *Romeo and Juliet*, the two young lovers Pyramus and his beloved Thisbe are forbidden to marry, victims of familial conflict (706–36). They conspire to run away together, whispering through a chink in the wall between their houses their plan for escape (737–92). Instead of romantic triumph, however, the lovers find tragedy: Pyramus kills himself because he believes a lion has devoured Thisbe, and she commits suicide upon discovering Pyramus's body. Chaucer's detailed attention to Thisbe's grief establishes her as a model of female suffering in love (869–82), and in her death, she proves herself the equal to a man: "Here may ye se, what lovere so he be, / A woman dar and can as wel as he" (922–23).

In the Legend of Dido, Chaucer continues his theme of women driven to suicide by love's despair, turning his attention to the passages from Virgil's *Aeneid* focusing on Aeneas's shameful treatment of his lover Dido. In this version of the tale, Dido is so beautiful that even God would be hard pressed to resist her charms:

> That, if that God, that hevene and erthe made,
> Wolde han a love, for beaute and goodnesse,
> And womanhod, and trouthe, and semelynesse,
> Whom shulde he loven but this lady swete? (1039–42)

Unfortunately for Dido, her lover is not God but Aeneas, who must fulfill his destiny of conquering Italy because his homeland Troy fell to the Greeks at the conclusion of the Trojan War. In contrast to Pyramus in the Legend of Thisbe, a male suitor wholly devoted to his beloved, Aeneas in the Legend of Dido is a cad, and the narrator describes him as an amatory charlatan: "This Troyan, that so wel hire plesen can, / That feyneth [feigns] hym so trewe and obeysynge [obedient]" (1265–66). Aeneas deserts Dido, despite the fact that she is pregnant with their child, and she throws herself on a funeral pyre while plunging his sword through her heart (1343–51). Through the reiteration of his themes, Chaucer imbues his dream vision with a strong sense of the power of female constancy, yet at the same time these women who are praised for their constancy must die to prove their command of this virtue.

The Legend of Hypsipyle and Medea presents a diptych of betrayal featuring the adventurer Jason, legendary leader of the Argonauts who faced numerous trials and escapades while retrieving the Golden Fleece, and two of the women in his life, Hypsipyle and Medea. In Chaucer's narrative, Jason exemplifies not heroism and derring-do but male treachery and betrayal. He is the "rote [root, source] of false lovers" (1368), the "sly devourere and confusioun / Of gentil wemen" (1369–70), and the prologue to this legend details his deceptiveness (1368–95). This dual legend first addresses his betrayal of Hypsipyle: with Hercules playing the role of pander and convincing her of Jason's worthiness, Hypsipyle falls to his charms and they marry, but he soon deserts her (1524–63). Proving her constancy in contrast to his fecklessness, she remains true to him until death: "Ne nevere hadde she joye at hire herte, / But deyede [died] for his love, of sorwes smerte" (1578–79). In the second half of this legend, Jason meets Medea, who explains to him how to win the Golden Fleece and thus saves his life (1611–36). They marry, and she abandons her home-land to be with him, presuming they will enjoy a life of domestic bliss together with their two children; Jason, however, betrays her and marries a third time. The legend ends with Medea pondering her attraction to Jason—"Whi lykede me thy yelwe her [yellow hair] to se / More than the boundes of myn honeste?" (1672–73)—but Chaucer whitewashes aspects of Medea's legend that showcase a more troubling image of this "heroine," such as her murder of her children to avenge herself against Jason. Tales often build meaning through what they do not narrate to readers, and Chaucer's refusal to recount the deaths of Medea's children recalibrates an understanding both of this legendary woman and of feminine virtue.

Similar to Chaucer's Physician's Tale in their mutual treatment of predatory male desire, female honor, and political authority, the Legend of Lucrece explores the ways in which a woman's honor brings about the end of the corrupt Roman monarchy. The legend begins with the king's son Tarquinius discussing the merits of women with his comrades: "And lat us speke of wyves, that is best; / Preyse every man his owene as hym lest, / And with oure speche lat us ese oure herte" (1702–4). Collatinus offers his wife Lucretia as a model of female virtue, and his words are proven true when the men silently sneak into their home and spy on her (1705–44). Inflamed with lust, Tarquinius rapes her (1745–1811), but Lucretia determinedly preserves her honor by killing herself:

"Be as be may," quod she, "of forgyvyng,
I wol not have noo forgyft for nothing."
But pryvely she kaughte forth a knyf,
And therwithal she rafte hirself hir lyf [took her own life]. (1852–55)

The Romans, outraged by Lucretia's rape and suicide, banish Tarquinius and praise the memory of Lucretia as a model of female virtue (1861–73). The Roman monarchy collapses due to Tarquinius's tyrannical behav-ior—"Ne never was ther kyng in Rome toun / Syn thilke [Since that] day" (1869–70)—and thus Lucretia's suffering not only proves the power of female virtue but connects it to foundational governmental reforms as well.

Much like Jason in the Legend of Hypsipyle and Medea, who relies on a woman's assistance to overcome an overwhelming obstacle and then forsakes her, Theseus plays the cad in the Legend of Ariadne (in contrast to his more heroic role in Chaucer's Knight's Tale). Ariadne's father Minos orders Theseus to be sacrificed to the Minotaur (1928–51), but, after consulting with her sister Phaedra, Ariadne instructs him how to defeat the beast and escape the labyrinth (1952–2156). Theseus rewards her for her assistance with a shockingly ugly act of betrayal—abandoning her on an island and running away with Phaedra. As Chaucer narrates, Theseus selects Phaedra for her physical beauty rather than Ariadne for her resourcefulness:

> Whan Adryane his wif aslepe was,
> For that hire syster fayrer was than she,
> He taketh hire in his hond and forth goth he
> To shipe, and as a traytour stal [stole] his wey. (2171–74)

As Lucretia in her legend is venerated as a saint for her unwarranted suffering, Ariadne is compensated for her lover's betrayal when the gods turn her into a constellation: "The goddes han hire holpen for pite [pity], / And in the signe of Taurus men may se / The stones of hire corone [crown] shyne clere" (2222–24). Like many of her fellow suffering heroines in the *Legend of Good Women*, Ariadne dies as a result of her blighted love, yet she glimmers in the heavens as a reminder to all of her steadfast devotion.

The Legend of Philomela returns Chaucer's collection of tales to the theme of rape first depicted in the Legend of Lucrece. It recounts the story of Tereus, who journeys to bring his wife Procne's sister Philomela to their home for a visit (2244–78). Upon viewing Philomela, Tereus is seized by lust—"He caste his fyry herte upon hyre [her] so / That he wol have hir, how so that it go" (2292–93)—and brings her to a cave where he rapes her (2308–26). Further proving the horrid cruelty associated with male sexual desire, Tereus cuts out her tongue so that she cannot expose his crimes (2330–41). Although bereft of speech, Philomela weaves the story of her rape into a tapestry, and Procne reunites with her:

> Allas! The wo, the compleynt, and the mone [moan, lament]
> That Progne upon hire doumbe [dumb, mute] syster maketh!
> In armes everych of hem other taketh,
> And thus I late hem in here sorwe dwelle. (2379–82)

Chaucer appends an anodyne moral to this tale—"Ye may be war of men" (2387)—but as he does in his editing of the story of Medea, in which he omits the murder of her children, here he elides the conclusion of the story of Procne and Philomela, in which Procne kills her son Itys and cooks him as dinner for Tereus. The legend of Procne and Philomela is traditionally an etiological tale, as the three main characters transform into birds at the myth's conclusion—Tereus into a hoopoe, Procne into a swallow, and Philomela into a nightingale. Chaucer, however, concludes his legend with female suffering rather than with revenge and magical transformations, thus preserving his depiction of woman as suffering steadfastly rather than avenging cruelly.

"Like father, like son": this axiom serves as, if not the moral, the theme of the Legend of Phyllis, in which readers meet Theseus's son Demophon, who equals his father in his shoddy treatment of women. The narrative pattern of the *Legend of Good Women*—in which a cad meets a virtuous woman, who falls for the cad, believes the cad loves her, and is then rejected by the cad—is well established at this point, and the Legend of Phyllis adheres to the familiar structure. After being tossed about by a storm at sea, Demophon and his ship land on Phyllis's island. She instantly feels a strong attraction to him—"This honurable Phillis doth hym chere; / Hire liketh wel his port [bearing, deportment] and his manere" (2452–53)—and he promises to marry her (2472–74). He then leaves, never to return, and she commits suicide (2475–86).

With this plotline in danger of devolving into the formulaic, Chaucer hints that he is growing weary of these tales:

But, for I am agroted [have had my fill] herebyforn
To wryte of hem that ben in love forsworn,
And ek to haste me in my legende,
(Which to performe God me grace sende)
Therfore I passe shortly in this wyse. (2454–58)

Indeed, acting almost as inappropriately as his character Pandarus in *Troilus and Criseyde*, Chaucer appears to flirt with the female members of his audience when he reports Phyllis's suicide:

She for dispeyr [despair] fordide [killed] hyrself, allas.
Swych sorwe hath she, for she besette hire so.
Be war, ye wemen, of youre subtyl fo [foe],
Syn yit this day men may ensaumple se;
And trusteth, as in love, no man but me. (2557–61)

The only man whom women can trust, Chaucer invites his female readers to take solace in him. (We have no record of how Chaucer's wife Philippa reacted to her husband's generous invitation.)

The last tale of the *Legend of Good Women* recounts the story of Hypermnestra, whose father Aegyptus marries her to his nephew Lynceus, the son of his brother Danaus. Aegyptus commands her to murder Lynceus on their wedding night, since he has dreamed that his nephew will destroy him (2653–62). Hypermnestra finds that she cannot kill her husband and warns Lynceus to flee, which he does—but without her (2678–2722). Again, Chaucer omits much of his mythical source materials, including that Aegyptus and Danaus have one hundred children between them and that Hypermnestra's forty-nine sisters heed their father's command on their wedding night to slay their husbands. He also switches the names Aegyptus and Danaus, as the former is typically the father of the sons and the latter the father of the daughters. The Legend of Hypermnestra is unfinished, breaking off as the narrator promises his moral (2723), and thus ends *Legend of Good Women*.

It is likely that additional legends of good women were lost, or at least planned, as Chaucer refers to his "book of the XXV. Ladies" in his Retraction to the *Canterbury Tales*. Furthermore, in the Introduction to the Man of Law's Tale, the Man of Law jests with Chaucer by mentioning "his large volume" of "noble wyves" (2.59–60), and he lists stories that have not survived as part of the *Legend of Good Women*, including narratives of Deianira, Hermione, Hero, Helen of Troy, Briseyde, Laodomia, and Penelope (2.66–76). Despite these missing wives, Chaucer's *Legend of Good Women* intriguingly exposes the gendered dynamics of mythic literature and its influence on his conception of himself as a writer of the fourteenth century. This collection of legendary materials presents womanly virtue as dependent upon suffering, betrayal, and passivity, as it concomitantly portrays masculine misconduct in amatory affairs. Regrettably, since *Legend of Good Women* lacks the expected ending of a dream vision—which here would likely see Chaucer returning to Cupid and Alceste's court, or at least waking and pondering the meaning of his dream—it is difficult to draw conclusions about Chaucer's personal stance in his treatment of these many good women. Yet there is much to admire in his select compendium of womanly virtue as inspired by the classical tradition, particularly his vivid descriptions of amatory conflict, the heartfelt scenes of betrayal, and Chaucer's ironic stance toward his own fiction as he turns various women of varying degrees of virtue into the stuff of legend.

Troilus and Criseyde

BOOK 1

For such a lively and engaging poem, *Troilus and Criseyde* begins rather mournfully. In this multigeneric masterpiece, Chaucer intermingles elements of romance, epic, comedy, and tragedy, but tragedy overshadows these other genres in the opening stanza:

> The double sorwe [sorrow] of Troilus to tellen,
> That was the kyng Priamus sone of Troye,
> In lovynge, how his aventures fellen
> Fro wo to wele, and after out of joie,
> My purpos is, er that I parte fro ye.
> Thesiphone, thow help me for t'endite [to compose]
> Thise woful vers, that wepen as I write. (1.1–7)

With these words, Chaucer encapsulates the Boethian tragedy unfolding for his protagonist: Troilus will rise from his current depths to enjoy the pleasures of love, but only to fall into utter anguish when his romance ends. Fate, as allegorized in Lady Fortune capriciously spinning her wheel, establishes a narrative pattern for *Troilus and Criseyde*, in which book 1 portrays Troilus as unsuccessful in love and ignorant of how to pursue his beloved, book 2 depicts his tentative courtship of Criseyde, and book 3 features the two lovers united in bliss; books 4 and 5, in contrast, depict Troilus's inexorable descent into heartache, misery, and death.

By invoking the Fury Thesiphone rather than one of the Muses in his opening lines, Chaucer's narrator further builds the tragic cast of the romance. The initial stanzas focus primarily on Troilus's incipient tragedy, but the narrator builds on the theme of sorrow's doubleness by mentioning Criseyde's death when concluding his introduction to the poem:

> For now wil I gon streght to my matere,
> In which ye may the double sorwes here
> Of Troilus in lovynge of Criseyde,
> And how that she forsook hym er she deyde. (1.53–56)

From this grim beginning, readers see that neither of the protagonists survives their love affair. Chaucer does not depict Criseyde's death in his account of this Trojan love story, but by reminding readers of her eventual demise, he further imbues his prologue with a sense of insurmountable sorrow.

When Criseyde is first introduced against the epic backdrop of the Trojan War, which the Greeks and Trojans have waged for years, her precarious situation shows her to be a woman both capable in her abilities and yet dependent on masculine forbearance. Her father Calkas has betrayed the Trojans and fled to the Greeks (1.64–91), and she is left to fend for herself among her countrymen, who share the general sentiment that Calkas's family are "worthi for to brennen [burn], fel [skin] and bones" (1.91). Criseyde escapes this threatened execution by petitioning Troilus's brother Hector, the king's eldest son, for mercy, which he grants (1.106–26). These early scenes emphasize Criseyde's tenuous circumstances among the Trojans: her father's treason casts her in mortal peril, yet her quick actions save her. At the same time, a woman's agency is circumscribed within Troy, as she must save herself by acting through a man. Criseyde's awareness of the dangers of living in Troy can never be discounted as a motivating factor in her decisions, especially when her behavior appears otherwise inscrutable. She is both the imperious courtly lady of the romance tradition, wielding amatory authority over Troilus's fate, and a woman often intimidated by those around her, who might view her as a traitor to their cause and execute or banish her.

While Criseyde manages a strategic reliance on others to assist her, Troilus is soon mired in passivity and thus serves as a suitable (if somewhat exaggerated) hero of courtly romance. Love so overwhelms him that he cannot act without his lady's love; in the scene when he first espies Criseyde, he is struck dumb by her attractiveness. As opposed to Troilus's stasis, Criseyde's reaction highlights her often indecipherable nature:

> To Troilus right wonder wel with alle
> Gan for [Began] to like hire mevynge [movement] and hire chere [appearance],
> Which somdel deignous [somewhat haughty] was, for she let falle
> Hire look a lite aside in swich manere,
> Ascaunces [as if to say], "What, may I nat stonden here?" (1.288–92)

Despite the slight arrogance in her pose, Criseyde piques Troilus's attention, but his burgeoning passion cannot save him from his striking ineptitude as a lover. Primarily, he hides his affections from Criseyde and all other Trojans, with the narrator repeatedly commenting on his antierotic affectations: "His woo he gan dissimilen and hide" (1.322); "Al feyneth he in lust [pleasure] that he sojorneth" (1.326); "First to hiden his desir in muwe [secret] / From every wight [person] yborn" (1.381–82). Within the romance tradition, lovers are frequently rendered passive by love's immobilizing force, yet Troilus appears to be an especially static suitor.

Given Troilus's inability to win Criseyde's love by himself, the plot requires a catalyst to advance the erotic action at the heart of its romance, and this catalyst is Pandarus. Few literary characters's names have entered the language as a noun and a verb, yet Pandarus's primary action—his pandering, or pimping—propels Troilus into amatory games the young Trojan would never undertake through his own volition. Pandarus finds Troilus "[b]ywayling in his chambre thus allone" (1.547) and determines to help his friend overcome his sorrow. Throughout their lengthy conversation (1.547–1061), readers learn much about Pandarus's character, especially through his relentless pursuit of Troilus's confidences. Foremost, Pandarus believes that love should be a delightful, if at times somewhat devious, pursuit. When he senses that Troilus will confess Criseyde's name, he cries out, "A ha! . . . Here bygynneth game" (1.868), a line suggesting that he views love as a pleasant and playful pastime rather than as a matter of profound and serious devotion. Toward the conclusion of their dialogue, in which Troilus has steadfastly refused to reveal the identity of his beloved, the young Trojan finally relents and names her:

> And with that word he [Pandarus] gan hym for to shake,
> And seyde, "Thef, thow shalt hyre [her] name telle."
> But tho [then] gan sely [innocent] Troilus for to quake
> As though men sholde han led hym into helle,
> And seyde, "Allas, of al my wo the welle [source],
> Thanne is my swete fo [foe] called Criseyde!"
> And wel neigh with the word for feere he deide [died]. (1.869–75)

The hyperbolic cast of the scene, with Troilus shaking in hellish dread and nearly dying for simply uttering Criseyde's name, highlights the comic excesses of the romance tradition that create an underlying thread of levity in matters of utmost seriousness. Troilus's heightened emotions indicate his sincere devotion to his beloved, yet they also gently mock the romance tradition for its overly passive lovers.

Romances frequently depict go-betweens arranging trysts for lovers, and although Pandarus assists both Troilus and Criseyde in their incipient relationship, his role in their affair is predicated more upon his devotion to Troilus than to Criseyde. Notwithstanding that he is her uncle (2.87, 2.98, and passim), he sides with Troilus throughout the relationship, scheming to promote his friend's suit in winning her hand. Pandarus's motivations are amorphous, but in an intriguing passage he implies that his role as an intermediary satisfies his own desires:

"Wherfore I am, and wol ben, ay redy [always ready]
To peyne me to do yow this servyse;
For both yow to plese thus hope I
Herafterward; for ye ben bothe wyse
And konne it counseil kepe in swych [such] a wyse
That no man shal the wiser of it be;
And so we may ben gladed alle thre." (1.988–94)

Pandarus suggests that, in helping his friend to seduce his niece, he too will find pleasure, and here Chaucer points to the tangled erotic work often glossed over in chivalric romances. Certainly, Troilus's words when he thanks Pandarus for his help—"Mi lif, my deth, hol [wholly] in thyn hond I leye" (1.1053)—reveal the deep bond between the two men. Bringing lovers together frequently requires duplicity and deviousness, and Pandarus proves readily capable of advancing this affair through unscrupulous tactics, yet it is enigmatically unclear how his desires are sated through matchmaking.

Because of Troilus's overwhelming passivity as a lover, it is easy for readers to overlook the ways in which Chaucer incorporates the masculine heroism expected of epic protagonists, along the lines of Achilles in Homer's *Iliad* and Aeneas in Virgil's *Aeneid*, into this character. At key points throughout *Troilus and Criseyde*, the narrator reminds readers that, despite the young knight's fecklessness in love, few men are braver on the battlefield than Troilus:

But Troilus lay tho [then] no lenger down,
But up anon upon his stede [steed] bay [brownish red],

And in the feld he pleyde tho leoun [lion];
Wo was that Grek that with hym mette a-day!
And in the town his manere tho forth ay
So goodly was, and gat hym so in grace,
That ecch hym loved that loked on his face. (1.1072–78)

Troilus's love, as yet undeclared to his beloved, inspires him to military and moral greatness. Here romance and epic blend to create the quintessential hero as a combination of lover and warrior, and Troilus embodies both the languishing passivity expected of a lover and the military activity expected of a hero. While enjoying the love games and military exploits of *Troilus and Criseyde*, however, readers should never forget what they know before beginning this narrative: the Greeks will win the Trojan War, and therefore any happiness experienced in Troy can only be temporary, as nearly all of the Trojans, including Troilus, will soon die. In this poetic masterpiece, tragedy should never be forgotten, although Chaucer frequently encourages readers to overlook its almost palpable presence in favor of the transitory pleasures of romance.

BOOK 2

For the romance between Troilus and Criseyde to flourish, she must first learn of his affections, and Pandarus energetically shuttles back and forth between the two. Visiting Criseyde, he encourages her to prepare herself for love, but she does not see herself as a romance heroine (such as Guinevere in the Arthurian legends or Tristan's Isolde); rather, she proclaims her desire for an introspective life as a widow. The lines of dialogue between uncle and niece contrast sharply, with Pandarus attempting to lure her into a world of romance and play, cajoling her, "Do wey [put away] youre book, rys up, and lat us daunce, / And lat us don to May som observaunce" (2.111–12); Criseyde, however, replies with mild consternation at such an idea: "I! God forbede! . . . Be ye mad? / Is that a widewes lif, so God yow save?" (2.113–14). Discerning Criseyde's true motivations throughout *Troilus and Criseyde* is difficult because her words and actions often fail to correspond, and such is the case in this scene, since she also tells Pandarus that it would be better for her to ensconce herself "in a cave / To bidde [pray] and rede on holy seyntes lyves" (2.117–18). If Criseyde believes she should lead a pious life of solitude while contemplating the moral examples espoused in hagiographies, it is ironic that, before Pandarus enters, readers see her enjoying with her girlfriends the rather lurid "romaunce . . . of Thebes" in which "kyng Layus deyde / Thorugh Edippus his sone" (2.100–102). Such a mild instance of hypocrisy does not necessarily malign Criseyde's character, but it highlights Chaucer's detailed attention to how his characters react to shifting circumstances.

The beginning of book 2 asks readers to gauge the actions of the characters in comparison to the truthfulness of their words, and numerous discrepancies arise. Criseyde presents herself as uninterested in love; however, when she sees Troilus on horseback while Trojans praise him for his prowess in battle, she becomes intoxicated with love, wondering to herself, "Who yaf me drynke?" (2.651). Pandarus declares to Criseyde that he would never act as a pimp for Troilus's pleasure: "And also think wel that this is no gaude [deception]; / For me were levere [I would prefer that] thow and I and he / Were hanged, than I sholde ben his baude [pimp]" (2.351–53). Readers soon perceive that Pandarus repeatedly manipulates Criseyde so that she will accept Troilus as her lover, and so it is hard to trust his repeated declarations of innocent intentions. Even Troilus engages in numerous deceptions in this romance. For example, Pandarus coaches him on the necessary rhetorical strategies for writing a letter to his beloved (2.1023–43), and Troilus employs this advice to advance his cause, even though he lies in the letter: "And after that he seyde—and leigh ful loude [blatantly lied]—/ Hymself was litel worth, and lasse he koude [less he could do]" (2.1077–78). Of course, Troilus is presenting himself modestly in this letter, but with the narrator describing his words as a lie, the scene presages the imminent deployment of even more deceptions in this game of love.

The escalating frisson of romance in *Troilus and Criseyde* is leavened with comic moments, especially Pandarus's frenetic shuffling between the two lovers, yet an undertone of impending tragedy further builds the amorous tension. Chaucer repeatedly rhymes the words *seye* and *deye* in his characters' voices, such as when Pandarus threatens Criseyde with Troilus's death, should she not agree to accept him as her lover: "Lo, here is al! What sholde I moore seye? / Doth what yow lest to make hym lyve or deye" (2.321–22). Pandarus's words are hyperbolic—lovesickness is rarely fatal—but he soon returns to this theme, warning Criseyde that not only Troilus but he too will die should she refuse the young man's love: "But sith I se my lord mot nedes dye, / And I with hym, here I me shryve [confess], and seye / That wikkedly ye don us bothe deye" (2.439–41). Passages similar to these achieve their intended effect, as Criseyde agrees to hear of Troilus's love, but they also remind the reader of the imminent defeat and death of all Trojans. The epic matter of the Trojan War provides a martial backdrop to Troilus and Criseyde's nascent love story, and this material encourages readers to consider whether an individual's pursuit of love is ethical while the community is struggling for survival.

In the overarching narrative trajectory, book 2 must bring Troilus and Criseyde together so that they can talk privately. To achieve this goal, Pandarus orchestrates a complex web of lies: he tells Troilus's brother Deiphebus that some men are harassing Criseyde and that she needs his help (2.1415–21); he tells Criseyde that a man named Poliphete plans to sue her, which, given her tenuous position in Trojan society, terrifies her (2.1464–70); and he convinces Troilus to malinger so that he, Pandarus, can arrange a moment of privacy for them (2.1513–26). These plans proceed smoothly, and Criseyde arrives in Troilus's sickroom so she can request his assistance in defending herself against Poliphete's supposed lawsuit. As the two meet face-to-face as potential lovers, book 2 ends with an emotional cliffhanger expressed in a *demande d'amour*:

> But now to yow, ye lovers that ben here,
> Was Troilus nought in a kankedort [tricky situation, predicament],
> That lay, and myghte whisprynge of hem here,
> And thoughte, "O Lord, right now renneth my sort [destiny]
> Fully to deye, or han anon comfort!"
> And was the firste tyme he shulde hire preye
> Of love; O myghty God, what shal he seye? (2.1751–57)

Throughout *Troilus and Criseyde*, the narrator asks readers to envision themselves as lovers and to imagine how they would react to circumstances similar to the ones facing Troilus. In the options Troilus sees before him—death or love—the plot of the poem is encapsulated in its naked simplicity. The climax of this scene, with the audience left to ponder how Troilus will represent himself as a lover, immediately closes off the question it has proffered, and the sweet delay of knowledge only sparks deeper anticipation for the erotic consummation depicted in book 3.

BOOK 3

The romance of *Troilus and Criseyde* climaxes as the lovers come together for a night of passion (and, for the reader, of rich humor). In the midst of romance, though, the pall of tragedy cannot be overlooked, as the text's concomitant interest in Boethian tragedy depicts Troilus at the height of happiness only to contrast it with his descent into despair in the fourth and fifth books. Notwithstanding the great joy depicted in the lovers' union, book 3 also offers numerous reasons why their love should not be consummated, as well as foreshadowings of its heartbreaking end.

Foremost, Criseyde does not desire a sexual relationship with Troilus. The courtly lady of romance frequently represents an ennobling yet ultimately chaste figure, one who inspires men to greatness with no expectation that she would degrade her pure love by engaging in its carnal enactments. While meeting Troilus at Deiphebus's house, Criseyde underscores the parameters of her love, as well as her determination to remain independent:

"But natheles, this warne I yow," quod she,
"A kynges sone although ye be, ywys,
Ye shal namore han sovereignete
Of me in love, than right in that cas is;
N'y nyl forbere [Nor will I forbear], if that ye don amys,
To wratthe yow; and whil that ye me serve,
Chericen yow right after ye disserve." (3.169–75)

Criseyde respects Troilus's secular position as a king's son, but she grants him no such accompanying authority in their amatory relationship. With her threat to "wratthe" him should he misbehave, it is clear that she establishes limits to their affair, reinforcing her position as the austere yet inspiring courtly lady of romance.

Criseyde's stance on a chaste relationship with Troilus necessitates that Pandarus and his young friend engage in yet more deceptions. Although Pandarus declared earlier that he would never act as a pimp, he now promises Troilus to play just such a role: "That is to seye, for the [you] am I bicomen, / Bitwixen game and ernest, swich a meene [mean, midpoint] / As maken wommen unto men to comen" (3.253–55). Given Criseyde's resistance to a love affair, maneuvering her into bed with Troilus requires much trickery, and even Fate's intervention. Pandarus invites Criseyde to dinner, telling her that Troilus is out of town (3.554–74), and when she plans to depart, Fortune, the "executrice of wierdes" (3.617), sends a rainstorm to trap her in Pandarus's house for the evening. Criseyde goes to bed in the supposed safety of a "myddel chambre" where her female companions will sleep nearby (3.666–72), but Pandarus sneaks into her bedroom by means of a "secre trappe-dore" (3.759) and tells her that Troilus is distraught because he believes she is betraying him with a man named Horaste (3.792–98). Thus misled and manipulated, Criseyde allows Troilus to enter her bedchamber (3.953–59). Her power as the courtly lady of romance has been tempered through Fate's intervention and Pandarus's prevarications, and it is difficult to assess her agency in the unfolding romance.

Troilus's arrival upsets Criseyde. He in turn becomes upset that she is upset, and thus Chaucer imbues the scene with a seriocomic tone that amuses readers while maintaining the tension inherent in their as yet unconsummated romance. This escalating emotional distress results in the comic climax of book 3: Troilus faints (3.1079–92). Pandarus immediately if improbably creates erotic possibilities out of a fainting lover:

This was no litel sorwe for to se;
But al was hust [quieted, hushed], and Pandare up as faste;
. . . .
And seyde, "O thef, is this a mannes herte?"   .
And of [off] he rente [tore] al to his bare sherte,

And seyde, "Nece, but ye helpe us now,
Allas, youre owen Troilus is lorn [lost]!" (3.1093–1101)

In such situations, love's curative powers are called for, and Criseyde graciously supplies her kisses to revive Troilus (3.1114–20), even though she still suspects that she is being duped. She has earlier warned Troilus not to press her beyond the chaste enjoyment of courtly love, and now she sternly asks him, "Is this a mannes game? / What, Troilus, wol ye do thus for shame?" (3.1126–27). In spite of her hesitations, Criseyde and Troilus share a night of passion, and the narrator provides luxurious descriptions of Troilus's enjoyment of her beautiful body in a highly eroticized blazon (3.1247–53).

Subverting the high romance of Troilus and Criseyde's love, which has been effected mostly through Pandarus's deceptions, numerous signs point ironically to the immediate undoing of their relationship. Chaucer refuses to paint these moments clearly, giving conflicting signals about the emotional importance and mutuality of the lovers' affections. For example, the narrator reports that, as part of their night of pleasure, they "pleyinge entrechaungeden hire rynges" (3.1368). An exchange of rings alludes to rites of marriage, and would be accepted as such according to medieval practice, but what does it signify that they did so in a "pleyinge" manner? Here the frequent Chaucerian tension between earnest and game, which is virtually ubiquitous in the *Canterbury Tales*, appears, and this tension complicates efforts to discern how seriously readers should view the lovers' actions. Also, Criseyde tells Troilus, "Now God, thow woost, in thought ne dede [deed] untrewe / To Troilus was nevere yet Criseyde" (3.1053–54). These words might convey Criseyde's heartfelt devotion to Troilus, but through the simple adverb "yet" they also convey her eventual betrayal by implying that she has been faithful to date but reserves the right to be unfaithful in the future.

Additional lines that give some readers pause narrate a scene between Criseyde and Pandarus, after Troilus has left his beloved the following morning:

I passe al that which chargeth nought to seye.
What! God foryaf [forgave] his deth, and she al so
Foryaf, and with here uncle gan to pleye,
For other cause was ther noon than so.
But of this thing right to the effect to go:
Whan tyme was, hom til here hous she wente,
And Pandarus hath fully his entente. (3.1576–82)

Do these lines obliquely hint at incest between uncle and niece? The opening line of the stanza declares that the narrator will pass over a matter he considers improper for the reader's attention, yet by telling the reader he will not address such a matter, he in fact addresses it tacitly. He then alludes to the "pleye" that the two share, and the word "pleye" often carries sexual connotations in Middle English. Chaucer refuses to signify clearly with these ambiguous lines, but this refusal leads some readers to suspect that Troilus and Criseyde's romance is undermined even more and that the climax of the romance is immediately subverted by signs of sexual betrayal.

Unaware of any potentially untoward acts between his lover and her uncle, Troilus reaches the heights of his happiness at the close of book 3.

He sings his "Canticus Troili," a song praising the power of love to ensnare him and other lovers:

"So wolde God, that auctour is of kynde,
That with his bond Love of his vertu liste
To cerclen hertes alle and faste bynde,
That from his bond no wight [person] the wey out wiste [knows]."
    (3.1765–68)

Love is a joyful prison, a blissful ensnarement, and Troilus seeks nothing more than to maintain the perfection of his life at this moment. The Trojan War proceeds apace outside the gates of the city, and Troilus continues to prove himself a mighty warrior of the epic tradition (3.1772–78). The narrator concludes book 3 with his protagonists secure in their love—"And Troilus in lust and in quiete / Is with Criseyde, his owen herte swete" (3.1819–20)—but within a Boethian worldview, happiness is a temporary moment of bliss in preparation for heart-wrenching loss, and book 4 begins the downward spiral destined to destroy Troilus's happiness.

BOOK 4

Since Fortune's wheel continually turns, Troilus, the devoted lover of romance and fearsome soldier of epic, soon faces unexpected challenges to his amatory bliss. This theme is proclaimed in the opening stanza of book 4's prologue:

But al to litel, weylaway the whyle [alas for that occasion],
Lasteth swich joie, ythonked be Fortune,
That semeth trewest whan she wol bygyle [deceive]
And kan to fooles so hire song entune
That she hem hent [seizes] and blent [blinds], traitour comune!
And whan a wight is from hire whiel ythrowe [thrown],
Than laugheth she, and maketh hym the mowe [grimace]. (4.1–7)

Fortune delights in inflicting life's vagaries on those whom she dupes into momentary happiness, and such is the case for Troilus. Following the structure of Boethian tragedy, Troilus must now suffer, and neither his successes as a lover nor as a warrior can prevent his downfall.

Troilus's troubles begin in the Trojan Parliament, which decides to send Criseyde to the Greeks in exchange for Antenor, a captured Trojan elder. In this scene the communal focus on an epic struggle eclipses Troilus's concern for his personal romance. (The trade was not a wise one: Antenor later betrayed the Trojans, leading to their cataclysmic defeat.) Hector honorably defends Criseyde: "Syres, she nys no prisonere," he points out, adding, "We usen here no wommen for to selle" (4.179, 182). Troilus, on the other hand, remains quiet:

> This Troilus was present in the place
> Whan axed [asked] was for Antenor Criseyde,
> For which ful soone chaungen gan his face,
> As he that with tho [those] words wel neigh [nearly] deyde.
> But natheles he no word to it seyde,
> Lest men sholde his affeccioun espye;
> With mannes herte he gan his sorwes drye [endure]. (4.148–54)

This is a puzzling moment in the text for many readers, as Troilus's silence can only increase his unhappiness. His affair with Criseyde has been cloaked in secrecy, but if Hector can speak up to defend her, there seems little reason for Troilus not to join his brother in advocating for her continued presence in Troy. This paradox in Troilus's character—valiant warrior, cowardly lover—is predicated upon the need for secrecy in courtly love affairs. In his declaration of the "rules" of courtly love, the twelfth-century author Andreas Capellanus notes, "When made public, love rarely endures,"[2] and Chaucer adheres to this trope of romance rather literally, even when it leaves his protagonist's inactivity unfathomable to readers.

Turning to Pandarus in his crisis, Troilus finds little solace because the two men hold conflicting views regarding love's value. For the pander, one woman is as good as another, and he believes Criseyde can be easily replaced: "Forthi be glad, myn owen deere brother! / If she be lost, we shal recovere an other" (4.405–6). He tries to convince Troilus to forget about Criseyde, telling him, "Absence of hire shal dryve hire out of herte" (4.427), but when Troilus demurs, he suggests an absurdly inappropriate solution: "Go ravysshe [abduct] here [her]!" (4.530). Given that the Trojan War is waged over Paris's abduction of Helen from her husband Menelaus (1.57–63), Pandarus's advice (as well as the Trojan parliament's decision) ironically shows how little Trojan men have learned about treating women properly, and about the brutal repercussions of their folly. From the traditions of both romance and epic, Pandarus's suggestions are shockingly misguided, and this mostly comic character can thus do little to assist Troilus with his imperiled romance.

Pandarus, with his blithe disregard for love, cannot empathize with Troilus, yet he continues to play his role as go-between for the two lovers. The romance that brought such delight in book 3, for the readers as well as for the characters, now devolves into a tragic and mournful affair. In his subsequent meeting with Criseyde, Pandarus witnesses her near-fatal suffering:

> She was right swich to seen in hire visage [face]
> As is that wight that men on beere [funeral bier] bynde;
> Hire face, lik of Paradys the ymage,
> Was al ychaunged in another kynde.
> The pleye, the laughter, men was wont to fynde
> On hire, and ek hire joies everichone,
> Ben fled; and thus lith now Criseyde allone. (4.862–68)

Criseyde's pain virtually palpitates in this scene, rendering her an image of the living dead. Momentarily overcoming her pain, she agrees to meet with Troilus to help him conquer his agonies, as Pandarus requests: "And shapeth yow his sorwe for t'abregge [abridge], / And nought encresse, leeve [dear] nece swete!" (4.925–26). Criseyde will soon jilt Troilus for Diomede, but these scenes establish her deep love for him, making her eventual betrayal of him all the more inexplicable and her character all the more inscrutable.

When the two lovers meet to discuss their sad fate, the tryst almost ends fatally in a scene similar to the legendary story of Pyramus and Thisbe, who slay themselves rather than live without each other (as told by Chaucer in *LGW* 706–923). In an inversion of Troilus's faint in book 3 (which led to the consummation of their love), Criseyde now faints, but Troilus believes that she has died. Seeing no hope for happiness in his future, he determines to join her in the afterlife:

> And after this, with sterne and cruel herte,
> His swerd anon out of his shethe he twighte [pulled]
> Hymself to slen [slay], how sore that hym smerte,
> So that his soule hire soule folwen myghte. (4.1184–87)

Troilus's death is delayed when Criseyde awakens from her swoon, but this reprieve is short-lived, as his tragedy draws ever nearer to its fatal conclusion in book 5. His faint in book 3 catalyzed sexual union with his beloved, but Criseyde's faint catalyzes only the lovers' desperate but ineffective attempts to remain together.

As much as the courtly lady of romance wields ultimate authority over her beloved, Criseyde can do little to alter the circumstances surrounding her trade for Antenor (and, concomitantly, her expulsion from Troy) because she is no longer in a romance in terms of genre. Now that tragedy and epic are subsuming romance and comedy, her authority dissipates. Book 4 concludes as the lovers plan for Criseyde to return from the Greeks, and she declares her emphatic intention to return:

> "Now, that I shal wel bryngen it aboute
> To come ayeyn, soone after that I go,
> Therof am I no manere thyng in doute [doubt];
> For, dredeles, withinne a wowke [week] or two
> I shal ben here; and that it may be so
> By alle right and in a wordes fewe,
> I shal yow wel an heep of weyes shewe." (4.1275–81)

Criseyde's optimism brightens the scene, as she elucidates the advantages of her plan: after she returns, the Trojans will have both Antenor and her (4.1310–16). The narrator defends Criseyde, saying that "al this thyng was seyd of good entente" and that "hire herte trewe was and kynde" (4.1416–17), but these defenses must stand against her betrayal coming shortly in book 5.

In this deteriorating situation, the courtly lady of romance and the valiant hero of epic are both powerless. Mulling their limited options, Troilus proposes that the two should run away together: "I mene thus: that syn we mowe er day / Wel stele awey and ben togidere so" (4.1506–7). It is a craven suggestion, and Criseyde rejects it because people would think him cowardly and her promiscuous:

> "They wolden seye, and swere it out of doute,
> That love ne drof [drove] yow naught to don this dede,
> But lust voluptuous and coward drede.
> . . . .
> And also thynketh on myn honeste,
> That floureth [flowers] yet, how foule I sholde it shende [ruin],
> And with what filthe it spotted sholde be,
> If in this forme I sholde with yow wende [depart]." (4.1571–79)

Criseyde appears the more confident of the lovers in her insistence that she can escape from the Greeks and return to her beloved Troilus. In an inverse scene to the conclusion of book 2, which ends with the cliffhanger of Troilus's imminent speech to Criseyde so that he can declare his love, book 4 concludes with the two lovers nervously awaiting their enforced separation.

BOOK 5

"Now holde youre day, and do me nat to deye" (5.84), Troilus beseeches Criseyde as she is traded to the Greeks, but the tragic cast of *Troilus and Criseyde* inescapably bears down upon the lovers. Book 5 moves with a sense of grim determination to Troilus's death, foreshadowed as it is in these words, and Criseyde's motivations in her love affairs become increasingly difficult to gauge. Upon joining the Greeks, she meets a new suitor, the suavely unctuous Diomede, who promises Criseyde that he will act as a brother to her (5.134). His fraternal protestations, however, are belied by his amorous advances. In contrast to Troilus's initial inability to pursue Criseyde (without Pandarus's assistance), Diomede is depicted as a relentless lothario masterfully playing the game of love "[w]ith al the sleghte [cunning] and al that evere he kan" (5.773). The narrator reports, "To fisshen hire he leyde out hook and lyne" (5.777), and the imagery of a sportsman setting out bait to trap his prey appropriately captures Diomede's predatory view of love.

As troubling as Diomede's lasciviousness is Criseyde's duplicity, as she baldly denies her love for Troilus in a discussion with her new suitor:

> "But as to speke of love, ywis," she seyde,
> "I hadde a lord, to whom I wedded was,
> The whos myn herte al was, til that he deyde;
> And other love, as help me now Pallas [the goddess Athena],
> Ther in myn herte nys [is not], ne nevere was." (5.974–78)

Her deceased husband, as Criseyde swears to Diomede, was the only lover in her life. Moreover, she realizes that, when her affair with Diomede becomes known, she will be disparaged for her decision to forsake Troilus—"No good word, for thise bokes [books] wol me shende [disgrace]. / O, rolled shal I ben on many a tonge!" (5.1060–61). Despite her fears for her reputation, she proceeds with her decision: "To Diomede algate [at any rate] I wol be trewe" (5.1071). In sum, Criseyde is an attractive but flawed heroine, one whose moral failings are marked on her body. Although she is peerless in her attractiveness, the narrator mentions one feature that mars her striking perfection: "And, save hire browes joyneden yfeere [together], / Ther nas no lak, in aught I kan espien" (5.813–14). The joining of the eyebrows—a "unibrow" in popular parlance—that sabotages her otherwise matchless beauty marks the inconstancy that tarnishes her character, and the narrator ends this passage by describing her as "[t]endre-herted, slydynge of corage" (5.825). These words emblematically capture her wavering spirit, in which fears incited by the precariousness of her position in both Trojan and Greek societies trump her affections for Troilus. Although Criseyde loves Troilus faithfully within the world of romance, the force of epic history overrides her amatory desires and renders her incapable of remaining true to him.

Much of book 5 addresses Troilus's growing despair, his dawning realization that Criseyde will not return to him, as the narrative increasingly focuses on its generic shift from romance to tragedy. Pandarus attempts to distract his friend's attention with a week's visit to Sarpedoun, a neighboring king, but Troilus incessantly concentrates on his absent Criseyde (5.400–504) to the point that he dreams that he finds her sleeping in the arms of a boar (5.1233–46). The boar symbolizes Diomede, as Troilus's sister Cassandra explains, and the dream simply signifies that "Diomede is inne, and thow art oute" (5.1519). Within the mythology of the Trojan War, Cassandra is cursed as the prophetess who predicts the future accurately, yet is never believed, and thus Troilus, adhering to this tradition, refuses to recognize the truth of her words. Receiving no comfort from Pandarus or Cassandra, Troilus sinks deeper into his melancholy.

Pandarus earlier taught Troilus how to write letters to his beloved (2.1023–43), and the young lover's epistolary skills are put to the test as he awaits his beloved's return. He begs to know when she will return, and the poem continues to forecast his imminent demise, this time in his own words:

> "Byseche I yow, myn owen lady free,
> That hereupon ye wolden write me,
> For love of God, my righte lode-sterre [guiding light, inspiration],
> That deth may make an ende of al my werre." (5.1390–93)

Again Criseyde promises to return, but her final letter to Troilus is a masterpiece of obfuscation and double meaning. She says, "Come I wole" (5.1618), but will not say when: "that what yer [year] or what day / That this shal be, that kan I naught apoynte" (5.1619–20). Troilus's response to her epistle—"This Troilus this lettre thoughte al straunge / Whan he it saugh, and sorwfullich he sighte [sighed]" (5.1632–33)—indicates his realization that the day or year of Criseyde's return is likely never to arrive. With its protagonist's love lost, the narrative hastens to its inevitable close because nothing is left to tell of the romance they shared.

Pandarus's comic pandering has injected much levity throughout the poem, but this amorous provocateur finds himself now incapable of lightening the impending tragic mood. In the end Pandarus offers only impotent anger toward his niece: "My brother deer, I may do the [for you] namore. / What sholde I seyen? I hate, ywis, Cryseyde" (5.1731–32). The rejection of familial affection for his niece is surprising, but Pandarus's final words in *Troilus and Criseyde* are even more so: "And fro this world, almyghty God I preye / Delivere hire soon! I kan namore seye" (5.1742–43). Damning Criseyde to her death, Pandarus exposes the depth of his contempt for his niece, but he also repudiates his own role throughout the narrative. A Pandarus who "kan namore seye," a Pandarus who will no longer glibly orchestrate words and actions for the pleasure of Troilus, bespeaks a fundamentally new vision of this character who has spurred the plot throughout its many twists and turns.

Troilus's death, the tragic climax of approximately eight thousand lines of poetry, is dealt with quickly, almost as an afterthought: "But— weilawey [alas], save only Goddes wille, / Despitously hym slough the fierse Achille" (1805–6). After Achilles kills him, Troilus's soul ascends to the "eighthe spere [sphere]" (5.1809), and he achieves a momentary vision of comic insight while gazing down upon his dead body:

And in hymself he lough [laughed] right at the wo
Of hem that wepten for his deth so faste,
And dampned al oure werk that foloweth so
The blynde lust, the which that may nat laste,
And sholden al oure herte on heven caste;
And forth he wente, shortly for to telle,
Ther as Mercurye sorted hym to dwelle. (5.1821–27)

It is an uncanny scene, with Troilus laughing at his own death and at those who mourn his passing, but it is a moment of deep insight as well, as the Trojan knight realizes that he has merely been following his "blynde lust." His earthly love for Criseyde is renounced in favor of divine insight, yet this moment of revelation is also coupled with loss, as he is then shuffled off to some vision of the pagan afterlife where Mercury places him for eternity. Through Troilus's laughter these lines create a comedy from the tragedy of his death, but they cannot wholly eclipse his suffering throughout the poem and into its afterlife. In many ways, effecting this shift of genre has been Chaucer's design behind *Troilus and Criseyde*, as he suggests in his valedictory to the narrative: "Go, litel bok, go, litel myn tragedye, / Ther God thi makere yet, er that he dye, / So sende myght to make in som comedye!" (5.1786–88).

Chaucer then ends his poem by redirecting its attention from a human love affair to his conception of eternal Christian truths:

And loveth hym the which that right for love
Upon a crois [cross], oure soules for to beye,
First starf [died], and roos, and sit in hevene above;
For he nyl falsen no wight, dar I seye,
That wol his herte al holly [wholly] on hym leye.
And syn [since] he best to love is, and most meke [meek],
What nedeth feynede [feigned] loves for to seke? (5.1842–48)

In the end, Troilus's love for Criseyde was a hollow pursuit, a "feynede love" that led him away from matters of spirituality into affairs of cupidity. A Christian moral concludes this pagan love story, anachronistically affixing a resolution impossible for its pre-Christian protagonists to achieve. *Troilus and Criseyde* melds the Christian and the classical in its closing consideration of Troilus's pain in love, but such a resolution cannot overshadow the narrative's primary motivating force throughout the previous five books, eclipsing even Pandarus and his many machinations: Lady Fortune, callously spinning her wheel and, in so doing, shifting the text among what one might term the various genres of life: comedy and tragedy, romance and epic.

Canterbury Tales

GENERAL PROLOGUE

Like the orchestral overture to a musical or opera, which strikes many of the themes and motifs running through the ensuing score, Chaucer's General Prologue to the *Canterbury Tales* captures the spirit of his bustling narrative of sacred and profane voices joining together on an ostensibly holy pilgrimage. Chaucer begins the General Prologue by establishing the theme of Nature's rebirth in the glorious season of spring:

> Whan that Aprill with his shoures soote [showers sweet]
> The droghte [drought] of March hath perced to the roote,
> And bathed every veyne [veins of plants and flowers] in swich licour
>   [liquid, rain]
> Of which vertu engendred is the flour [flower]. (1.1–4)

These four lines (indeed, the first eighteen) rank as some of the most famous in English literature, and they quickly set the stage for the unfolding narrative: it is springtime, and the earth shakes off the vestiges of its winter slumber. Against this backdrop of nature's rebirth, people from various levels of English society join together on a pilgrimage to Canterbury Cathedral to pray at the shrine of St. Thomas à Becket, the "hooly blisful martir . . . / That hem hath holpen [helped them] whan that they were seeke [sick]" (1.17–18).

In this light, the Canterbury pilgrimage represents a holy journey undertaken to honor a martyred saint, but, as soon becomes apparent, many of the pilgrims travel for reasons other than spiritual devotion. To suggest a connection between this pilgrimage and the spring-break revels of college students would be to overstate the parallels, yet "spring fever"—that delicious season of high spirits and unbridled inhibitions— cannot be discounted as a motivating factor for the less devout members of the pilgrimage. Indeed, the Wife of Bath is described as "wandrynge by the weye" (1.467) on her many pilgrimages, but should not one travel in a straight line when undertaking a holy journey? With this festive air, the Canterbury pilgrimage takes on the atmosphere of the carnivalesque, with the rules of everyday life suspended in a spirit of mutual fun and transgression.

The first character whom readers encounter in the General Prologue is Chaucer himself in his role as first-person narrator of the unfolding story. While staying at the Tabard Inn on his journey to Canterbury, he encounters numerous travelers who come from various levels of English culture and society (1.19–42), and the bulk of the General Prologue details Chaucer's initial reactions to these pilgrims and the ironic discrepancies between Chaucer's descriptions of them and the truth lying underneath the surface. He introduces them in miniature portraits arranged in loose clusters according to social class, in the following order: the Knight, with his Squire and Yeoman, representing the aristocracy (1.43–117); the Prioress (who travels with another nun and three priests), Monk, and Friar, who belong to religious orders (1.118–269); the Merchant, Clerk, Sergeant of Law, Franklin, five Guildsmen (whose occupations are Haberdasher, Carpenter, Weaver, Dyer, and Tapestry-Weaver), Cook, Shipman, Physician, and Wife of Bath, who collectively represent the middle-class, or bourgeois, members of medieval English society, including both self-interested businesspeople and educated professionals (1.270–476); the Parson and Plowman, who are brothers and honest men representing the beneficial harmony between the clergy and peasantry (1.477–541); the Miller, who is so "byg . . . of brawn, and . . . bones" that he appears to stand off by himself (1.545–66); and the Manciple, Reeve, Summoner, and Pardoner, who are administrators in courtly and ecclesiastical contexts (1.567–714). One of the great pleasures of the *Canterbury Tales* is becoming acquainted with these many distinct characters, who variously represent the best and the worst of their professions. The General Prologue is typically referred to as an estates satire, a genre in which the author presents the reader with representatives of various levels of society and comments on how well they meet their responsibilities to their occupations and to society as a whole.

In his role as narrator, Chaucer introduces the various pilgrims with brief sketches, and the humor of the General Prologue arises in discerning the disjunctions between the narrator's naive description of a character and the truth that ironically shines through his words. Chaucer's portrait of the Prioress, a masterpiece of pert ironies, highlights this technique:

> Ther was also a Nonne, a PRIORESSE,
> That of hir smylyng was ful symple and coy;
> Hire gretteste ooth was but by Seinte Loy;
> And she was cleped [called] madame Eglentyne.
> Ful weel she soong the service dyvyne,
> Entuned in hir nose ful semely;
> And Frenssh she spak ful faire and fetisly [elegantly],
> After the scole [school] of Stratford atte Bowe,
> For Frenssh of Parys was to hire unknowe. (1.118–26)

By the second line of this portrait, readers see behaviors not typically expected from prioresses. Should nuns smile coyly? Chaucer hints throughout this portrait that Madame Eglentine is a flirt, as is also suggested by her brooch that bears the inscription "*Amor vincit omnia* [Love conquers all]" (1.162) and her wimple that is pleated in a "[f]ul semyly [very comely]" (1.151) manner, despite the fact that wimples are designed to cloak, not to accentuate, female attractiveness. He praises her singing of the liturgy, but a person need never have taken voice lessons to understand that the finest vocalists do not sing through their noses. Also, Chaucer compliments Madame Eglentine's fluency in French, but a latent insult arises in that her French is not the French of Paris. In light of such ironies, readers must continually scratch beneath the surface of Chaucer's apparent compliments to dig out the hidden truth.

Given Chaucer-as-narrator's unrelieved naiveté, readers of the *Canterbury Tales* must in many ways work as literary detectives, looking for gaps between his words and what the portraits nonetheless describe. To take another brief example, Chaucer calls the Shipman "a good felawe" (1.395), but the ensuing description hints that the man is more likely a pirate than an honest captain:

Ful many a draughte [drink] of wyn had he ydrawe [taken]
Fro Burdeux-ward, whil that the chapman [merchant] sleep.
Of nyce conscience took he no keep.
If that he faught and hadde the hyer hond [higher hand, advantage],
By water he sente hem [them] hoom to every lond. (1.396–400)

From these lines it is clear that this "good felawe" steals wine while merchants nap, and it also appears that he forces his defeated enemies to walk the plank. Chaucer's line "By water he sente hem hoom to every lond" does not definitively state that the Shipman drowns his foes, but the contextual clues point in this direction. Learning to read Chaucer requires that one look at the wider social milieu of his characters, since he so frequently refrains from commenting on their faults forthrightly. As narrator of the *Canterbury Tales*, Chaucer's observational skills are humorously superficial; to counter his assumed air of credulity, readers must interpret these passages with care, lest they accept the surface portrayal as a reliable assessment of a pilgrim's character.

Not all of the portraits in the General Prologue are satiric, and many critics agree that the descriptions of the Knight (1.43–78), Parson (1.477–528), and Plowman (1.529–41) represent ideal figures.[3] These men embody the three primary social classes of medieval England—those who fight (the aristocracy), those who pray (the clergy), and those who work (the serfs). This simplistic breakdown of English society mostly overlooks both women and the rising merchant class: such figures as the Wife of Bath, the Miller, and the five Guildsmen represent social castes not included within the old rubric, and Chaucer frequently depicts his characters chafing against this social structure. Much of the tension between and among the social classes is illustrated in the prologues to the various tales, and Chaucer frequently incorporates specific characteristics outlined in the portraits of the General Prologue within these subsequent prologues, providing his pilgrims with consistency of character. For the most part, the characters described in the General Prologue do not yet interact with one another, but the tensions inherent in such a diverse group of pilgrims simmer under the surface of their portraits, waiting to spring out with unrestrained comic effect throughout the remainder of the narrative, such as in the Miller's vulgar reimagination of the Knight's Tale or in the Wife of Bath's lengthy prologue, in which she rails against the patriarchal structures and sexual mores of medieval life.

In his representation of himself in the General Prologue, Chaucer assumes a journalistic position from which he reports what he sees without attempting to color the reader's perception of the person or events. As the examples of the Prioress and the Shipman show, this disingenuous pose reveals far more than its literal expression. Yet Chaucer repeatedly proclaims that, should his fictions offend the sensibilities of his readers, he is not at fault because he merely transcribes events that he witnessed firsthand:

> But first I pray yow, of youre curteisye,
> That ye n'arette [not attribute] it nat my vileynye,
> Thogh that I pleynly speke in this mateere,
> To telle yow hir words and hir cheere [appearance],
> Ne thogh I speke hir wordes proprely.
> For this ye knowen al so wel as I:
> Whoso shal telle a tale after a man,
> He moot reherce as ny [nearly] as evere he kan
> Everich a word, if it be in his charge,
> Al [although] speke he never so rudeliche and large,
> Or ellis [else] he moot telle his tale untrewe,
> Or feyne thyng, or fynde wordes newe. (1.725–36)

Such a defense of the *Canterbury Tales* is utterly preposterous: Chaucer is not reporting facts, he is creating fictions, and it is within his power as author and as narrator to tell any story he desires. At the same time, this lie reveals one of the great truths of fiction: to be true to the characters he invents, Chaucer must let them speak as he believes they would, even if some prove themselves prone to vulgarities or otherwise indecorous speech. Through this rhetorical strategy, Chaucer frees himself to tell his myriad tales in the voices most appropriate for their delivery, no matter how churlish, crude, or blasphemous such voices might be.

The General Prologue concludes with Chaucer introducing readers to the Host, Harry Bailly, proprietor of the Tabard Inn and the man who proposes the taletelling game that guides the remainder of the *Canterbury Tales*. Harry suggests that, to pass the time during their long journey, each pilgrim tell four stories—two on the way to Canterbury, two on the way home:

> "This is the poynt, to speken short and pleyn,
> That ech of yow, to shorte with oure weye,
> In this viage [voyage] shal telle tales tweye [two]
> To Caunterbury-ward, I mene it so,
> And homward he shal tellen othere two." (1.790–94)

Intriguingly, such a plan would necessitate that Chaucer write at least 120 tales, four for each of the pilgrims and for himself, and possibly for Harry Bailly as well. This framework indicates that Chaucer set himself the task of surpassing Boccaccio's *Decameron*, the fourteenth-century Italian masterpiece in which ten noblepersons each tell a story for each of the ten days they spend waiting for the plague to pass, resulting in a collection of one hundred tales. Both Boccaccio's and Chaucer's collections of tales prove the importance of establishing a frame narrative to unite what would otherwise devolve into apparently haphazard anthologies. It is to be regretted that Chaucer died before he could complete his *Canterbury Tales*; he finished only twenty-four (and some of these, including the Cook's Tale and the Squire's Tale, trail off inconclusively).

The General Prologue winds down as the pilgrims draw straws to determine who will tell the first tale. The Knight wins the draw:

> And shortly for to tellen as it was,
> Were it by aventure [fortune], or sort [fate], or cas [chance],

The sothe [truth] is this: the cut fil to the Knyght,
Of which ful blithe and glad was every wyght [person]. (1.843–46)

Of course, the Knight's good fortune is not really the work of Providence but of Chaucer's design. The *Canterbury Tales* is Chaucer's fiction, and it suits his authorial purposes to depict this member of the aristocracy leading the taletelling competition. As readers see throughout the prologues to the tales, members of various levels of society clash through their respective narratives, and the first such instance of this tension arises after the Knight concludes his aristocratic tale, as the Miller speaks up, drunkenly and crudely, to debase its romance themes.

KNIGHT'S TALE

Is it better to have loved and lost than never to have loved at all? Concerning the characters in the Knight's Tale, the answer to this clichéd yet intriguing question would likely depend on whom one asks. The story's three main characters—the young knights Palamon and Arcite and their mutual beloved Emily—face strikingly different endings in this epic romance: Palamon happily looks forward to marrying Emily, Emily prepares to marry Palamon (despite her prayers for lifelong virginity), and Arcite dies. As much as this tale celebrates love and knightly honor as the noblest of virtues, it also exposes the ways in which they create bitter hostilities that undermine longstanding relationships. The intermingling of epic and romance storylines shifts standard expectations for both genres, and Chaucer investigates how epic and romance build conflicting goals of military victory and of love, as well as the repercussions of these pursuits for his protagonists.

Certainly, many conventional features of romance appear in the Knight's Tale: love is an ennobling force, one that inspires a man to great feats of arms for his lady fair; he fights to defend her honor and to win her love; and he proves his merit as a knight by undertaking combats in grand tournaments and quests. Chaucer celebrates romance in the Knight's Tale, but he simultaneously questions its values when depicting how private love affairs conflict with other courtly responsibilities and relationships. Foremost, Chaucer stresses that Palamon and Arcite are united through a bond deeper than mere friendship: they are cousins, related by blood, and they have also sworn oaths of brotherhood to each other, and thus have publicly professed their commitment to advance each other's causes (1.1128–51). Love's power to inspire is coupled with love's power to destroy, and its double edge undermines efforts to read the Knight's Tale as a straightforward homage to romance values.

The tale begins against an epic backdrop as Duke Theseus returns home to Athens with his bride Hippolyta and her sister Emily after conquering the Amazons (1.859–92); on this journey, he encounters a company of mourning women, who bemoan their husbands' deaths at the hands of Creon, the ruler of Thebes (1.893–951). Moreover, Creon will not allow the men to be buried and "maketh houndes ete hem [eat them] in despit" (1.947). At these women's behest, Theseus kills Creon and, after the ensuing carnage, sends the wounded Theban knights Palamon and Arcite to Athens to dwell in prison forever (1.952–1032). With Theseus dominating the tale's beginning, the epic focus on martial masculinity as a civilizing force—defeating Amazons and delivering justice for the afflicted—appears to exalt the just use of violence to ensure proper governance. At the same time, Theseus's position in a romance of courtly love is suspect, for Chaucer narrates how he "conquered al the regne of Femenye" (1.866), proving the duke's ready use of violence to achieve his desired goals, even in amatory affairs.

From their jail cell, cut off from opportunities to prove their masculine worth (as Theseus has), Palamon and then Arcite espy Emily. Quickly their alliance dissolves as they debate the nature of love and romance (1.1033–1186). Arcite resorts to rather shoddy argumentation to convince his sworn brother that he, Arcite, is more deserving of Emily's love:

"For paramour I loved hire first er [before] thow.
What wiltow seyen? Thou woost [know] nat yet now
Wheither she be a womman or goddesse!
Thyn is affeccioun of hoolynesse,
And myn is love as to a creature." (1.1155–59)

Arcite's sophistry in contending that Palamon's love for Emily is less true because he cannot determine whether she is a woman or a goddess fails to carry his case. True, Palamon did "mistake" Emily for Venus (1.1101–2), but he could hardly have imagined that praising her beauty would be cast back at him to suggest that he is therefore unworthy of her love.

After Palamon and Arcite squabble over their mutual beloved, the plot moves quickly forward: Arcite is freed and exiled after his ally Duke

Perotheus pleads to Theseus on his behalf (1.1187–1208), while Palamon remains imprisoned. The first part of the romance concludes by asking readers to ponder which of the two knights suffers more:

> Yow loveres axe [ask] I now this questioun:
> Who hath the worse, Arcite or Palamoun?
> That oon may seen his lady day by day,
> But in prison he moot dwelle alway;
> That oother wher hym list [it pleases him] may ride or go,
> But seen his lady shal he nevere mo [more]. (1.1347–52)

This conundrum that the Knight poses for his audience is an example of the literary technique of the *demande d'amour*, a common feature of courtly romances and debate poetry that directly engages the text's audience in the issues under consideration. In this instance, Chaucer's *demande d'amour* encourages readers to ponder love's effects on Palamon and Arcite and their suffering, but since the two men are virtually identical, distinguishing between them is difficult. In many ways, the interpretive crux of the Knight's Tale arises in the distinct endings that the two protagonists eventually face, even though much of the story treats them almost interchangeably. It is tempting to align Palamon with the romance tradition and Arcite with the epic tradition in accordance with their respective prayers to Venus, Goddess of Love, and Mars, God of War, later in the poem, but at this point in the narrative, they appear more similar than not.

A dominant trope of medieval romance is its depiction of love's torments. Part 2 of the Knight's Tale begins with Arcite returning to Athens, after several years have passed and in violation of his exile, and taking work as Emily's page because he cannot live without hope of seeing his beloved (1.1355–1449). Intermingled with these plot points are numerous passages concentrating on his "loveris maladye" (1.1373), to the extent that the narrator almost exasperatedly cuts off this mournful description with a terse "What sholde I al day of his wo endite [write]?" (1.1380). Similar to Arcite in his amatory pains, Palamon likewise languishes in love, with the narrator describing him as a martyr: "Who koude ryme in Englyssh proprely / His martirdom?" (1.1459–60). Martyrs more typically belong to the genre of hagiography, with its depictions of saints patiently (and often gruesomely) suffering for their faith, but Chaucer employs this exaggerated metaphor to link spiritual and secular loves as similarly ennobling passions. When Palamon escapes from his prison, he encounters Arcite, and the two men prepare to fight (1.1451–1662), their hatred for each other overshadowing their mutual love for Emily. Theseus discovers the men and orders their execution, but, again bowing to women's pleas for mercy, he decrees instead that a tournament be held in which the two men will fight for Emily's hand. "Thanne shal I yeve [give] Emelya to wyve [as a wife] / To whom that Fortune yeveth so fair a grace," Theseus proclaims (1.1860–61). Despite Emily's unwanted status as a prize to be won, the Knight's Tale appears to be moving to the climactic feature of many courtly romances: the tournament, in which the victorious combatant wins both the honors of battle and the hand of his beloved.

The third section of the Knight's Tale focuses on prayers, with Palamon, Emily, and Arcite each seeking divine assistance to achieve their objective of winning (or, in Emily's case, eschewing) love. The participation of the classical gods is a standard element of epic, and these prayers highlight the ways in which earthly events resonate with cosmic significance. Palamon, Emily, and Arcite respectively pray to Venus (1.2209–70), Diana, goddess of chastity (1.2271–366), and Mars (1.2367–2437), and Chaucer describes these supplicants' rituals in the lavish yet grim settings of the gods' temples. Palamon beseeches Venus that, regardless of the outcome of the combat, she will grant him Emily: "I recche [care] nat but it may bettre be / To have victorie of hem, or they of me, / So that I have my lady in myne armes" (1.2245–47). Emily prays to Diana to help her escape the bonds of matrimony: "Chaste goddesse, wel wostow [you know] that I / Desire to ben a mayden [virgin] al my lyf, / Ne nevere wol I be no love ne wyf" (1.2304–6). Arcite prays to Mars to win the impending combat with Palamon:

"I moot [must] with strengthe wynne hire [her] in the place,
And wel I woot [know], withouten help or grace
Of thee ne may my strengthe noght availle.
Thanne help me, lord, tomorwe in my bataille." (1.2399–402)

Palamon's and Arcite's prayers are virtually identical, as the former prays for Emily and the latter prays for victory in battle, presumably so he can win Emily's hand. The Knight's Tale, until now a romance of earthly lovers, takes on a deeper epic significance as the gods enter the fray: Venus and Mars respectively provide signs that they will grant Palamon's and Arcite's prayers (1.2261–70, 1.2421–37), but Diana rejects Emily's petition

(1.2346–66). Venus and Mars argue over their apparently conflicting promises to Palamon and Arcite, but Saturn—who represents earthly death in his declaration, "My lookyng is the fader [father] of pestilence" (1.2469)—promises to resolve their dispute.

In part 4 of this epic romance, the conflict between Palamon and Arcite (and hence between Venus and Mars) is resolved, and it appears that one of the lessons of the Knight's Tale is to be careful what one wishes for. Arcite wins the battle, and thus appears to have won Emily in marriage, but he then dies in a horse accident (1.2676–2815). With his final words, he bequeaths Emily to Palamon, and the two prepare to live happily ever after (despite Emily's desire to remain a virgin all her life). Theseus pronounces his conclusion to the tale:

> "Thanne is it wysdom, as it thynketh me,
> To maken vertu of necessitee,
> And take it weel that we may nat eschue [avoid],
> And namely that to us alle is due." (1.3041–44)

Theseus's words are a bit sterile here, focusing on how people must accept rather than fight their lot in life, but then again, his words are painfully true, for railing against one's fortune will not alter it. It is a somewhat austere ending for a romance, one that couples the expected happiness of an amorous ending with sadness for the conditions that enabled it. Both a celebration and a critique of epic and romance values, the Knight's Tale asks probing questions about the meaning of knightly honor and earthly love, and in so doing it achieves a level of philosophical depth by celebrating love while simultaneously exposing the pains left in its wake.

MILLER'S PROLOGUE AND TALE

The opening lines of the Miller's Prologue suggest that the Knight's audience has greatly enjoyed his tale, but Chaucer hints that social-class hostilities quietly fester among the company:

> Whan that the Knyght had thus his tale ytoold,
> In al the route [company] nas ther yong ne oold
> That he ne seyde it was a noble storie
> And worthy for to drawen to memorie,
> And namely the gentils everichon. (1.3109–13)

The pilgrims unanimously appreciate the story, Chaucer tells his readers, but the gentlefolk—the wellborn aristocrats and other upper-class members of society—enjoy it especially, presumably because it reflects their tastes and values. However, many of the pilgrims, including the Wife of Bath, the Guildsmen, the Cook, the Shipman, and the Plowman, cannot reasonably be construed as "gentils," and so Chaucer's phrasing insinuates that, although bourgeois folk appreciate the tale, they do so less than their social superiors. Chaucer uses his characters' prologues to bind together the overarching narrative of the *Canterbury Tales* by allowing the pilgrims to speak to one another, often with undisguised hostility. In this instance, when Harry Bailly invites the Monk to tell the next tale, the Miller rudely interrupts and promises to tell his own story, one that will retaliate against the Knight's genteel romance: "By armes, and by blood and bones, / I kan a noble tale for the nones [occasion], / With which I wol now quite [pay back, avenge] the Knyghtes tale" (1.3125–27). The Miller's hostility is somewhat surprising, since no specific reason motivates his outburst, aside possibly from his drunkenness (1.3138). It thus appears that he dislikes the Knight's rarefied romance because it does not suit his coarse sensibilities, and his tale subverts and ridicules the values of courtly love celebrated in this aristocratic narrative.

Before proceeding to the coarse humor of the Miller's Tale, Chaucer employs his position as narrator of the Miller's Prologue to reiterate his regret that he must repeat the stories as they have been told. He calls the Miller's impending story a "cherles [churl's] tale" (1.3169) and declares that he "moot [must] reherce / Hir tales alle, be they bettre or werse, / Or elles falsen som of my mateere [material]" (1.3173–75). Building on this theme, Chaucer addresses another motif repeated throughout the Canterbury pilgrimage, that of the tension between seriousness and play: "Avyseth yow, and put me out of blame; / And eek men shal nat maken ernest of game" (1.3185–86). The tension between earnest and game, seriousness and play, captures the Canterbury pilgrimage as a whole: this spiritual journey purportedly represents an endeavor of moral gravity and contemplation, but many of the pilgrims are motivated more by play than by piety, which further contributes to the carnivalesque themes throughout the *Canterbury Tales*.

To denigrate the Knight's romance, the Miller employs the genre of fabliau in his tale, and no genre better encapsulates the term "cherles tale" than fabliau. Romances and fabliaux could not be more dissimilar in their thematic elements: romances glorify courtly love and the aristocrats who engage in it, while fabliaux feature raw concupiscence and sexually voracious clerks (or peasants, or priests) who seek fornication—often despite rather squalid conditions—over more ennobling forms of love. The knight of a romance frequently undertakes a quest to prove his worth as a lover and a warrior, but the protagonist of a fabliau is more often a trickster figure, one who succeeds in his sexual pursuits by deceiving others through his quick wit. The comic climax of the Miller's Tale depicts the most famous fart in all of English literature, but this is not merely a ribald interjection of bawdy humor into the the *Canterbury Tales*; on the contrary, this fart structures the Miller's recasting of the great romance of the Knight's Tale into a debasement of its most esteemed values through the fabliau's focused attention on the human body and its embarrassments.

The Miller's Tale is rather simple in structure, although it depends on a fabliau tendency for outlandish plot devices. Nicholas, a young student, lives with the carpenter John, who is an old man married to a young woman, Alison (1.3187–3220). John thus represents the stock figure of the *senex amans*, the amorous old man whose young wife will sexually betray him for comic effect as the plot unfolds. Nicholas determines to seduce Alison and succeeds quickly: after her initial shock at his advances (1.3280–87), it requires only three additional lines for her to acquiesce (1.3288–90). At several points in his tale the Miller ironically refers to Nicholas as "hende" (1.3199, 1.3272, and passim), which is a word bearing connotations of well-bred behavior; in clear contrast, Nicholas's comportment does not resemble the courtesy expected of a knight of romance but rather the untamed sexuality of a fabliau protagonist, one who reveals his affections for Alison by aggressively accosting her: "As clerkes ben ful subtile and ful queynte [clever] / And prively he caughte hire by the queynte [crotch]" (1.3275–76).

A further complication to these erotic shenanigans arises in that Alison has attracted yet another suitor for her affections, Absolon, who parallels Nicholas in numerous key details (1.3312–38). In one of the most obvious yet humorous instances of foreshadowing in English literature, the Miller notes one of Absolon's defining personality traits: "But sooth [truth] to seyn, he was somdeel squaymous [squeamish] / Of fartyng" (1.3337–38). A dislike of farts is so nearly universal that it does not warrant mentioning, but these lines lay the foundation for the tale's explosive climax. As much as Nicholas and Absolon resemble each other, Nicholas wields an unbeatable advantage over his rival because, as the narrator notes, he lives nearer to her than does Absolon (1.3386–96). The Miller's fabliau thus bears numerous typical features of the genre, including an amorous competition for the privilege of bedding a young woman, the structural deployment of vulgarity to mark the plot's incipient climax, and a female protagonist eager to cuckold her husband.

To arrange a night of passion, so that Alison "sholde slepen in his arm al nyght" (1.3406), Nicholas pretends to receive a heavenly vision and tricks John into thinking that God will flood the world (1.3513–600). To save them from impending death, the hapless carpenter builds three tubs—one each for Nicholas, Alison, and himself—to hang from the ceiling as they await the cataclysm. Once John falls asleep in his tub, Nicholas and Alison steal away for their adulterous pleasures, only to be interrupted by her other suitor, Absolon, who requests a kiss from Alison at her bedroom window (1.3671–3729). In fabliau fashion, she grants him an unexpected and unwelcome surprise:

> And at the wyndow out she putte hir hole [anus],
> And Absolon, hym fil no bet ne wers,
> But with his mouth he kiste hir naked ers [ass]
> Ful savourly, er he were war [aware] of this.
> Abak he stirte [jumped], and thoughte it was amys,
> For wel he wiste a womman hath no berd.
> He felte a thyng al rough and long yherd [haired],
> And seyde, "Fy! allas! what have I do?"
> "Tehee!" quod she, and clapte the wyndow to. (1.3732–40)

Were this the comic climax of the Miller's Tale, with Absolon kissing Alison's ass and her silly giggle in response, one would already be well reimbursed for the efforts it takes to read Middle English. But Chaucer lays on even more vulgar pleasures. Absolon resolves to avenge himself on Alison, borrows a heated coulter from a blacksmith, and returns, pleading again for a kiss but poising himself to implant a searing revenge on his ex-beloved's backside (1.3747–89). Nicholas, having risen to urinate, decides to duplicate Alison's scatological trickery, a decision that he soon regrets:

And therwith spak this clerk, this Absolon,
"Spek, sweete bryd, I noot nat [do not know] where thou art."
    This Nicholas anon leet fle a fart
As greet as it had been a thonder-dent [thunderclap],
That with the strook he was almoost yblent [blinded];
And he was redy with his iren hoot,
And Nicholas amydde the ers [ass] he smoot [struck]. (1.3804–10)

At this point in the story, Absolon and Nicholas have respectively endured the painful humiliations of butt-kissing and butt-burning, and
now it is John's turn to suffer his fabliau fate. After being poked with
the hot iron, Nicholas screams, "Water! Water!" (1.3815). John hears his
cry, but he thinks that Nicholas's scream refers to God's flood, not to a
branded tush. John cuts the cords from his tub, falls to the floor, and
breaks his arm, with his neighbors coming by to laugh at his sorry condition (1.3816–49).

    Certainly, the Miller succeeds in his goal of "quiting," or repaying,
the Knight for his tale, as his fabliau upends the courtly values of the
Knight's romance. In the Knight's Tale, two noble and valiant knights
fight for the pure love of a beautiful virgin; in the Miller's Tale, two licen-
tious clerks fight for the impure love of a married woman. The Knight's
Tale ends with the marriage of Palamon and Emily, in which the union
is likely consummated in the narrative's undepicted afterlife but is not
depicted in the tale itself. In contrast, the Miller's Tale shows Nicholas
and Alison fornicating in bed, or, as Chaucer euphemistically phrases
it, "In bisynesse of myrthe and of solas" (1.3654). He also satirically ad-
umbrates Nicholas and Absolon's potential homosexual union when the
latter graphically assaults the former's rear end with an "iren hoot" in a
parody of sodomy, and thus this scene reconfigures Palamon and Arcite's
chaste brotherhood into a tableau of humorous yet gruesome violence
with sexual undertones. Intriguingly, another contrast suggests the Miller's attention to the gender politics of romance and fabliau as well: Emily
wields little agency in her amorous dealings in the Knight's Tale, as she
must yield to the will of the gods and accept Theseus's pronouncements
about her choice of a husband. Alison, on the other hand, triumphs at
the conclusion of the Miller's Tale: the three men who desire her all suffer
painful humiliations, but she sates her sexual desires without paying any
penalty for her adulterous transgressions.

REEVE'S PROLOGUE AND TALE

The Reeve's Prologue begins in a fashion similar to the Miller's Prologue: most of the pilgrims enjoyed the Miller's bawdy story, but again Chaucer shows that such good humor does not extend uniformly throughout the company. In particular, the Reeve bristles at the Miller's humor, as Chaucer as narrator reports:

> Whan folk hadde laughen at this nyce [silly] cas
> Of Absolon and hende [noble] Nicholas,
> Diverse folk diversely they seyde,
> But for the moore part they loughe and pleyde.
> Ne at this tale I saugh no man hym greve [aggrieved],
> But it were oonly Osewold the Reve. (1.3855–60)

Why would Oswald the Reeve dislike the Miller's raunchy tale? In the General Prologue, Chaucer remarks that the Reeve is "a wel good wrighte [workman], a carpenter" (1.614, cf. 1.3861, 1.3914), and so it appears that the Reeve feels insulted by the Miller's fabliau depiction of the carpenter John and his adulterous young wife. In his tale, he avenges himself on the Miller by depicting a miller whose wife and daughter inadvertently succumb to the "seductions" of two young university students. The Miller degraded the Knight's Tale by responding to romance with fabliau, and the Reeve likewise deploys the raunchy genre of fabliau to attack his enemy: "And, by youre leve, I shal hym quite anoon; / Right in his cherles termes wol I speke" (1.3916–17). "Cherles termes" can be read as a synonym for fabliau in this passage (cf. "cherles tale," 1.3169), and it also presages Chaucer's use of dialect humor in this tale, in which the protagonists Allen and John talk like northern yokels instead of southern sophisticates.

The Reeve's Tale begins with a lengthy description of the miller Symkyn and his wife, and key details in their combined portraits include his violent temperament, as evidenced by the many weapons he carries (1.3929–33), his jealous fear that other men might approach his wife (1.3955–68), and the family's aspiration to marry their daughter Maline into the aristocracy (1.3981–82). Here the Reeve foreshadows his fabliau's conclusion, and readers should therefore expect a violent yet humorous scuffle, and a failure by Symkyn's wife and daughter to preserve the family's sexual honor. Furthermore, the family's lofty ambitions for Maline reveal their disregard for social propriety due to their suspect ancestry: Symkyn's wife's father is the town's parson, in obvious violation of his priestly calling (1.3942–43).

After the introduction of Symkyn's family and its suspect lineage, readers meet Allen and John, two students at Cambridge University who discover that Symkyn is cheating their school because the administrator has fallen ill (1.3897–4001). In a comic aside, the Reeve notes that, prior to this administrator's sickness, the miller "stal [stole] but curteisly," but he is "now . . . a theef outrageously" (1.3997–98). Allen and John decide to monitor Symkyn to prevent subsequent thefts, but when they visit him and his family, he unties their horse, and as they chase the animal down, he cheats them even more than before (1.4046–4113). Because of the late hour, the two students must spend the night at Symkyn's house once they have captured their runaway horse, and Allen decides to copulate with Maline in recompense for their mistreatment at Symkyn's hands, as he explains to John. His logic is grossly inappropriate as a basis for any legal remedies, yet it is congruent with the tale's fabliau sensibility, which prizes sexual conquest and masculine aggrandizement over ethical conduct:

"For, John," seyde he, "als evere moot I thryve,
If that I may, yon wenche wil I swyve [screw].
Som esement [easement, redress] has lawe yshapen us,
For, John, ther is a lawe that says thus:
That gif [if] a man in a point be agreved [injured],
That in another he sal be releved." (1.4177–82)

Allen quickly succeeds in "seducing" Maline: "And up he rist [rose], and by the wenche he crepte / . . . / And shortly for to seyn, they were aton [as one, coupled]" (1.4193–97). By stealing her virginity, Allen effectively forecloses Symkyn's plan to marry his daughter to the aristocracy, and thus the clerk's fabliau revenge is achieved, if as yet incomplete.

Meanwhile, John frets that his fellow students will deride him for his celibate night in contrast to Allen's frisky adventuring, and he devises a plan to preserve his wounded sexual pride that should never succeed: he moves the cradle holding his hosts' baby from the foot of their bed to the foot of his bed, with the goal of luring Symkyn's wife into his arms (1.4199–4212). Fortunately for John, Symkyn's wife needs to urinate, and afterwards she mistakenly climbs into bed with him. With the randiness often associated with fabliau protagonists, he immediately takes advantage of the situation:

> Withinne a while this John the clerk up leep [leaped],
> And on this goode wyf he leith on soore.
> So myrie a fit ne hadde she nat ful yoore [not for a long time];
> He priketh harde and depe as he were mad. (1.4228–31)

In typical fabliau fashion, John and Allen achieve their revenge through cleverness and a bit of luck, but their victory lacks a crucial element because they have not yet humiliated Symkyn with the knowledge of how they passed the night with his wife and daughter. While searching for John in the dark to boast about his conquest, Allen finds the bed without the crib at its foot—the bed that should therefore be John's—and mistakenly tells Symkyn, with ungentlemanly detail, how he has greatly enjoyed Maline's company: "I have thries in this shorte nyght / Swyved the milleres doghter bolt upright" (1.4265–66). The tale concludes violently, as the opening descriptions of Symkyn's fierce nature hinted it would, but Allen and John escape, while Symkyn's wife accidentally smites her husband on the head (1.4268–4312).

The Reeve attaches a moral to his fabliau—"A gylour [beguiler, deceiver] shal hymself bigyled be" (1.4321)—and it applies well. But it is hard to imagine that he told his tale simply to illustrate this proverb. His deeper reason was, quite simply, revenge. At the end of the Reeve's Tale, Oswald proclaims, "Thus have I quyt [repaid] the Millere in my tale" (1.4324), and again readers see the aggressive dynamics latent throughout the taletelling game and the ways in which genres are conscripted as weapons in an ongoing narrative battle. In Chaucer's hands, the fabliau is not merely a humorous genre but a rhetorical weapon with which the pilgrims undertake skirmishes.

COOK'S PROLOGUE AND TALE

With the taletelling game devolving into a fabliau exchange, the Cook excitedly anticipates contributing to the vulgar fun. Such a crude side to his character is in keeping with his portrayal in the General Prologue for, despite his affiliation with the culinary arts, Roger the Cook is somewhat of an unsavory fellow. Chaucer first compliments his cooking skills before observing the man's disgusting affliction:

He koude rooste [roast], and sethe [simmer], and broille, and frye,
Maken mortreux [stews], and wel bake a pye.
But greet harm was it, as it thoughte me,
That on his shyne [shin] a mormal [boil] hadde he. (1.383–86)

Here again readers see Chaucer's pattern of seeming to compliment a
character while deftly revealing his flaws, as few patrons of a culinary
establishment would appreciate the gourmet skills of a chef with an open
sore. The Cook's Prologue further exposes Roger's suspect culinary practices, as Harry Bailly accuses him of selling pies that "hath been twies
[twice] hoot and twies coold" (1.4348) and of allowing flies to buzz about
his shop (1.4352).

Harry's playful insults touch upon Chaucer's theme of the thin line between earnest and game, and readers must evaluate how seriously Harry
intends for the Cook to respond. In this regard, the two men debate the
meaning of seriousness and play:

"Now telle on, gentil Roger by thy name.
But yet I pray thee, be nat wroth [angry] for game;
A man may seye ful sooth [truth] in game and pley."
       "Thou seist ful sooth," quod Roger, "by my fey!
But 'sooth pley, quaad [bad] pley', as the Flemyng seith." (1.4353–57)

Roger agrees with Harry that truths may be addressed in play, yet he
immediately refutes this through his citation of the Flemish proverb.
Similar to the antagonism between the Miller and the Reeve, aggression
escalates between Roger and Harry, and Roger hints that his story will
lampoon Harry:

"And therfore, Herry Bailly, by thy feith,
Be thou nat wrooth, er we departen heer [here],
Though that my tale be of an hostileer [innkeeper].
But natheleess I wol not telle it yit;
But er [before] we parte, ywis [certainly], thou shalt be quit."
   (1.4358–62)

Although Roger suggests that one of his subsequent narratives will al-
legorize Harry in order to satirize him, his current tale is set "in Chepe"
(1.4377), where Harry resides (1.754). It appears that, in congruence with
the hostility evidenced in the Knight-Miller and Miller-Reeve interac-

tions, the Cook's story will target Harry Bailly for the sheer fabliau fun of such attacks.

Roger's tale addresses the antics of one Perkyn Revelour, a name that could be loosely modernized as Peter Party-Boy. Less than sixty lines long, the unfinished Cook's Tale describes Perkyn's riotous ways and his employer's decision to fire him from his apprenticeship (1.4365–4413), and it ends with the young hedonist moving in with a friend whose wife is a prostitute (1.4414–22). Chaucer likely envisioned a fabliau through which Roger would insult Harry by depicting him as a cuckold. It is also possible that the Cook's Tale would build upon the Miller's Tale and the Reeve's Tale, but given its truncation, readers can only conjecture just how delightfully vulgar this fabliau was to have been.

MAN OF LAW'S INTRODUCTION, PROLOGUE, TALE, AND EPILOGUE

In the Introduction to the Man of Law's Tale, Harry Bailly frets over the passing of time, advising the pilgrims that "tyme wasteth nyght and day" (2.20) and that, like Maline's maidenhead, lost time can never be regained (2.29–32). Harry's concern for time allows him to reassert his authority over the pilgrims in their taletelling game, and the Man of Law bows to Harry's governance, saying, "Biheste [a promise] is dette" (2.41). In his Prologue, he declares his theme will be the burdens of poverty: "O hateful harm, condicion of poverte! / With thurst, with coold, with hunger so confoundid!" (2.99–100). His tale, however, does not primarily illustrate the difficulties created by a life of poverty; rather, he tells the story of Custance, a young woman confronting dire circumstances due to the wickedness of those around her. In terms of its genre, the Man of Law's Tale combines elements of folklore, hagiography, and romance, enfolding them into an intriguing narrative of the rewards eventually earned by suffering patiently for one's faith.

In a manner similar to the wicked stepmothers of fairy tales, mothers-in-law are frequently caricatured as evil women, and such is the case in the Man of Law's Tale, which features the travails of Custance, an unfortunate woman whose two mothers-in-law sabotage her desire for happiness in marriage. These women's hatred for Custance arises from their religious prejudices against Christianity, which thus paints them as spiritual villainesses within the narrative's worldview; in contrast, the descriptions of Custance, as articulated by "the commune voys of every man" (2.155), emphasize her desirability as a model of numerous saintly qualities:

"In hire is heigh beautee, withoute pride,
Yowthe, withoute grenehede [immaturity] or folye;
To alle hire werkes vertu is hir gyde;
Humblesse hath slayn in hire al tirannye.
She is mirour of alle curteisye;
Hir herte is verray chambre of hoolynesse,
Hir hand, ministre of fredam for almesse." (2.162–68)

Given this idealized portrait that stresses her beauty, modesty, virtue, humility, and sanctity, it is difficult to fathom the villainy of Custance's mothers-in-law, but through this conflict the Man of Law's Tale addresses the ways in which religious tensions spawn abhorrent cruelty, and such a clash of religious cultures is a frequent narrative element in hagiographies that concentrate on the truth of the Christian faith. (Hagiography, it should be noted, is not a genre given to ecumenical celebrations of diverse beliefs.) Custance's first fiancé, the Muslim sultan of Syria, converts to Christianity to marry her, but his mother slaughters him and other Christians at the banquet celebrating the impending nuptials (2.414–34). The narrator refers to the sultan's mother as the "welle of vices" (2.323) and explains her murderous rage as resulting from her son's conversion (2.324–27), as well as her desire to rule (2.434). Although the Man of Law proclaims in his Prologue that he will speak of poverty, in truth religious conflict, with Christianity depicted as wholly good and Islam as wholly evil, provides the tale's major theme, as Custance owes her eventual triumph to her unswerving adherence to her faith.

Exiled from Syria (although, somewhat inexplicably, not executed with the other victims of the sultan's mother's murderous rampage), Custance is set out to sea and drifts for three years until she washes ashore in England, surviving this ordeal (and a subsequent period of five years adrift) through God's assistance (2.470–504). Beyond representing the ideal of virtue in poverty, Custance embodies the religious virtues of constancy and patience, of suffering yet never wavering in one's beliefs, and this aspect of her character is captured in her name with its play on "constancy." Upon arriving in England, she is taken in by a constable and his wife Hermengild, and the saintly Custance succeeds in converting Hermengild and then the constable, although other Christians have fled that pagan land (2.540–46). In a scene that further establishes Custance as a paragon of Christian virtue, Satan inspires a knight with lust for her;

upon being rejected, the knight slays Hermengild and frames Custance for the crime (2.582–602). When he swears that Custance is guilty of Hermengild's murder, he is immediately struck down through divine (and bloodily eye-popping) retribution and then executed (2.666–93). Following this miraculous event, Custance converts King Alla and many others to Christianity, and she then marries the king (2.673–93). Historically, a king named Aella ruled in Northumbria during the middle years of the ninth century, but in the fiction of the Man of Law's Tale, the king's name alludes to Allah, and thus metaphorically suggests that Custance succeeds in converting the Muslim god to Christianity.

The Man of Law's Tale returns to the folkloric plot device of the evil mother-in-law, as Alla's mother Donegild attempts to trick her son into abandoning his wife by replacing a letter announcing the birth of their healthy son Mauricius with accounts of an elfish monster (2.722–56). Alla accepts these falsehoods with equanimity of spirit (2.757–70), but Donegild then tricks her son's constable into banishing Custance and Mauricius by casting them adrift in the same ship on which Custance arrived years earlier (2.771–875). Custance miraculously floats to Rome, where she eventually reunites with Alla, who has come to Rome to seek absolution for killing his mother. In terms of the tale's hagiographic message, the trip to Rome symbolizes Custance's fulfillment of her Christian destiny, as she returns to the location of the Church's authority. Indeed, the plot of the Man of Law's Tale borders on soap-operatic, as it details the various difficulties Custance overcomes through her unswerving devotion to her Christianity. Remaining true to her faith, as her name promises, Custance can finally live free from poverty—and mothers-in-law. In this hagiographic romance, readers observe the moral example of Custance's saintly virtue coupled with the amatory elements of courtship and marriage. True to her faith, true to her husband, and witnessing her son Mauricius crowned emperor by the pope, Custance reaps the earthly rewards granted to the faithful, as the tale concludes with her death as a foreshadowing of the redemptive potential of "Joye after wo" (2.1161).

In the Man of Law's Epilogue, more dissension erupts among the pilgrims, and thus Chaucer keeps his readers' attention on the aggressive valence of the storytelling competition. Harry asks the Parson to tell the next tale, but the Parson is offended by the Host's swearing (2.1170–71); fearing that the Parson will preach a sermon to the pilgrims, the Shipman interrupts and promises that he will tell a tale that "schal not ben of philosophie" (2.1188). Typically, the Shipman's Tale comes much later in the generally agreed arrangement of the *Canterbury Tales*, which suggests that Chaucer was continually reordering his tales until his death. The Wife of Bath's Prologue resumes the narrative, and her lusty voice offers as powerful a rebuttal to the Parson's potential preaching as the Shipman's delayed fabliau possibly could.

WIFE OF BATH'S PROLOGUE AND TALE

With her sharp wit and bawdy humor, Chaucer's Wife of Bath expresses numerous ideas that undermine the social assumptions of the Middle Ages. The opening lines of her Prologue might not appear terribly incendiary at first glance, but by exploring their repercussions throughout her Prologue and Tale, we see how she riotously reimagines women's place in medieval society: "Experience, though noon auctoritee [authority] / Were in this world, is right ynogh [sufficient] for me / To speke of wo that is in mariage" (3.1–3). In the masculine milieu of the Middle Ages, men controlled virtually every social structure, and thus in large measure determined how women lived their lives; despite the patriarchal nature of this society, Alison of Bath asserts her right to speak for herself through her personal experience, which, she argues, teaches her more about life than do men's sterile proclamations. In establishing an opposition between experience and authority, Alison privileges her personal knowledge over the dictates of men who, despite their holding a near monopoly on governance in the Middle Ages, can never experience life as women. These weighty themes might suggest an exegesis of deep philosophical seriousness, but the Wife of Bath's Prologue crackles with humor due to Alison's fabliau sensibility, which infuses her argument with vulgar hilarity as she dismantles masculine prerogatives in her household.

The Wife of Bath's Prologue is approximately twice as long as her corresponding Tale, and it can be subdivided into six discrete units: Alison's views on marriage and virginity (3.1–162); the Pardoner's interruption with a question about his impending marriage (3.163–92); Alison's methods for managing her first three husbands (3.193–451), and then her fourth (3.452–502); Alison's courtship and marriage to her fifth husband Jankyn (3.503–828); and finally a spat between the Summoner and the Friar (3.829–56). (These two men's fractious interjection continues the focus of the *Canterbury Tales* on rivalries between men, such as those between the Miller and the Reeve, and this new rivalry is developed considerably in their taletelling exchange, which follows the Wife of Bath's Tale.) In its entirety, and despite some interruptions, the *Prologue* focuses squarely on Alison and her indefatigable assault on medieval cultural mores requiring feminine submissiveness.

Alison's opening discussion of marriage and virginity contains some of the most bawdy and hilariously sacrilegious commentary in all of literature. At times she assumes a naive persona, such as when she expresses difficulty in understanding the meaning of Jesus's words in the New Testament (3.14–20). Contradicting herself soon after, she also states that she does not need masculine authorities to interpret texts for her when she brazenly reinterprets them according to her protofeminist worldview: "But wel I woot [know, understand], expres, withoute lye [deception], / God bad us for to wexe [grow] and multiplye; / That gentil text kan I wel understonde" (3.27–29). In her argument against virginity and for marriage, Alison makes an obvious point: since humans cannot multiply themselves without engaging in sexual intercourse, and since, according to medieval Christian thought, one should have sex only within marriage, one should marry in order to procreate. But if Alison's defense of marriage depends on the possibility of procreation, it is certainly ironic that she never mentions having mothered any children. She also displays sound, if somewhat bawdily blatant, logic in her argument rebutting the necessity of virginity:

"For hadde God comanded maydenhede [virginity],
Thanne hadde he dampned weddyng with the dede.
And certes, if ther were no seed ysowe [sown],
Virginitee, thanne wherof sholde it growe?" (3.69–72)

Truly, virgins cannot produce the next generation of virgins without losing their virginity, and thus the propagation of the human species depends on sexual activity. For a woman married five times and looking forward to her sixth husband (3.45–46), virginity represents the antithesis of her excessive amatory desires.

In its deflation of lofty Christian ideals, Alison's fabliau sensibility is congruent with numerous bawdy stories depicting the moral failings of the clergy, but Alison escalates such satire by mocking Jesus's morals in her diatribe. With a rather shocking metaphor, Alison compares virgins and wives to white and brown breads, and concludes by implicitly comparing Jesus to a pimp:

"Lat hem [virgins] be breed of pured whete-seed [refined white
   bread],
And lat us wyves hoten [be called] barly-breed [barley bread];
And yet with barly-breed, Mark telle kan,
Oure Lord Jhesu refresshed many a man." (3.143–46)

The pun on "refresshed" suggests both Jesus's feeding of the crowd in
the miracle of the loaves (Mark 6.30–44; cf. Matthew 14.13–21, Luke
9.10–17, John 6.1–14) and his providing of wives for sexual pleasure; this
pun is not an isolated incident in Alison's bawdy vocabulary, as she uses
the same word to describe her envy of King Solomon's active sex life
(3.35–38). Transforming Jesus's miracle of the loaves into a metaphor for
copulation, Alison resignifies biblical events of spiritual inspiration into
fabliau celebrations of carnality.

For many readers, the Wife of Bath's lascivious nature builds much
of her appeal, but one should not overlook the serious import of her
Prologue. Throughout her monologue, she pays keen attention to a
woman's tenuous position in medieval society and, in particular, how
she gained and lost control of her own estate. Scrutinizing her relationship with her fifth husband Jankyn, Alison realizes that she erred in
trusting him too much. She reports that she "hym yaf [gave] . . . al the
lond and fee [property] / That evere was me yeven [given] therbifoore"
(3.630–31), and in so doing she ceded governance over her own destiny. Alison's troubles with Jankyn extend beyond his control over her
property, as he delights in reading his "book of wikked wyves" (3.685),
a misogynist compendium detailing women's failings as recounted in
numerous biblical and classical sources (3.711–87). Jankyn's literary
amusements drive Alison into such a fury that she rips three pages
from the book and then decks him; he strikes her in retribution, and
she, after feigning impending death, lands a sucker punch to avenge her
injury (3.788–812). Despite the violence of the scene, which deafens her
in one ear (1.446, 3.668), Alison succeeds in regaining control of her
property and her husband:

"He yaf [gave] me al the bridel in myn hond,
To han the governance of hous and lond,
And of his tonge, and of his hond also;
And made hym brenne [burn] his book anon right tho." (3.813–16)

As much as the Wife of Bath's Prologue trumpets a woman's ability to interpret her life and culture according to her own values, it is also the story of a woman who corrects and learns from her marital mistakes. Should Alison find the sixth husband to whom she earlier alludes, it is certain that she will not make the same mistake twice in ceding conrol of her life to a masculine authority.

The protofeminist message cloaked under the fabliau humor of Alison's Prologue is encapsulated in her rhetorical question "Who peyntede the leon [lion], tel me who?" (3.692). These words allude to an old fable in which a lion sees a painting of another lion killed by a human, and its question underscores the ways in which perspectives influence interpretations. Had a lion painted the encounter between man and beast, this provocative query suggests, the picture would emphasize different aspects of the conflict leading to the animal's demise, or perhaps depict an altogether different vision of human-animal relations, with the lion triumphant over the remains of a devoured man. Similarly, Alison's Prologue allows a woman to speak, to "paint the lion," of women's experience in medieval England, and as Alison progresses into her tale, she assumes the narrative voice necessary to tell a romance rather than the fabliau that one might expect from such a bawdy figure.

On the surface, the Wife of Bath's Tale is a rather typical romance: a knight undertakes a quest, and he succeeds through the assistance of an old woman who appears both recognizably human and also fairylike in her supernatural powers. The two marry, and they live happily ever after. But if one peers beneath the surface, numerous aspects of this story question, if not undermine, the typical values of a chivalric romance. Foremost, the knightly protagonist is a rapist. He is a "lusty bacheler" (3.883) who spies a virgin walking alone and preys upon her: "By verray force, he rafte [stole] hire maydenhed" (3.888). King Arthur's court condemns the knight to death, but the ladies of the court—inexplicably, to many modern readers—intercede on his behalf; to escape punishment, he is required to discover what women want most in the world (3.899–912). One would think, given the context, that the answer is obvious: women do not want to be raped, preferring to wield personal authority in their amatory affairs. With breathtaking ignorance, this knight cannot solve the riddle by himself, but he stumbles across an old woman who promises him the answer on the condition that he grant her an unspecified future request (3.1009–13). The knight returns to the queen and answers the question that motivated his quest, in language more poetic than the blunt statement that women do not want to be raped, while nonetheless clearly expressing this idea:

> "My lige lady, generally," quod he,
> "Wommen desiren to have sovereynetee
> As wel over hir housbond as hir love,
> And for to been in maistrie [control] hym above." (3.1037–40)

Given the knight's transgression, he must learn to respect women's autonomy and their agency in love. Although he succeeds in his quest by suggesting his understanding of his culpability, his words are not yet matched by deeds. Within the world of romance, he now appears to have redeemed himself and to display the attractive and courtly masculinity expected of knights and the aristocracy, but the Wife of Bath has not completed her protagonist's amatory education.

As a rapist, the knight forced sex upon a woman who did not desire him, and in a fitting punishment, the old woman who saved him from execution demands his hand in marriage and his body in bed. In Chaucer's hilarious depiction of their first night together as husband and wife, the knight squirms at the prospect of consummating their marriage, and the old woman sarcastically asks, "Is this the lawe of kyng Arthures hous? / Is every knyght of his [beloved] so dangerous [aloof]?" (3.1089–90). The knight confesses to his bride that he finds her hideously unattractive, old, and lowborn. In her lengthy reply, as she refutes his claims about her suitability as a wife, one can readily locate similarities with the arguments in Alison's Prologue. Primarily, the old woman focuses on the concept of gentility, reminding him that an aristocratic lineage does not guarantee meritorious behavior: "For, God it woot, men may wel often fynde / A lordes sone do shame and vileynye" (3.1150–51). These words remind the knight of his own transgressions and conclusively demonstrate the wisdom of her argument.

The old woman concludes her excursus by offering the knight a choice:

> "Chese [choose] now," quod she, "oon of thise thynges tweye:
> To han me foul and old til that I deye,
> And be to yow a trewe, humble wyf,
> And nevere yow displese in al my lyf,

Or elles ye wol han me yong and fair,
And take youre aventure [chance] of the repair [change]
That shal be to youre hous by cause of me." (3.1219–25)

Which will it be: a wife old and ugly yet faithful, or young and beautiful yet promiscuous? The knight, unwilling to choose, asks his wife to make the decision for the two of them. She forgives him and grants the best of both options, transforming into a beautiful young lady who will remain forever faithful to him. The story concludes with the knight's "herte bathed in a bath of blisse" (3.1253), and the romance ending subsumes the irony of a rapist knight rewarded for his transgressions.

The end of the Wife of Bath's Tale, however, indicates that Alison sees through the courtly values upheld in her tale, that she muffled but did not fully quell her rebellious spirit while narrating this romance. In her valediction, her fabliau voice reemerges to curse men who will not be ruled by their wives, and it is truly an anomalous moment in literature, as few storytellers finish their narratives by damning members of their audience with the plague:

"And thus they lyve unto hir lyves ende
In parfit joye; and Jhesu Crist us sende
Housbondes meeke, yonge, and fressh abedde,
And grace t'overbyde [outlive] hem that we wedde;
And eek I praye Jhesu shorte hir lyves
That noght wol be governed by hir wyves;
And old and angry nygardes [stingy men] of dispence,
God sende hem soone verray pestilence!" (3.1257–64)

If the old woman's submission to her husband in marriage upholds typical ideals of romance, Alison's closing curse renders this value system and the genre that extols it highly suspect. Indeed, the Friar's response to Alison's tale—"Us nedeth nat to speken but of game" (3.1275)—suggests his discomfort with her curse, as he attempts to return the taletelling competition to a spirit of levity rather than imprecations, but the subject is then dropped as the antagonism between the Friar and the Summoner takes center stage. In this light, Alison's romance resembles the sucker punch with which she tamed Jankyn in her Prologue—a fabliau-style trick devised to put women back on top in a world designed to keep them subservient to men.

FRIAR'S PROLOGUE AND TALE

Similar to the Miller and the Reeve in their mutual animosity, the Friar and the Summoner detest each other, as we saw in their exchange between the Wife of Bath's Prologue and Tale (3.829–56). Now that their turns to tell tales have arrived, the men attack each other's moral failings in their respective stories. Chaucer offers no specific reason to explain the two men's vicious quarrel, but both of these spiritual charlatans exploit religious belief for financial gain, and so they would likely view each other as competitors threatening their potential profits. As the Friar's Tale makes clear, summoners were charged with calling transgressors to church courts, a practice conducive to bribes and extortion, and as the Summoner's Tale demonstrates, friars often sought generous contributions to maintain their supposedly spartan lifestyles with surprising luxuries. Perhaps more important in the narrative development of the Canterbury pilgrimage, their shared animosity is quite amusing. Indeed, the Friar's Prologue begins with the Friar making a face at the Summoner (3.1265–67), a juvenile moment that prepares the reader for another round of satiric narratives designed primarily for the pleasures of insulting an enemy.

The Friar's Tale recounts the story of a sinful summoner damned to hell, and the tale is designed as a negative example of how to behave in accordance with Christian values. As such, it is an exemplum, a genre frequently used by medieval preachers to illustrate the moral themes of their sermons; with its religious inflections, an exemplum is thus a particularly apt genre for Chaucer to put in his Friar's mouth. The Friar's opening lines describing this summoner stress his corrupt lifestyle, complete with a network of spies (3.1323–24) and prostitutes (3.1355–58) for purposes of blackmail. His current plan for pecuniary gain involves extorting money from a poor old woman (3.1375–78), but on his journey he encounters a yeoman, with whom he immediately swears an oath of brotherhood (3.1403–6). This brotherhood oath recalls the similar pledge between Palamon and Arcite in the Knight's Tale, and it thus exposes the summoner's preference for courtly relationships over religious ones. This "yeoman" soon confesses his true identity as a devil, but the summoner's reaction—instead of shock and horror—only accentuates his own moral turpitude:

"A!" quod this somonour, "benedicite [bless you]! What sey ye?
I wende [thought] ye were a yeman trewely.
Ye han a mannes shap as wel as I;
Han ye a figure thanne determinat
In helle, ther ye been in youre estat?" (3.1456–60)

The heavy irony of a summoner blessing a devil underscores the moral bankruptcy of the man and his position in the Church. Furthermore, he evinces more interest in the devil's manipulation of his body than in his evil nature, which reveals that he values physical form over spiritual virtue. This summoner should not express wonder and admiration at meeting such an impressive fellow; he should flee immediately to protect the sanctity of his soul.

As the Friar's negative exemplum progresses, readers should expect this summoner to make immoral decisions, and in this regard he does not disappoint. He lies to the devil and claims to be a yeoman as well (3.1524) because he is ashamed to be identified in the unsavory role of a summoner (3.1393–94). In addition to their brotherhood oaths, the two men now agree to share each other's winnings:

"Taak thou thy part, what that men wol thee yive [give],
And I shal myn; thus may we bothe lyve.
And if that any of us have moore than oother,
Lat hym be trewe and parte it with his brother." (3.1531–34)

This agreement lays the foundation for the summoner's fall at the story's end, and the moral lesson of this exemplum appears to be, quite simply, that one should not make a deal with the devil. The tale is also concerned with the significance of language and intention, as the brief interlude in which a man curses his horses allows the devil to explain to the summoner the necessity for a person to truly mean his words. The horses' owner spoke in a fit of pique, not with true conviction, and he soon praises the beasts for their work. The devil concludes, "The carl [churl] spak oo [one] thing, but he thoghte another. / Lat us go forth abouten oure viage; / Heere wynne I nothyng" (3.1568–70). Spoken words are exterior expressions of thought, but they do not always indicate a person's feelings. One must peer beneath the surface to learn the truth because, like this devil camouflaged as a yeoman, the exterior can be deceiving.

When the summoner confronts the old woman whom he plans to extort, he accuses her of fornicating with priests (3.1583) and of cursing (3.1586–87), and he then offers her the opportunity to bribe him to overlook these trumped-up charges (3.1598–1603). In return the woman, declaring her innocence, damns the summoner to hell unless he repents his sins: "Unto the devel blak and rough of hewe / Yeve [Give] I thy body and my panne also!" (3.1622–23). Unlike the man who cursed his horses, this woman's words reflect her true intentions, and so when the summoner refuses to atone for his misdeeds, the fiend fulfills the woman's damning words:

> "Now, brother," quod the devel, "be nat wrooth;
> Thy body and this panne been myne by right.
> Thou shalt with me to helle yet tonyght,
> Where thou shalt knowen of oure privetee [private doings]
> Moore than a maister of dyvynytee." (3.1634–38)

The summoner's greed is punished by his damnation, but ironically, his desire to learn about the ways of hell—as evidenced in his earlier questions about the devil's terrestrial and infernal forms—is fulfilled. Promising that the summoner will surpass the earthly knowledge of spiritual men, the devil grants him the knowledge that he sought, although it is at the expense of his soul.

Through this exemplum the Friar teaches a lesson on the evils of greed and hypocrisy, but if one reviews the depiction of the Friar in the General Prologue, it becomes evident that the Friar hypocritically chastises the summoner of his tale (and thus the Summoner of the pilgrimage) for sins that he himself commits. For example, Chaucer recounts how the Friar wheedles money from poor old women: "For thogh a wydwe hadde noght a sho [shoe], / So plesaunt was his 'In principio,' / Yet wolde he have a ferthyng, er he wente" (1.253–55).[4] Perhaps a shade less deceitful than the summoner in his tale, the Friar nonetheless hypocritically concerns himself more with financial gain than spiritual growth, and although his exemplum teaches a valuable lesson, the source from which this moral comes is muddied with similar transgressions.

SUMMONER'S PROLOGUE AND TALE

After the Friar completes his tale of a damned summoner, the Summoner, greatly offended, undertakes to humiliate his foe. His narrative revenge begins prior to his tale, as he includes a short dream vision in his prologue in which a friar falls asleep and experiences a vision of hell. This friar is delighted not to see any of his brethren in Satan's realm and interprets it as a sign of their special grace. His guide, however, to correct this erroneous assumption, says to Satan: "Shewe forth thyn ers [ass], and lat the frere se / Where is the nest of freres in this place!" (3.1690–91). At this command, twenty thousand friars fly out of Satan's rectum, swarm around the rest of the damned, and then return to their home: "And in his ers they crepten everychon [each one]" (3.1698). With its filthy excess, this dream vision is suffused with fabliau elements, yet it would be remiss not to see its connections—tenuous though they may be—to the exemplum tradition as well. With the final lines of his Prologue, the Summoner suggests that this friar might reform himself, since "was the develes ers ay [always] in his mynde" (3.1705). As with the Friar's Tale, a moral lesson can be gleaned from the Summoner's Prologue, but again the moral is secondary to the insult in which it is couched.

Given the fabliau sensibility of the Summoner's Prologue, it is not surprising that the Summoner's Tale builds up to an equally riotous climax. This fabliau features a greedy friar attempting to wheedle money out of a sick man named Thomas, all the while flirting with his wife (3.1802–9) and mistreating his cat (3.1775). He also sermonizes to Thomas, exhorting him to avoid the sin of anger (3.1992–2093). Like the old woman in the Wife of Bath's Tale, who offers a long litany of biblical and classical sources to justify her argument to the rapist knight, the friar patiently cites numerous authorities as he explains to Thomas why he must relinquish his anger (and, concomitantly, open his purse). He urges Thomas to heed the advice of Seneca (3.2017–42) and to learn from the story of Cambises, the king of Persia (3.2043–88), along with other such instructive tales. This friar displays his wide knowledge of the classical tradition in these passages, and in distilling a moral congruent with his avaricious objectives, he perverts the exemplum tradition by devising lessons directed to his personal gain rather than to Thomas's spiritual needs.

The tables are turned, and the tale's fabliau sensibility comes to the forefront when Thomas tricks the friar into excavating for treasure in his buttocks:

"Now thanne, put in thyn hand doun by my bak,"
Seyde this man, "and grope wel bihynde.

Bynethe my buttok there shaltow fynde
A thyng that I have hyd in pryvetee." (3.2140–43)

It is surely a sign of the friar's greed, as well as of his great stupidity, for it strains the imagination—even in these days of drug trafficking—to guess what he hopes to find there. And these lines contain a deeper irony: the friar who earlier criticized curates who are "ful necligent and slowe / To grope tendrely a conscience" (3.1816–17) now readily displays his preference to grope a sick man's body for treasure rather than to tend to the health of his soul. His reward, reminiscent of the thunderclap of a fart that humiliated Absolon in the Miller's Tale, is blasted upon him in an impressive explosion of flatulence: "Ther nys no capul [horse], drawynge in a cart, / That myghte have lete a fart of swich a soun [sound]" (3.2150–51).

In many ways, the thematic cores of the Friar's Tale and the Summoner's Tale parallel each other, as the narratives hinge on philosophical issues absurdly removed from their plots and yet central to their unfolding. The summoner of the Friar's Tale was more concerned with the devil's shape in hell than with the fact that he had sworn a brotherhood oath with a manifestation of evil, and the friar in the Summoner's Tale professes great distress because he cannot divide his reward—the fart—with his fellow friars, which was a condition of Thomas's bequest (3.2129–36). After receiving this gaseous gift, the friar retreats to the lord of the village to pose the riddle of how to share a fart, a vexing problem requiring deep knowledge of "ars-metrike [the art of measuring]" (3.2222). Chaucer's pun on "arse" nicely encapsulates his thematic attention to merging fabliau vulgarity and philosophical musings on issues of form and meaning. The lord's squire solves Thomas's riddle, with the ingenious suggestion that the farter should stand on the center of a wheel and then allow the stinky vapors to be equally disbursed down the wheel's spokes (3.2253–86). Although the squire is described as a "cherl" (3.2290), he proves himself capable of outsmarting the humiliated friar, and his triumph fulfills the narrative expectations of fabliaux, in which the clever are lionized for outwitting the foolish.

CLERK'S PROLOGUE AND TALE

Although not as pronounced as the hostility between the Miller and the Reeve, or between the Friar and the Summoner, tension simmers between Harry Bailly and the Clerk in the Clerk's Prologue, likely due to their differences in class and status as tradesman and student. Chaucer foreshadows the antagonism between the two men in the General Prologue when the Host chastises the Clerk for his studious manner, ordering him to "lat be youre shamefastnesse [modesty], / Ne studieth noght" (1.840–41), and this friction continues in the Clerk's Prologue when Harry impugns his masculinity: "'Sire Clerk of Oxenford,' oure Hooste sayde, / 'Ye ryde as coy and stille as dooth a mayde [maiden, virgin] / Were newe spoused, sittynge at the bord [reception table]'" (4.1–3). Goading the Clerk into telling his tale, Harry reasserts his governance over the Canterbury pilgrims, but the Clerk's response highlights that the pilgrims need not acquiesce to the Host's somewhat minatory posturings. His response models the ways in which the pilgrims resist Harry's authority while appearing to submit:

> This worthy clerk benignely [graciously] answerde:
> "Hooste," quod he, "I am under youre yerde [authority];
> Ye han of us as now the governance,
> And therfore wol I do yow obeisance,
> As fer as resoun axeth, hardily." (4.21–25)

Through the Clerk's caveat—that he will obey Harry only as far as reason requires—it appears that the two men are wrestling to control the Clerk's place in the taletelling competition. In the end the Clerk refuses to conform to the Host's desires: he tells a tale, but it is not the "murie [merry] thyng of aventures" (4.15) that the Host requests. Rather, the Clerk's Tale is generally agreed to be one of the most disturbing of the *Canterbury Tales*, with its detailed focus on its suffering heroine, Griselda, and the torment she endures at the hands of her cruel husband, Walter.

The beginning of the Clerk's Tale might remind readers of the fairy tale *Cinderella* in their shared rags-to-riches plots, in which Griselda is plucked from poverty to marry the marquis Walter. *Cinderella* ends with its protagonist living "happily ever after," but the Clerk's Tale continues well beyond the point of marriage to puncture any idealized romanticism in wedlock. On the contrary, Harry Bailly refers to the tale as a "legende" (4.1212d), a term that typically denotes a saint's life, and thus readers should be prepared to witness Griselda's exemplary behavior in the face of great adversities. When Walter proposes to Griselda, he demands that she sacrifice her personal desires in the service of his:

"I seye this: be ye redy with good herte
To al my lust [pleasure], and that I frely may,
As me best thynketh, do yow laughe or smerte [hurt],
And nevere ye to grucche [begrudge] it, nyght ne day?
And eek whan I sey 'ye,' ne sey nat 'nay,'
Neither by word ne frownyng contenance?
Swere this, and heere I swere oure alliance." (4.351–57)

This demand for Griselda to vanquish any sense of interior will or desire in favor of his is certainly not the most romantic of marriage proposals. Nonetheless, she agrees, they marry, a daughter is born, and then the story degrades into a series of cruel tests of Griselda's ability to patiently endure emotional torments. As Custance of the Man of Law's Tale was persecuted by her mothers-in-law so that she could prove her mettle as a hagiographical heroine, so too must Griselda embody the virtues of patience and constancy in her marriage if she is to triumph and be rewarded at the narrative's end.

Walter, determined to test Griselda's unwavering obedience, convinces her that he has ordered their daughter to be executed. Even when Griselda pleads with the supposed executioner to bury the girl's body after her murder, this slight comfort is denied her:

"Gooth now," quod she, "and dooth my lordes heeste [command];
But o [one] thyng wol I prey yow of youre grace,
That, but my lord forbad yow, atte leeste
Burieth this litel body in som place
That beestes ne no briddes [birds] it torace [tear it apart]."
But he no word wol to that purpos seye,
But took the child and wente upon his weye. (4.568–74)

It is a rather gruesome scene, one that Walter repeats after their second child, a son, is born (4.610–86). Once again, Griselda's shocking display of patience provides no relief for her suffering, and the narrator concludes that she succeeds in evacuating herself of any desires unsanctioned by her husband: "She shewed wel, for no wordly unreste / A wyf, as of hirself, nothing ne sholde / Wille in effect, but as hir housbonde wolde" (4.719–21). Griselda reflects Walter's desires to him, proving the intransigence of her will in allowing his every desire, no matter how abhorrent, to be fulfilled.

To achieve the hagiographical potential in her suffering, Griselda must face additional torments, and Walter sends her back to a life of poverty with her father, returning her with nothing but the clothing on her back (4.785–896). As a final insult, he then requests that she return to his court to prepare for his new bride (4.939–80). Griselda patiently carries out these domestic chores, and in the tale's climax, Walter reveals that his new "bride" and her little brother are actually their own children (4.1065–71). The family is reunited, and everyone lives happily ever after, achieving the fairy-tale ending so long delayed by Walter's sadistic tests of Griselda's constancy: "Thus hath this pitous day a blisful ende, / For every man and womman dooth his myght / This day in murthe and revel to dispende" (4.1121–23). Griselda's suffering is stitched over and resignified as an unfortunate prelude to her present happiness, but the bulk of the Clerk's Tale, having portrayed so excruciatingly the pains she has endured, argues against accepting this merry ending. Who would desire to spend the rest of her life married to a man like Walter, and what must the children think of their father's cruel treatment of their mother?

If Harry Bailly is correct that readers should interpret the Clerk's Tale as a legendary saint's life, Griselda should stand as a role model for all to emulate; Chaucer, however, troubles such a reading. The Clerk first rejects this interpretation—"This storie is seyd nat for that wyves sholde / Folwen Grisilde as in humylitee" (4.1142–43)—but he then appends a religious moral to his tale: "For sith a womman was so pacient / Unto a mortal man, wel moore us oghte / Receyven al in gree [graciously] that God us sent" (4.1149–51). This moral smooths over the painful nature of Griselda's experiences, but the happy ending rings false in many ways, especially with such interpretive waffling: if one should not follow Griselda "in humylitee," and yet one should, by extrapolating from her example, accept cheerfully "all . . . that God us sent," what precisely is the moral and spiritual message to be gleaned from this tale that exalts Griselda and her inhuman patience? Readers frequently chafe at the ostensible joy depicted in the tale's dénouement, as it celebrates Griselda's eventual triumph, yet this triumph is predicated upon her continued allegiance to a man who has proved himself monstrous. In some ways, her story resembles the biblical book of Job, whose eponymous protagonist suffers greatly as a result of God's wager with Satan, and the Clerk encourages his audience to interpret his story through Job's experiences (4.932–38). The analogy, however, is a frustrating one because, if Walter metaphorically represents God, God is thus depicted as needlessly cruel and arbitrary in his relationship with humanity. Within the *Canterbury Tales*, the Clerk's Tale rebuts Alison of Bath's depiction of female sovereignty in marriage, as Griselda's subservience forcefully contrasts with Alison's independence. Many of the *Canterbury Tales* address the conditions of medieval marriage, and the Clerk's Tale espouses feminine submission in marriage while simultaneously criticizing the men who would make it so excrutiatingly odious.

At the end of the Clerk's Tale, Harry Bailly expresses his desire for sovereignty in his own marriage: "By Goddes bones, / Me were levere than a barel ale / My wyf at hoom had herd this legende ones!" (4.1212b–d). Harry insulted the Clerk's masculinity at the beginning of the tale, but his own masculinity now appears under duress at the tale's conclusion. Within the rough-and-tumble taletelling of the Canterbury pilgrimage, the Clerk appears to have won this round in his fight against Harry's blustering governance. Through the complex example of Griselda's suffering in this secular saint's life, the ideals of gender in marriage—masculine authority and feminine submission—are revealed as unnecessarily constrictive and harmful, and the Clerk deploys his tale in such a manner that Harry then confesses his inability to compel his wife to suffer as patiently as the exemplary Griselda.

MERCHANT'S PROLOGUE, TALE, AND EPILOGUE

The Wife of Bath's Prologue and Tale and the Clerk's Tale address the trials and tribulations of marriage, and the Merchant continues this theme, introducing his tale by telling the pilgrims about his wife: "I have a wyf, the worste that may be; / For thogh the feend to hire ycoupled were, / She wolde hym overmacche [defeat], I dar wel swere" (4.1218–20). The Merchant concludes his Prologue by directing attention away from his troubles in marriage (4.1243–44). After witnessing the insulting allegories encoded in the Miller's, Reeve's, Friar's, and Summoner's tales, he concentrates on the fabliau humor of marital difficulties but directs his audience's attention away from any similarities between himself and his cuckolded protagonist. With this rhetorical play, he dampens the tale's metatextual relevance to his marriage but maintains its participation in Chaucer's frame narrative, in which conflicting perspectives of love, marriage, and sexuality have enlivened the taletelling game.

In many ways, the fabliau plot of the Merchant's Tale matches the

Miller's Tale: both stories focus on older men married to younger, adulterous wives. Instead of John, Alison, and Nicholas, readers meet January, May, and Damian in this fabliau, but they fulfill roughly the same roles of cuckold, adulteress, and randy youth. Despite his advanced years, and despite the wisdom one might assume to correlate with age, January proves himself foolish by marrying a woman so much younger than himself; the narrator cannot tell readers whether the old man decides to wed "for hoolynesse or for dotage [senility]" (4.1253). The narrator extols the virtues of wedlock in a lengthy passage often referred to as the "marriage encomium" (4.1263–1392), and these lines are replete with ironies. When he innocently wonders, "How myghte a man han any adversitee / That hath a wyf? Certes, I kan nat seye" (4.1338–39), it is apparent that Chaucer is setting up January for a riotous comeuppance. Even when the marriage encomium focuses on the biblical examples of such wives as Rebecca, Judith, Abigail, and Esther (4.1362–74), it is unclear whether the narrator's celebration of marriage should be believed, for these women are known more for their disobedience and trickery of their husbands than for adhering to their wishes.

After convincing himself of the merits of his pro-marriage argument, January turns to his allies Placebo and Justinus for their opinions, and these characters' names indicate their respective positions. "Placebo" translates from Latin into "I will please," which underscores his unctuous and toadying nature as January's sycophant, whereas the name "Justinus" captures the justice and truthfulness of his opinions. Here Chaucer plays loosely with the genre of debate poetry, in which opposing sides, often cast as allegorical figures, argue their respective opinions. Placebo confesses to January that he only states what he believes his superiors wish to hear: "I woot wel that my lord kan [knows] moore than I. / With that he seith, I holde it ferme and stable; / I seye the same, or elles thyng semblable" (4.1498–1500). Justinus, on the other hand, warns January of the disasters to be found in marriage, telling him that a wife may do him unthinkable harm: "Paraunter [perhaps] she may be youre purgatorie! / She may be Goddes meene and Goddes whippe" (4.1670–71). January describes marriage as an earthly paradise (4.1265), and thus the Merchant's Tale puts forth competing views of marriage and its religious significance. Since this story is a fabliau, Justinus's view of marriage and its woes will be proven true when May cuckolds her husband.

May marries January and finds herself the object of sexual desires she does not share, and the description of her wedding night is a masterpiece of Chaucer's fabliau poetics, capturing the raw carnality of January's raunchy desire. The descriptions focus on the physicality of January's rough and elderly body and its impositions on May:

> And Januarie hath faste in armes take
> His fresshe May, his paradys, his make [mate].
> He lulleth hire; he kisseth hire ful ofte;
> With thikke brustles of his berd [beard] unsofte,
> Lyk to the skyn of houndfyssh [shark], sharp as brere [briars]—
> For he was shave al newe in his manere—
> He rubbeth hire aboute hir tendre face. (4.1821–27)

January's tight grasp, his demanding kisses, and his rough, bristly beard against May's smooth young face: Chaucer paints this scene in stark colors to align readers' sympathies with May. Also, despite his years, January persists in his matrimonial pleasures throughout the night, rewarding May with a deliciously unsexy sight as he sings in joy: "The slakke skyn aboute his nekke shaketh / Whil that he sang, so chaunteth he and craketh" (4.1849–50). Within a wider moral universe, adultery violates oaths of deep spiritual meaning, but within a fabliau, such sexual transgressions against May's body must be avenged through additional erotic antics.

The fabliau plot takes an unexpected turn when Fortune blinds January (4.2057–71), a moment which proves ironically true the narrator's assertion that "love is blynd" (4.1598). Rather than freeing May from his control, January literally keeps his hands on her at all times (4.2072–91), which makes a dalliance with Damian difficult to schedule and thus focuses the narrative on the tricksters' need for cunning to pursue their erotic goals. They pass notes, and when May reads one and then tears it up and tosses it into the privy (4.1950–54), the Merchant debases their nascent romance by imbuing it with an excremental stench. May and Damian meet in January's garden for a tryst in a pear tree, but their plans are interrupted by the arrival of the Roman god Pluto and his wife Proserpina. Much as Placebo and Justinus debated earlier in the narrative, Pluto and Proserpina argue over January's and May's respective rights regarding the impending adulterous affair. In contrast to January and May, however, Pluto and Proserpina successfully resolve their disagreement: Pluto plans to restore January's sight and thereby reveal May's adultery to him (4.2237–63), but Prosperpina defends May, promising to give her ready excuses for her deceitful actions (4.2264–2310). Their argument ends amicably with mutual compromise, as Proserpina declares: "Lat us namoore wordes heerof make; / For sothe, I wol no lenger yow contrarie [contradict]" (4.2318–19). In this tale that mercilessly ridicules marriage, Chaucer's depiction of Pluto and Proserpina tempers the satire through this pagan union of mutual respect, yet simultaneously subverts marriage even more through Proserpina's successful defense of May's adultery.

The Merchant pleads modesty in detailing the comic climax of his fabliau, in which May and Damian achieve their goal by escaping up a pear tree for an erotic rendezvous. It is a somewhat surprising moment rhetorically, for he has not shied away at other moments in the tale from frank depiction of sexual activity, yet he now says:

> Ladyes, I prey yow that ye be nat wrooth;
> I kan nat glose, I am a rude man—
> And sodeynly anon this Damyan
> Gan pullen up the smok, and in he throng. (4.2350–53)

Like Chaucer (both as narrator of the *Canterbury Tales* and in his own voice in the Retraction), the Merchant apologizes for a story that he completely controls. His apology rings a bit hollow, especially given the candid descriptions of May and January's wedding night, but the action continues apace: Pluto restores January's eyesight, and the old man, to his horror, sees his wife copulating in a pear tree with his squire. May quickly rebuts January's accusations in the tale's final debate scene, in accordance with Proserpina's declaration that May would always have a ready reply, and convinces January that his newly restored sight has deceived him. With a rhetorical flourish that heightens the fabliau climax, May warns her husband that such sights are likely to continue: "Til that youre sighte ysatled [settled] be a while / Ther may ful many a sighte yow bigile [deceive]" (4.2405–6). In contrast to the Miller's Tale and Reeve's Tale, in which John and Symkyn are confronted with the humiliating evidence of their wives' extramarital escapades, January remains oblivious to May's adultery: "This Januarie, who is glad but he?" (4.2412). This fabliau's conclusion posits the possibility of a cheerful cuckold, one whose sense of masculine sexual prerogatives remains unchecked simply because he cannot (or refuses to) confront the evidence of his wife's infidelity.

Building on the conclusion of the Clerk's Tale, the Epilogue to the Merchant's Tale offers readers further insight into Harry Bailly's home life. Harry seizes this opportunity to comment on his shrewish spouse, reporting that she is a "labbyng [blabbering] shrewe" with a "heep of vices" (4.2428–29). He closes this short interruption to the taletelling game with an intriguing line—"And eek my wit suffiseth nat therto / To tellen al; wherfore my tale is do [completed]" (4.2439–40). It is unclear whether this reference to a tale should be construed as Harry's contribution to the pilgrims' narrative game. If so, its abbreviated and confessional qualities indicate that, like many critics, Harry may be better at discerning the merits of other people's narratives than creating his own.

SQUIRE'S INTRODUCTION AND TALE

The portrait of the Squire in the General Prologue suggests a rather effete young man, one whose masculinity and martial capabilities do not match those of his father, the Knight:

> Embrouded [embroidered] was he, as it were a meede [meadow]
> Al ful of fresshe floures, whyte and reede.
> Syngynge he was, or floytynge [playing the flute], al the day;
> He was as fressh as is the month of May. (1.89–92)

It is hard to imagine any type of effective soldier as "fressh as is the month of May," and thus the portrait of the Squire suggests his inability to live up to his family's military traditions. Likewise, his tale reveals his failure to match his father's skill in telling courtly romances, as the Squire's Tale is inferior to the Knight's Tale by virtually any literary standard.

The Squire quickly confesses his rhetorical failings: "Myn Englissh eek is insufficient" (5.37). Truly, his romance, with its convoluted and apparently endless plotline, displays none of the masterful and symmetric construction of his father's romance epic. In the introduction, readers meet the main characters: Cambyuskan (Genghis Khan), his wife Elpheta, his sons Algarsif and Cambalo, and his daughter Canacee. The romance begins appropriately enough, with a scene similar to those in such medieval romances as Chrétien de Troyes's *Lancelot* and the fourteenth-century masterpiece *Sir Gawain and the Green Knight*, in which a stranger rushes into King Arthur's court and disrupts the festivities. In this instance, the intruder rides in on a steed of brass and gives Cambyuskan and his family an array of magical gifts (5.110–67). The astonished court marvels at the magic, but also expresses trepidation that the brass horse might be a trick, similar to the famed Trojan horse, to conquer them: "I trowe som men of armes been therinne, / That shapen hem this citee for to wynne," one courtier cautions (5.213–14). But when Canacee uses her gift of a ring that allows her to speak with birds, readers encounter a long-winded and mopey falcon lamenting over her duplicitous boyfriend who jilted her for a kite (in this instance a type of hawk, not a child's toy). After this preliminary material, the Squire prepares his audience for a virtually interminable tale, which will detail Cambyuskan's military victories, Algarsif's marriage (maneuvered with the assistance of his brass horse), and Cambalo's combats (5.661–70).

The promise of such a long romance, told by such a poor taleteller, eventually overwhelms the pilgrims, and the Franklin politely asks the Squire to end his tale:

> "In feith, Squier, thow hast thee wel yquit
> And gentilly. I preise wel thy wit,"
> Quod the Frankeleyn, "considerynge thy yowthe,
> So feelyngly thou spekest, sire, I allow the!" (5.673–76)

One would expect the Franklin to speak in such a gracious manner: in the General Prologue, he is compared to St. Julian, the patron saint of hospitality (1.340). Franklins owned their lands without concomitant obligations to their lords, and, although their precise social status is the subject of debate, they would likely participate in or emulate aristocratic social rituals. It appears part of the Franklin's congenial character to firmly yet gently keep the taletelling game progressing by ending the Squire's turn; by concentrating on the more elevated aspects of the Squire's performance, the Franklin praises his courtly masculinity while sparing the pilgrims the continuation of such an elaborate romance by a young man who is insufficiently skilled in the rhetorical arts.

Somewhat surprisingly, Harry Bailly takes offense at the Franklin's courteous words, particularly his defense of the virtue of gentility. Gentility ostensibly represents an aristocratic virtue, and Harry—certainly no aristocrat—explodes in anger: "Straw for youre gentillesse!" (5.695). Within this mixed social grouping, the concept of gentility exposes fault lines among the pilgrims, with Harry demanding that the more aristocratic members of the pilgrimage expand their narrow view of such cultural values as belonging exclusively to the elite. Here again Harry reasserts his control of the taletelling competition, and the Franklin patiently accepts Harry's governance: "'Gladly, sire Hoost,' quod he, 'I wole obeye / Unto your wyl; now herkneth what I seye'" (5.703–4). With the Squire's turn ending prematurely, the Franklin now undertakes his own tale, one that addresses the meaning of gentility in marriage.

FRANKLIN'S PROLOGUE AND TALE

In his Prologue, the Franklin claims to be a simple man, one who "lerned nevere rethorik [rhetoric]" (5.719), yet he succeeds in telling a charming if melancholy story, one that meditates on the meaning of love, honor, and fidelity in marriage. In many ways, the Franklin's Tale concludes the debate about marriage engaged in by the Wife of Bath, Clerk, and Merchant because it demonstrates a mutually satisfying resolution to marital conflict. The marriage between the protagonists Arveragus and Dorigen, although it faces a difficult and emotionally torturous test, is predicated on mutual love and respect. The Franklin identifies his tale as a Breton lay (5.709–15), a genre that, in its typical incarnation, narrates a relatively short romance.

This Breton lay begins with the knight Arveragus marrying the beautiful Dorigen (5.729–805). He fulfills the role of the subservient male suitor—"Ther was a knyght that loved and dide his payne / To serve a lady in his beste wise" (5.730–31)—and she accepts him as her husband for his admirable performance of this role:

> But atte laste she, for his worthynesse,
> And namely for his meke obeysaunce,
> Hath swich a pitee caught of his penaunce
> That pryvely she fil of his accord
> To take hym for hir housbonde and hir lord. (5.738–42)

In the Franklin's argument against the Wife of Bath's suggestion that women should seek mastery over their husbands, his narrator declares, "Love wol nat been constreyned by maistrye. / Whan maistrie comth, the God of Love anon / Beteth his wynges, and farewel, he is gon!" (5.764–66). The depiction of Arveragus and Dorigen's marriage stresses their mutual compatibility and affection (5.787–805), but, to fulfill his responsibilities as a knight, Arveragus must depart for England and "seke in armes worshipe and honour" (5.811). Here Chaucer employs a standard plot device of romance, in that knights cannot remain perfectly true to their military responsibilities and to their ladies simultaneously (such as in Chrétien de Troyes's *Yvain*, in which Yvain neglects his lady Laudine when he travels with Gawain and other knights, and is duly punished for this transgression against love). Dorigen pines for Arveragus during his absence, and in her melancholy mood she fears that, even should he attempt to return to her, he would likely die because of the "grisly rokkes blake" (5.859) that line the shore and cause many shipwrecks. She muses that these black rocks appear to have no purpose other than causing death and despair: "But wolde God that alle thise rokkes blake / Were sonken into helle for his sake! / Thise rokkes sleen [slay] myn herte for the feere" (5.891–93).

Chaucer deploys the familiar yet protean plot structure of the love triangle, in which two men compete for the affections of one woman, in his Franklin's Tale. This device escalates the fabliau comic potential in the Miller's Tale and Merchant's Tale, but in the romance of the Franklin's Tale, all characters of the love triangle are esteemed for their inherent nobility. Thus even Aurelius, the young man who adores Dorigen despite her being married to Arveragus, is not a rake but a sincere and devoted lover. Because of her anxieties over the black rocks and her constant worrying over Arveragus's safety, Dorigen makes an extravagant vow to Aurelius:

> "Aurelie," quod she, "by heighe God above,
> Yet wolde I graunte yow to been youre love,
> Syn I yow se so pitously complayne.
> . . . .
> I seye, whan ye had maad the coost so clene
> Of rokkes that ther nys no stoon ysene,
> Thanne wol I love yow best of any man." (5.989–97)

Dorigen's words exemplify the folkloric motif of the rash promise, which is a frequent plot device in fairy tales. For example, in *Rumplestiltskin*, the young maiden promises her firstborn child to the mysterious dwarf who appears before her when she is faced with the impossible task of spinning straw into gold, but she does so with little idea that her words could ever come back to haunt her. Likewise, Dorigen's promise commits her to actions that she would never undertake under normal circumstances; her words do not so much betray Arveragus as show her painful fears for his safe return, as well as her confidence that she would never be called on to fulfill her vow, for how could these black rocks possibly be removed?

Within the supernatural world of medieval romance, magic often resolves impossible situations, and Aurelius finds a magician who will "maken illusioun" (5.1264) that the rocks have disappeared; then, to Dorigen's horror, he comes to claim his reward (5.1311–38). A moral quandary thus stands at the heart of this Breton lay: should Dorigen maintain her fidelity to her husband Arveragus, or should she keep her promise to Aurelius? She considers suicide as a virtuous escape from her dilemma, citing numerous examples from the past of women who preserved their honor by killing themselves (5.1355–1456). This passage shares many of the same themes and motifs of Chaucer's *Legend of Good Women*, in which women are praised for choosing death over dishonor, and Dorigen decides that, to preserve her honor as a woman and a wife, she must conform her actions to their exemplary behavior: "I wol conclude that it is bet [better] for me / To sleen [slay] myself than been defouled thus" (5.1422–23). Given the weight of these moral examples, it is then surprising that Dorigen abstains from suicide and instead shares her dilemma with her husband. Arveragus, in a scene virtually unimaginable given medieval concerns about masculine identity and cuckoldry, nobly suggests that she should be true to her word and give herself to Aurelius: "Ye shul youre trouthe holden, by my fay! / . . . / Trouthe is the hyeste thyng that man may kepe" (5.1474–79).

Learning of Arveragus's noble spirit, Aurelius releases Dorigen from her promise (5.1526–50), and in the end the magician releases Aurelius from paying for the illusion. The Franklin ends his tale with a rhetorical question, a *demande d'amour*, to his audience: "Lordynges, this question, thanne, wol I aske now, / Which was the mooste fre, as thynketh yow? / Now telleth me, er that ye ferther wende" (5.1621–23). The beauty of the Franklin's Tale in many ways is that no single answer can fully respond to his question. Each character has acted nobly, and their faults (if they can even be considered faults, rather than minor and momentary lapses in judgment) fade away as they act with magnanimity of spirit toward one another in a manner that becomes almost infectious.

PHYSICIAN'S TALE

Without a prologue to the Physician's Tale, readers gain little additional insights into this character. In the General Prologue, Chaucer characteristically praises him—"He was a verray, parfit praktisour" (1.422)—yet he also hints that this doctor cheats his patients through a conspiracy with his pharmacists:

Ful redy hadde he his apothecaries
To sende hym drogges [drugs] and his letuaries [medicines],
For ech of hem made oother for to wynne—
Hir frendshipe nas nat newe to bigynne. (1.425–28)

Healing his patients while lining his wallet, the Physician thus appears to be another of the hypocrites among the Canterbury pilgrims. Likewise, his tale superficially displays a veneer of morality, but its moral is not structurally maintained to its conclusion.

When a woman's sense of integrity in love was put to the test in the Franklin's Tale, she escaped unscathed, but in the Physician's Tale, readers see a contrasting account of how women must suffer to protect their honor. The Physician establishes the genre of his tale by declaring that it "is no fable, / But knowen for historial thyng notable" (6.155–56), but he uses history not merely to record a story of the past but to teach a moral in the manner of an exemplum. His historical narrative retells the legend of Virginia, whose name encapsulates the defining feature of her character: she is a virgin, and an exemplary young woman in all aspects of her life (6.5–71). As the Physician describes her, "And if that excellent was hire beautee, / A thousand foold moore vertuous was she" (6.39–40). Unfortunately for Virginia, her beauty attracts the attentions of the unscrupulous judge Apius, who hires a churl named Claudius to accuse her father Virginius of kidnapping her from him when she was a young child (6.118–90). Apius rules in favor of Claudius in a travesty of justice (6.191–202), and Virginius realizes that Apius's lust motivates the lawsuit (6.203–12). As he explains to Virginia, two ugly options lie before her: "'Doghter,' quod he, 'Virginia, by thy name, / Ther been two weyes, outher deeth or shame, / That thou most suffre; allas, that I was bore [born]!'" (6.213–15). Calling her thus by name, Virginius concomitantly reminds his daughter—and the reader—of her virginity.

Following the expected gendered dynamics of this historical exemplum, as well as the narrative pattern of Chaucer's Legend of Good Women, Virginia decides to protect her virginity rather than her life: "Blissed be God that I shal dye a mayde! / Yif me my deeth, er that I have a shame; / Dooth with youre child youre wyl, a Goddes name!" (6.248–50). The

Physician imbues his moral tale with a lurid edge, focusing on Virginius's gruesome decapitation of his daughter; the father then takes her severed head to court and delivers it to Apius (6.251–57). Ultimately, Virginia's sacrifice of herself to the ideal of virginity purges the town: Virginius is held blameless, Apius is imprisoned and commits suicide, and Virginius intercedes on Claudius's behalf so that the conspirator is exiled instead of executed (6.258–76). In its emphasis on the necessity of sacrifice for maintaining moral virtue and honor, the Physician's Tale parallels the Legend of Lucrece, in which Lucrece's suicide topples the Roman monarchy (*LGW* 1680–1885), and contrasts with the argument of the Franklin's Tale, in which Dorigen preserves her honor while nonetheless escaping suicide.

The Physician concludes his hortatory tale with an axiomatic moral: "Therfor I rede [advise] yow this conseil take: / Forsaketh synne, er synne yow forsake" (6.285–86). This moral, however, does not capture the narrative that has preceded it in a particularly apt manner. Virginia, an exemplary character in all ways, avoided sin assiduously, yet she dies as a result of others' transgressions. The Physician's words more readily apply to the devious Apius who perverts justice, but this secondary character would then metamorphose into the narrative's focal point. A woman pays the highest price imaginable to maintain her honor in this tale, yet her sacrifice is then eclipsed as the Physician urges readers to find a moral inapplicable to her constant virtue.

PARDONER'S INTRODUCTION, PROLOGUE, AND TALE

Harry Bailly, whose blustering masculinity has wavered through his confessions of his wife's domineering temperament, confesses himself distraught over Virginia's fate in the Physician's Tale. He requires the immediate remedy of a humorous tale and turns to the Pardoner for narrative relief:

> "By corpus bones! but I have triacle [medicine],
> Or elles a draughte [drink] of moyste and corny ale,
> Or but I heere anon a myrie tale,
> Myn herte is lost for pitee of this mayde.
> Thou beel amy [good friend], thou Pardoner," he sayde,
> "Telle us som myrthe or japes [jokes] right anon." (6.314–19)

Harry's affective response exposes a soft side to his blustering masculinity, but when he tries to return the pilgrimage to more comic affairs by requesting from the Pardoner "som myrthe or japes," the pilgrims clamor instead for a "moral thyng, that we may leere / Som wit" (6.325–26). Perhaps the most important detail of this introductory passage is not Harry and the pilgrims' debate over a mirthful or a moral tale, but the Pardoner's drinking (6.320–22, 327–38). Chaucer does not conclusively declare that the Pardoner is drunk in this scene, but as this unsavory and hypocritical character prepares his sermon against such sins as drinking, it would be quite appropriate for him to act out one of the evils against which he rails.

The Pardoner in his prologue shocks his fellow Canterbury pilgrims with his brutal honesty, as few literary characters so blatantly expose their own hypocrisy. As a representative of the Christian Church, the Pardoner should help sinners overcome their transgressions, but he does not merely reveal his own sins, he revels in them. With breathtaking candor, the Pardoner explains how he preaches a message of modesty, yet lives a life of deception and excess. The theme of his sermons is *Radix malorum est Cupiditas* (6.334), which is taken from the New Testament, 1 Timothy 6.10, and which translates as "the root of evils is greed." This moral lesson could effectively serve as the theme for any churchman's sermon, but the Pardoner is more interested in separating believers from their money than in helping them to atone for their misdeeds—and he shamelessly exposes his ploys designed to this end. He sells ridiculous relics, including the shoulder bone of a holy sheep that cures livestock disease and jealousy (6.350–71) and a miraculous mitten that increases grain production (6.372–76). At church services, he compels the parishioners to give him money through a clever rhetorical trap, telling them:

> "Goode men and wommen, o [one] thyng warne I yow:
> If any wight [person] be in this chirche now
> That hath doon synne horrible, that he
> Dar nat, for shame, of it yshryven [confessed] be,
> Or any womman, be she yong or old,
> That hath ymaked hir housbonde cokewold,
> Swich folk shal have no power ne no grace
> To offren to my relikes in this place.
> And whoso fyndeth hym out of swich blame,
> He wol come up and offre a Goddes name,
> And I assoille [absolve] him by the auctoritee

Which that by bulle [papal authority] ygraunted was to me."
    (6.377–88)

Given these terms, all parishioners who do not want their neighbors to think they are egregious sinners must open their purses. The people in the pews cannot win, for the wording forces them to give whether they were sinful or not. The Pardoner is an intriguing character because he is such an honest liar, declaring his debauched lifestyle openly and without apology, even admitting that he would gladly allow children to starve if their deaths would increase his purse (6.447–51). At the conclusion of his prologue he declares, "For though myself be a ful vicious man, / A moral tale yet I yow telle kan" (6.459–60), and, indeed, these words are true: from such a vicious man comes a sermon of moral depth and insight.

The Pardoner's Tale takes the form of a sermon with two distinct yet interrelated components: the explication of his sermon's themes and an exemplum to illustrate them. The opening lines of the sermon establish its moral basis, which includes exhortations against the sins of gluttony (6.463–588), gambling (6.589–628), and swearing (6.629–59). Certainly the Pardoner is a compelling rhetorician, and he describes these sins and their deleterious effects with lurid attention to detail. He takes his examples from the Judeo-Christian Bible, including the stories of Adam (6.505–11) and Jeremiah (6.631–37), and from history, including the stories of Seneca (6.492–97) and Attila the Hun (6.579–82).

After introducing these themes of his sermon, the Pardoner illustrates them with an exemplum portraying three ignorant and literal-minded revelers who live a dissolute and gluttonous lifestyle complete with gambling and swearing. They learn that one of their friends has died, and they make an unwise decision:

"Lat ech of us holde up his hand til oother,
And ech of us bicomen otheres brother,
And we wol sleen this false traytour Deeth.
He shal be slayn, he that so manye sleeth,
By Goddes dignitee, er it be nyght!" (6.697–701)

Although stupidity is not a sin, it surely does not speak well of these young men that they decide that they can kill Death, mistaking the allegorical figure for a person. Chaucer also satirizes their social pretensions in undertaking a brotherhood oath, a type of ritual more appropriate in the aristocratic milieu of courtly romance than in a tavern.

While searching for Death, the young men encounter a old man, perhaps Death himself, who tells them that they can find what they seek under a nearby tree (6.711–67). To their surprise and delight, the rioters find a trove of gold rather than Death, and they decide to wait until nightfall to take the treasure home. When one leaves to buy bread and wine, the other two conspire to kill him and to divide his portion of the gold between them; meanwhile, the lone man similarly determines that he would prefer to keep the gold to himself, and he therefore poisons his friends' wine. This exemplum quickly approaches its fatal conclusion, and, as the Pardoner says, "What nedeth it to sermone of it moore?" (6.879). The two men stab their friend upon his return, and they then die from drinking the poisoned wine (6.880–88). The Pardoner has convincingly demonstrated the perils of gluttony, gambling, and swearing, as he has also incorporated his preferred preaching theme of *Radix malorum est Cupiditas*. Greed is the root of evils, the wages of sin are death, and the Pardoner's sermon powerfully illustrates these messages.

After concluding his moral tale, the Pardoner shocks his fellow pilgrims yet again by trying to sell them his relics, even though he has already confessed that they are shams. That is to say, after he confesses his hypocrisy, he hopes to profit from the pilgrims by convincing them now to overlook it. The Pardoner invites Harry Bailly to make the first purchase, but Harry replies with great anger, cursing him roundly:

> "Nay, nay," quod he, "thanne have I Cristes curs!
> . . . .
> I wolde I hadde thy coillons [testicles] in myn hond
> In stide of relikes or of seintuarie [relic box].
> Lat kutte hem of, I wol thee helpe hem carie;
> They shul be shryned in an hogges toord [pig shit]!" (6.946–55)

In proposing to castrate the Pardoner, Harry might be suggesting what has already been accomplished. The portrait of the Pardoner in the General Prologue hints at his sexual indeterminacy: "No berd hadde he, ne nevere sholde have; / As smothe it was as it were late shave. / I trowe he were a geldyng or a mare" (1.689–91. Harry also dismisses the Pardoner's claims regarding his holy relics, positing their value to be excrementally worthless rather than spiritually priceless.

With Harry and the Pardoner engaged in this vulgar, comic, and pointed exchange, the pilgrimage faces a crisis of leadership, and the Knight steps in to restore order. According to medieval social structure, he is one of the leading figures among the pilgrims, and so it is appropriate that he reconcile the two fighting men:

"Namoore of this, for it is right ynough!
Sire Pardoner, be glad and myrie of cheere;
And ye, sire Hoost, that been to me so deere,
I prey yow that ye kisse the Pardoner.
And Pardoner, I prey thee, drawe thee neer,
And, as we diden, lat us laughe and pleye."
Anon they kiste, and ryden forth hir weye. (6.962–68)

Despite their animosity these two kiss each other, but they do so while acting under the Knight's authority, as neither man makes any effort to resist his commands. Ironically, the Pardoner earlier requested Harry to kiss his relics—"Com forth, sire Hoost, and offre first anon, / And thou shalt kisse the relikes everychon" (6.943–44)—and so he wins the kiss he requested, if not in the manner that he expected. The Knight restores peace to the Canterbury pilgrimage, but only after riotous insults are hurled at the Pardoner for his startlingly honest hypocrisy.

SHIPMAN'S TALE

Are successful businessmen—the Carnegies, Rockefellers, Gettys, and Trumps of the medieval world—smart? The Shipman addresses this question in his fabliau of familial and sexual economics, in which matrimonial affections are entangled with erotic deceptions in the quest for financial gain. The tale begins with the narrator's ironic observation concerning how money clouds people's perceptions: "A marchant whilom [once] dwelled at Seint-Denys, / That riche was, for which men helde hym wys" (7.1–2). Given the fabliau sensibility of the Shipman's Tale, readers can rest assured that this merchant will receive a comic comeuppance, and the narrator proceeds to introduce the cause of his troubles, which is his "compaignable and revelous" wife (7.4). Adultery is a staple plot device of Chaucer's fabliaux, and so readers should expect this wife, admired for her "excellent beautee" (7.3), to incite amatory attentions from men other than her husband. Some puzzling lines then disrupt the opening of the Shipman's Tale:

the narrator, who should be the Shipman, begins to speak in the voice of a woman (7.11–19). For example, this narrator declares,

> The sely housbonde, algate [always] he moot paye,
> He moot us clothe, and he moot us arraye,
> Al for his owene worshipe richely,
> In which array [clothing] we daunce jolily. (7.11–14)

Most scholars agree that the Shipman's Tale was originally intended for the Wife of Bath, which would explain these odd lines that Chaucer likely failed to revise prior to his death. Also, readers could assume that the Shipman speaks these words while mimicking a woman's voice, perhaps in a manner to ridicule his fellow pilgrim Alison of Bath.

In Chaucer's fabliaux the humor often depends on two men fighting for the sexual favors of one woman (or some permutation of this basic scenario) and, in so doing, seeking to prove their masculinity by defeating their foe; in the Shipman's Tale, the merchant's competitor for his wife's affections is a monk named John. Chaucer adds further irony in this depiction of adultery and cuckoldry by describing the merchant and John as cousins who have sworn a brotherhood oath:

> The monk hym claymeth as for cosynage [cousinage, kinship],
> And he agayn; he seith nat ones nay,
> But was as glad therof as fowel [fowl, rooster] of day,
> For to his herte it was a greet plesaunce.
> Thus been they knyt with eterne alliaunce,
> And ech of hem gan oother for t'assure
> Of bretherhede whil that hir lyf may dure [endure]. (7.36–42)

The Shipman expends this detailed attention on the bonds between the men to increase the humor when John so quickly breaks them. After some flirtatious banter with the merchant's wife (7.100–123), the monk reveals to her that his friendship with her husband is designed solely so that he can spend time with her:

> "He is na moore cosyn unto me
> Than is this leef that hangeth on the tree!
> I clepe hym so, by Seint Denys of Fraunce,
> To have the moore cause of aqueyntaunce
> Of yow, which I have loved specially

Aboven alle wommen, sikerly [certainly].
This swere I yow on my professioun." (7.149–55)

Any vow this man makes appears to be immediately undone, as his oath
of brotherhood to the merchant is forsaken in this passage, and he similarly renounces his religious vows as a monk, simply to advance his seduction of his friend's wife. In many fabliaux, erotic satisfaction trumps
all other commitments, and John sacrifices his fraternal and spiritual
bonds to bed this merchant's comely wife.

The merchant's wife has more pressing matters at hand than sex: her
clothing bill is due, and she needs a hundred franks to pay it (7.178–81). In
her conversation with the monk, she accuses her husband of being a horrible person—"Myn housbonde is to me the worste man / That evere was
sith that the world bigan" (7.161–62)—but little evidence supports this
assertion within the tale, as readers never observe her being mistreated
in any way. The monk devises a clever scheme to sleep with her that will
sate his sexual and her financial desires: he borrows a hundred franks
from the merchant, gives the money to the wife, and enjoys his night
of passion with her (7.269–319). Then, when he next sees the merchant,
he tells him that he returned the hundred franks to her (7.349–64). The
merchant confronts his wife about the missing money, but in a final irony
surrounding the bond between the two men, she blames their fraternal
relationship for her failure to remit the funds:

"He took me certeyn gold, that woot I weel—
What! Yvel thedam [bad luck] on his monkes snowte!
For, God it woot, I wende, withouten doute,
That he hadde yeve it me bycause of yow
To doon therwith myn honour and my prow [benefit],
For cosynage, and eek for beele cheere
That he hath had ful ofte tymes heere." (7.404–10)

The wife then offers a dreadful pun (and, of course, dreadful puns are
often the best puns) when she tells her husband how to recoup his losses:
"I am youre wyf; score it upon my taille, / And I shal paye as soone as ever
I may" (7.416–17). The pun arises in the play between "taille" as a tally of
debts and as a crude euphemism for her genitalia, as in the slang phrase
"a piece of tail." The merchant appreciates his wife's solution, and forgives
her for the lost money. In the end, he has paid a hundred franks for his

wife to cheat on him, but since he never learns of his cuckoldry, perhaps it is money well spent within the carnivalesque world of the fabliau; like January in the Merchant's Tale, this merchant has been spared knowledge of his wife's transgressions, and thus his own sense of masculine authority is unthreatened, despite readers' clear understanding of the betrayal.

The Shipman concludes his fabliau with a short and bawdy prayer: "Thus endeth my tale, and God us sende / Taillynge ynough unto oure lyves ende. Amen" (7.433–34). The Shipman repeats his character's ribald pun, praying for sufficient sex to last all of his days. The fabliau is not a genre particularly conducive to prayer, and the Shipman's mock petition to heaven further contrasts the spiritual sensibility of religion with the sexual antics of his tale. Not surprisingly, Harry Bailly appreciates this naughty story, thanks the Shipman for it, and then asks the Prioress to contribute to the taletelling game (7.443–51). Her story proves to be one of the more disturbing of the *Canterbury Tales* to modern eyes.

PRIORESS'S PROLOGUE AND TALE

The Prioress opens her Prologue with a prayer to "O Lord, oure Lord" (7.1) and introduces the theme of her tale that young children, in their innocence, can perform holy acts: "But by the mouth of children thy bountee / Parfourned [performed] is, for on the brest soukynge [suckling] / Somtyme shewen they thyn heriynge [praise]" (7.457–59). Invoking the aid of the Virgin, she then builds the thematic link between her prologue and tale by comparing herself to a child:

But as a child of twelf month oold, or lesse,
That kan unnethes [hardly] any word expresse,
Right so fare I, and therfore I yow preye,
Gydeth [guide] my song that I shal of yow seye. (7.484–87)

Claiming such childlike sanctity, the Prioress positions herself as a voice of innocence and purity; however, this stance appears incongruous when compared with her portrait in the General Prologue. There Chaucer portrays her as a woman with aristocratic pretensions (1.137–41) and affected table manners (1.127–36), and he remarks casually regarding her size, "For, hardily, she was nat undergrowe" (1.156). By contrasting these visions of the Prioress—as Chaucer slyly presents her in the General Prologue and as she presents herself in her tale's prologue—the reader sees a large, secularly minded woman naively assuming the persona of a holy child. In terms of genre, the Prioress's story is identified as a miracle (7.691), a narrative form that inspires spiritual devotion through its depiction of marvelous events revealing God's intercession in human affairs.

Despite the ostensible piety of this tale's speaker, many modern readers find her story rather odious because it is steeped in anti-Semitic rhetoric. Her miracle concerns a young Christian boy, a widow's son, who sings a Marian hymn, the "Alma redemptoris" (Sweet [Mother] of the Savior), as he walks through a Jewish neighborhood (7.488–557). Satan incites the Jews to exact a bloody vengeance for the child's innocent devotion to Christianity:

> Oure firste foo, the serpent Sathanas,
> That hath in Jues herte his waspes nest,
> Up swal [swelled], and seide, "O Hebrayk peple, allas!
> Is this to yow a thyng that is honest,
> That swich a boy shal walken as hym lest
> In youre despit, and synge of swich sentence,
> Which is agayn youre lawes reverence?" (7.558–64)

Following Satan's evil seductions, the Jews hire an assassin to murder the child. After the boy is killed and his body tossed into a privy, his distraught mother desperately seeks him, and he miraculously begins to sing the "Alma redemptoris" (7.565–613). The Christians find his body and slaughter the Jews in revenge, with the Prioress detailing their deaths in gruesome detail:

> With torment and with shameful deeth echon [each one],
> This provost dooth thise Jewes for to sterve [die]
> That of this mordre wiste [knew], and that anon.
> He nolde no swich cursednesse observe.
> "Yvele shal have that yvele wol deserve";
> Therfore with wilde hors he dide hem drawe,
> And after that he heng hem by the lawe. (7.628–34)

With the Jewish characters so violently ejected from the story, the narrator turns her attention to the dead child, who miraculously continues his praise of Mary with his final words (7.649–69). A monk takes a mysterious grain, likely symbolizing the Eucharist, out of the boy's mouth, and then the child "yaf up the goost ful softely" (7.672).

The Prioress's miracle succeeds in displaying the Christian God's sal-vific intervention in human affairs, but it is difficult in modern times to read the story as an affirmation of religious faith rather than as an ugly example of anti-Semitic bigotry. The connection between Chaucer's voice and that of his Prioress intrigues many readers, and some theorize that Chaucer reveals the shallow morals of the Prioress in her choice to tell this miracle. Although this may well be the case, her anti-Semitism is not questioned by any of the other pilgrims, whose reaction to the tale is one of sober reverence (7.691–92). Furthermore, the Parson, one of the ideal pilgrims, expresses similar anti-Semitic thoughts (10.599). King Edward I expelled Jews from England in 1290, and this order was not rescinded until 1656, which illustrates the extent of anti-Semitism throughout the Middle Ages and Renaissance.

PROLOGUE AND TALE OF SIR THOPAS

Chaucer's self-deprecating sense of humor is readily apparent in the Prologue to Sir Thopas, and this introduction allows him to join in the antagonistic posturings among the pilgrims. Harry Bailly abruptly takes notice of him by barking, "What man artow [are you]?" (7.695), and then insults Chaucer for his chubbiness, pointing out that they share a waist size although Chaucer is the smaller man (7.700–701). He then refers to him with such effeminizing terms as "popet" and "elvyssh" (7.701–3). Cowed by the Host's attention, Chaucer promises to tell a story he learned long ago (7.708–9); the resulting tale, a romance of knightly adventure, is dreadful—so bad it's good—as it parodies, rather than simply portrays, the traditional characteristics of courtly romance.

The titular hero Sir Thopas, who should be a brave and daring knight, is instead effeminate and ineffective. Chaucer's initial description of the character underscores his beauty rather than his bravery:

> Sire Thopas wax [grew up to be] a doghty swayn;
> Whit was his face as payndemayn [white bread],
>   His lippes rede as rose;
> His rode [complexion] is lyk scarlet in grayn,
> And I yow telle in good certayn
>   He hadde a semely nose. (7.724–29)

This type of literary description, known as a blazon, typically details the attractiveness of a female beloved, but here it is directed to the story's male protagonist. His nose, no matter how seemly it might be, could never assist him in his knightly endeavors against giants and dragons, and it is merely an early sign of the comic misadventures that will befall him and his inability to respond effectively. Mention is also made of Thopas's meticulous attention to his dress, casting him as a medieval dandy (7.730–35).

Furthermore, Thopas's quest represents not the typical knightly adventure of seeking the Holy Grail or of rescuing a damsel in distress, but of finding love with an elf-queen (7.784–96). His predilection for amatory adventures over martial ones structures the tale's parodic humor, and when Thopas meets his adversary, the evil giant Sir Olifaunt whom he must battle to win his beloved, his response is to retreat quickly:

> Sire Thopas drow abak ful faste;
> This geant at hym stones caste
> Out of a fel [terrible] staf-slynge [slingshot].
> But faire escapeth child Thopas. (7.827–30)

Not yet ready for battle, Thopas returns to town and assembles his minstrels (7.833–56), although it is unclear how these musicians would commemorate his knightly bravery in song, since he has displayed only cowardice.

This parodic romance continues with detailed descriptions of Thopas's armor and weapons (7.857–90), but as Chaucer prepares to continue his tale, Harry Bailly interjects, "Namoore of this, for Goddes dignitee" (7.919). His patience has been sorely tested by this ridiculous story told in a grating singsong meter, and it is also likely that he does not recognize the rich humor of this parody of courtly romance: Harry might see it as simply awful. Chaucer protests that he is performing to the best of his abilities (7.926–28), but Harry refuses to allow him to recommence:

> "By God," quod he, "for pleynly, at a word,
> Thy drasty rymyng is nat worth a toord!
> . . . .
> Or telle in prose somwhat, at the leeste,
> In which ther be som murthe or som doctryne." (7.929–35)

Chaucer grants Harry his wish and embarks on his Tale of Melibee, but this too is perhaps not what the Host desires to hear. Although it contains a moral, this prose treatise is one of the less lively narratives recited during the Canterbury pilgrimage, and so while apparently acquiescing, Chaucer resists Harry's commands by failing to fulfill his desire for narrative fun.

TALE OF MELIBEE

Chaucer's Tale of Melibee, a moral treatise in the form of a dialogue between husband and wife, addresses the meaning of human suffering and forgiveness. Chaucer describes Melibeus or Melibee as "yong . . . myghty and riche" (7.967), but his happy life is turned upside-down when some old enemies attack his house, beat his wife Prudence, and almost murder their daughter Sophie (7.968–73). No compelling reason explains these brutal assaults, and Melibee passionately desires vengeance. Prudence, however, as her allegorical name suggests, explains why Melibee must act with restraint. In the debate genre, advocates of the winning position typically argue slowly yet surely in demonstrating their adversary's errors, and in Chaucer's tale, Prudence eventually triumphs as she rebuts Melibee's arguments and backs up her plea for mercy.

Prudence, in relation to the Canterbury pilgrims, resembles the Wife of Bath in several ways, as both women build their arguments by carefully citing respected authorities; at the same time, Prudence stands as Alison of Bath's inverse in her calm restraint, as opposed to Alison's unrestrained passion. At one point Melibee worries that if he listens to her advice he will be seen as a milksop: "And also, certes, if I governed me by thy conseil, it sholde seme that I hadde yeve [given] to thee over me the maistrie, and God forbede that it so weere!" (7.1058). The critical issue of a husband's and his wife's respective authority over each other in marriage, a recurrent theme of the *Canterbury Tales*, reappears in the Tale of Melibee, and Melibee must learn the wisdom of heeding his wife's wise counsel. Unlike the Wife of Bath, who won mastery over Jankyn through cunning and violence, Prudence proves her worth through her superior rhetorical skills. Citing classical, biblical, and exegetical authorities to bolster her position, as Alison did before her, Prudence relies on male authorities to encourage her husband to make peace with their enemies.

In their lengthy dialogue, Prudence consistently urges restraint, deliberation, and equanimity. First, she must convince him to abandon his grief over their suffering, and she does so by citing Ovid and comparing her husband to a weeping mother; she also reminds him of the story of Job, who exemplifies the virtue of patiently withstanding adversity (7.974–1001). Following Prudence's suggestion, Melibee calls together a "greet congregacion of folk" to discuss his situation, but he decides to follow the general opinion of the young men who cry for combat (7.1002–49). Because of Melibee's reluctance to follow a woman's advice, Prudence must first defend women's wisdom (7.1050–1114) before explaining the difference between good and bad advisors (7.1115–1231). Prudence must also rebut Melibee's counselors, pointing out that he called too many men into too large an assembly and that many of them lack wisdom because of their youth (7.1232–1354), and she must examine the reasons behind her husband's agony (7.1355–1426). At the heart of her argument is her advocacy of patience over vengeance, despite Melibee's fear that if he does not punish his enemies, other men might be emboldened to do harm (7.1427–1545). She also admonishes him to be careful of his good reputation and to avoid the vagaries of conflict (7.1546–1670). Prudence succeeds in convincing Melibee to reconcile with his enemies (7.1671–1725), and she then convinces these men to seek forgiveness from him (7.1726–69). The tale concludes by addressing the power of forgiveness (7.1770–1887), as Melibee meets and reconciles with his attackers: "Wherfore I receyve yow to my grace / and foryeve yow outrely alle the offenses, injuries, and wronges that ye have doon agayn me and myne" (7.1881–82).

Chaucer's Tale of Melibee ends with the protagonist grateful, which powerfully highlights the virtue of forgiveness extolled throughout Prudence's speeches. Melibee "thonked God, of whom procedeth al vertu and alle goodnesse, that hym sente a wyf of so greet discrecioun" (7.1873). Among the Canterbury narratives depicting wives, including the Miller's Tale, Wife of Bath's Prologue and Tale, Clerk's Tale, Merchant's Tale, and Franklin's Tale, Prudence exemplifies feminine virtue and patience, and, because she speaks so eloquently, she appears a much stronger character than passive Griselda. This moral treatise allows women a voice of wisdom, and Prudence fully realizes the allegorical qualities embedded in her name. A treasure trove of proverbs and wisdom, Chaucer's Tale of Melibee likely offers insufficient "solaas" to win Harry Bailly's prize for the taletelling competition, yet it lays out a bounteous fare of "sentence" for readers seeking to understand the necessity of patience and forgiveness.

MONK'S PROLOGUE AND TALE

After Chaucer concludes his Tale of Melibee, Harry Bailly again comments on his troubles at home, and the Monk's Prologue thus keeps readers' attention on the confessional qualities of Harry's discourse. His wife's
bullying contrasts sharply with Prudence's patience, and the blustering
leader of the pilgrimage now presents himself as a henpecked husband:
"For I am perilous with knyf in honde, / Al be it that I dar nat hire withstonde, / For she is byg in armes, by my feith" (7.1919–21). Throughout the
prologues of the *Canterbury Tales*, Harry's masculinity proves itself to be
more hollow bravado than mighty manhood. Turning to the Monk to tell
his story, Harry compliments this man's readily apparent virility, which is
an unusual way to greet a member of a religious order:

> "I pray to God, yeve [give] hym confusioun
> That first thee broghte unto religioun!
> Thou woldest han been a tredefowel [chicken-fucker, cock] aright.
> Haddestow as greet a leeve [desire] as thou hast myght
> To parfourne al thy lust in engendrure,
> Thou haddest bigeten ful many a creature." (7.1943–48)

As the chinks in his masculinity are increasingly exposed, Harry turns
his attention to those pilgrims who would likely be more successful lovers, even if their religious vocations render such erotic pastimes illicit.
The indecorous term "tredefowel," suggestive of the energetic copulating
of birds, is an ironic compliment to a monk who should never "bigeten
ful many a creature." Chaucer's description of the Monk in the General
Prologue indicates that this man prefers life outside the monastery to
life inside and that he especially enjoys hunting (1.166, 177–92), and so
it seems that Harry envies the worldly attributes of this ostensibly clois-
tered man.

The Monk listens patiently to Harry's humorous yet inflammatory
words (7.1965) and then introduces his story. He declares that he will
speak of tragedies and defines this genre for his audience:

> "Tragedie is to seyn a certeyn storie,
> As olde bookes maken us memorie,
> Of hym that stood in greet prosperitee,
> And is yfallen out of heigh degree
> Into myserie, and endeth wrecchedly." (7.1973–77)

The Monk's Tale is a collection of such tragedies, recounting the sad fates of Lucifer, Adam, Samson, Hercules, Nebuchadnezzar and his son Belshazzar, Zenobia, Pedro of Castile, Pierre de Lusignan, Bernabò Visconti, Ugolino of Pisa, Nero, Holofernes, Antiochus, Alexander, Julius Caesar, and Croesus. These stories are collected from a range of sources, including the Judeo-Christian Bible, classical literature, and historical sources, but they all share the same theme of a wealthy and powerful man (or, in the case of Zenobia, a woman) who falls from glory to an abysmal end. At the height of their power, Fortune turned her wheel, and their suffering ensued.

The Monk's tragedies are relatively short—four of them consist solely of one stanza—and they all reflect a Boethian conception of fate, in which Lady Fortune spins her wheel and the mighty fall while the powerless rise. Chaucer translated Boethius's *Consolation of Philosophy*, and its influence on the Monk's Tale is evident in the treatment of its tragic theme. The Monk's definition of tragedy mirrors Boethius's analysis of the genre:

> What other thynge bywaylen the cryinges of tragedyes but oonly the dedes [deeds] of Fortune, that with an unwar strook overturneth the realmes of greet nobleye? (*Glose. Tragedye is to seyn a dite [literary work] of a prosperite for a tyme, that endith in wrecchidnesse.*) Lernedest nat thow in Greek whan thow were yong, that in the entre [entry] or in the seler [cellar] of Juppiter ther ben cowched two tones [vats], the toon [one] is ful of good, and the tother [other] is ful of harm? (*Boece*, book 2, prosa 2)

Notably, Chaucer's conception of tragedy differs from that of the dramatic tradition. In classical dramas (which influenced Shakespeare's conception of the theater in such plays as *Hamlet* and *Othello*), the protagonist is typically a man who is neither overly good nor bad, but who sparks the tragic events by committing or embodying an error, a dramatic structure that Aristotle refers to as *hamartia* in his *Poetics*. In consequence of this failing, he suffers greatly and typically dies violently (as do many of the other characters with whom he shares the stage). The Monk's Boethian conception of tragedy features the simpler narrative structure of a fall from prosperity, and this is the sole essential element of the plot. Indeed, it is rather jarring to consider some of these brief tales, particularly Lucifer's and Nero's, as tragedies, for the Monk appears not to draw any distinction among his various protagonists as to moral culpability for their actions.

The Monk's tragedies include numerous lurid details, including Ugolino of Pisa's children begging their father to eat them—"ete the flessh upon us two. / Oure flessh thou yaf us, take oure flessh us fro, / And ete ynogh" (7.2450–52)—and Nero's disemboweling of his mother to view his place of origin, as well as his incestuous affair with his sister and the murder of his brother (7.2479–86). Readers, however, should forgive themselves if they find the Monk's Tale one of their least favorite narratives of the *Canterbury Tales*; Chaucer intends his audience to dislike this virtually endless parade of such tragedies, as the Prologue to the Nun's Priest's Tale makes clear. The Monk's Tale is nonetheless worthy of appreciation for the insight it provides into Chaucer's view of tragedy, as well as his continued interest in writers and legends from the classical tradition.

NUN'S PRIEST'S PROLOGUE, TALE, AND EPILOGUE

The Monk's virtually endless litany of tragedies frustrates and bores the pilgrims, and so the Knight abruptly cuts him off:

> "Hoo!" quod the Knyght, "good sire, namoore of this!
> That ye han seyd is right ynough, ywis,
> And muchel moore; for litel hevynesse
> Is right ynough to muche folk, I gesse." (7.2767–70)

Again, readers see a skirmish over who controls the pilgrims and their taletelling, and Harry Bailly chimes in to agree with the Knight (7.2780–2805). Harry informs the Monk that his story "anoyeth al this compaignye" (7.2789) and requests a story about hunting (7.2805). The Monk petulantly refuses Harry's request—"'Nay,' quod this Monk, 'I have no lust to pleye. / Now lat another telle, as I have toold'" (7.2806–7)—and the Nun's Priest agrees to recite the next tale, although he warns his audience of his "myrie" spirit. The pilgrims have learned by this time that merry spirits often spark vulgar tales, but except for chickens debating the merits of laxatives and indulging in excessive sexual pleasures, the Nun's Priest relies less on crudeness and more on irony, satire, and parody to create his mirthful tale. One of the true gems of the *Canterbury Tales*, this fable of a rooster named Chauntecleer, his beloved wife Pertelote, and a dastardly fox determined to enjoy a feast of poultry parodies numerous medieval genres, including epic, tragedy, and romance. This hodgepodge of literary influences results in a narrative both silly in its chickens and profound in its multilayered discourses.

On its surface level, the Nun's Priest's Tale is a simple beast fable, and the story is set in the modest surroundings of a poor widow's cottage. The opening lines stress her limited means and the necessary economies of her life (7.2821–46), and this mundane setting is ironically contrasted to the glories of Chauntecleer's "court," which is treated as if it were the height of aristocratic grandeur. Chaucer again uses the literary tradition of the blazon satirically, as he did in the description of Sir Thopas, and this time he accentuates its potential for comic effect by directing it to a rooster (7.2859–64). Chauntecleer may indeed represent a "gentil cok" (7.2865), but the image of a noble rooster cannot uphold gentility as an aristocratic virtue as much as undermine it. Furthermore, Chauntecleer's active sex life, with "Sevene hennes for to doon al his plesaunce" (7.2866), strips him of the elevated aspects of courtly love and renders him a promiscuous rather than an ennobled lover.

If this fable were insufficiently humorous in its treatment of the courtly love shared between two exemplary chickens, it reaches new heights of intellectual silliness when the lovers discuss the meaning of dreams. Chauntecleer dreams of a fiendish beast attacking him, and he fears that this vision bodes ill for his future. Taking a more pragmatic view of the prophetic power of dreams, Pertelote calls Chauntecleer a coward—that is, a chicken—for his fright:

> "For certes, what so any womman seith,
> We alle desiren, if it myghte bee,
> To han housbondes hardy, wise, and free,
> And secree—and no nygard, ne no fool,
> Ne hym that is agast of every tool [weapon],
> Ne noon avauntour [boaster], by that God above!
> How dorste ye seyn, for shame, unto youre love
> That any thyng myghte make yow aferd?" (7.2912–19)

In her demand that her husband adhere to the standards of manliness typical of romance narratives, Pertelote recalls for readers the opinions of the Wife of Bath. She insists that Chauntecleer live as the hero of a courtly romance, that he exhibit the type of martial masculinity shown by Palamon and Arcite in the Knight's Tale, yet all the while he is merely a rooster a bit shaken by a nightmare. Her closing advice to him—"For

Goddes love, as taak som laxatyf" (7.2943)—dismisses his manliness and paints him as a dyspeptic worrywart.

Through Chauntecleer's long-winded reply to Pertelote (7.2970–3171), the Nun's Priest satirizes the learned discourses of the educated and deploys many of the rhetorical strategies used by other pilgrims and the characters in their tales. Chauntecleer cites exemplary stories illustrating his belief in the prophetic nature of dreams, including the tale of a murdered traveler (7.2984–3063), a prophetic sea-voyager (7.3064–3109), and St. Kenelm, who saw his impending death in a vision (7.3110–21). He also cites a long litany of biblical and classical authorities and their examples, including Macrobius (the preeminent authority on dreaming in the Middle Ages), Daniel, Joseph, Croesus, and Andromache (7.3122–56). Chauntecleer wins his debate with Pertelote, but he concludes his discourse with an error that illustrates his scholastic ignorance, thus proving that his oratory rings loudly yet with shallow understanding:

"Now let us speke of myrthe, and stynte [stop] al this.
. . . .
For al so siker as *In principio,*
Mulier est hominis confusio—
Madame, the sentence of this Latyn is,
'Womman is mannes joye and al his blis.'
For whan I feele a-nyght your softe syde—
Al be it that I may nat on yow ryde,
For that oure perche is maad so narwe, allas—
I am so ful of joye and of solas,
That I diffye both sweven and dreem." (7.3157–71)

Chaucer punctures the elevated discourse of courtly romance in these lines, as the devotion of a knightly protagonist to his beloved is here reconfigured into words of amorous praise from a rooster to his hen. Notable, too, is the devolution of romance ideals in the rooster's lascivious language. He makes his sexual intentions unmistakably clear in his lamentations that the tight quarters of their night roost render mounting her unmanageable. (The following morning, Chauntecleer and Pertelote manage to indulge their desires for each other many times [7.3177–78]). Also amusing is the rooster's shaky command of Latin. Although his Latin sounds sufficiently authoritative, his translation of *Mulier est hominis confusio* is blatantly incorrect. It more accurately translates as "woman is man's undoing," and this error points to Chauntecleer's inflated sense both of his intelligence and of his understanding of women—or perhaps to his purposeful mistranslation of a misogynist bromide to facilitate his seduction of his wife.

The humor of the Nun's Priest's Tale continues developing through its mock treatment of grave themes when the narrator satirizes epic in the tale's climax. Chauntecleer's nightmare comes true when a fox enters the chicken yard, and the Nun's Priest paints this dastardly character as the embodiment of traitorousness:

> O false mordrour, lurkynge in thy den!
> O newe Scariot, newe Genylon,
> False dissymulour [deceiver], o Greek Synon,
> That broghtest Troye al outrely to sorwe! (7.3226–29)

Although a rooster being eaten by a fox may indeed be a tragedy for the fowl in question, it can hardly be considered a traitorous or duplicitous act. The comparisons that the Nun's Priest establishes between his fox and Judas Iscariot (who betrayed Jesus), Ganelon (who betrayed Roland in the French epic *The Song of Roland*), and Sinon (who betrayed the Trojans in accounts of the Trojan War) elevate a rooster to the level of Christian and military heroes. Even though Chauntecleer is presented as the most illustrious of fowl, the reader is always aware that he is merely another rooster in a farmyard, and the Nun's Priest relies on this disjunction between ideal and actuality to heighten the satiric effect of his mock-epic similes.

To seduce his prey, the fox praises Chauntecleer's singing, and when the rooster crows in a display of vanity, the fox seizes the opportunity to capture his dinner (7.3282–3337). Here Chaucer incorporates the moral of his fable—a requirement of the genre—about the follies of pride, and pride also frequently catalyzes the downfall of the protagonist of a tragedy. But Chauntecleer is indeed a clever rooster, and he turns the tables by appealing to the fox's sense of pride to maneuver his escape: the bird urges his enemy to revel in his victory by taunting those who would rescue him, and when the fox opens his mouth, Chauntecleer flies to safety (7.3402–37). At the conclusion of this light yet learned fable, the Nun's Priest declares that it bears a worthy moral and advises the pilgrims, "Taketh the fruyt, and lat the chaf be stille" (7.3443). In many ways his tale more focuses on parodying romance, epic, debate, and other genres than on instructing his audience about spiritual virtue, but a moral regarding the sin of pride can be distilled through the levity: the fox captures Chauntecleer not so much through violence as through ravishing him with flattery, and Chauntecleer likewise finagles his escape by playing to his captor's pride.

In the Epilogue to the Nun's Priest's Tale, Harry Bailly makes an arch comment to the teller of the tale, and his words continue his pervasive interest in the respective masculinities of the pilgrims as they respond to one another's narratives:

> "Sire Nonnes Preest," oure Hooste seide anoon,
> "I-blessed be thy breche [buttocks, rear end], and every stoon
> [testicle]!
> This was a murie tale of Chauntecleer.
> But by my trouthe, if thou were seculer,
> Thou woldest ben a trede-foul [chicken-fucker] aright." (7.3447–51)

Harry's speech inverts the dynamics of his earlier confrontation with the Pardoner at the conclusion of the Pardoner's Tale, in which he similarly paid attention to the genitals of a fellow pilgrim, although in a markedly menacing fashion in that instance. Praising the Nun's Priest's genitalia, Harry links the fable's success to the ostensible pleasures the priest would enjoy while copulating with chickens, a comically vulgar yet thematically appropriate ending to a tale that has depicted so forthrightly the erotic escapades of courtly chickens.

SECOND NUN'S PROLOGUE AND TALE

The prologue to the Second Nun's Tale does not depict any petty quarreling among the pilgrims; on the contrary, in this prayerful monologue the Second Nun outlines the themes of her upcoming tale without any dissenting voices interrupting her. She first discusses the spiritual perils of idleness, which she refers to as the "ministre and the norice [nurse] unto vices" (8.1) and offers St. Cecilia as an example of a "mayde [virgin] and martyr" (8.28) who eschewed this sin. By retelling the life of a saint, the Second Nun offers a specific kind of exemplary narrative, the hagiography, or saint's life. She proceeds to offer an Invocation to Mary (8.29–84) and then discusses the etymological roots of the name Cecilia (8.85–119). The prologue ends by foreshadowing Cecilia's gruesome martyrdom:

And right so as thise philosophres write
That hevene is swift and round and eek brennynge [burning],
Right so was faire Cecilie the white
Ful swift and bisy evere in good werkynge,
And round and hool in good perseverynge,
And brennynge evere in charite ful brighte. (8.113–18)

The repetition of "brennynge" captures how Cecilia eschews idleness throughout her life—she metaphorically burns with charity and activity—yet it also alludes to how Cecilia's persecutors torment her at the narrative's end. Torture and martyrdom are essential features of most hagiographies, and such violent finales exemplify the necessity of suffering for one's faith.

As is the case with many female saints, Cecilia resolutely protects her virginity, and this feature, along with her energetic efforts to convert others to Christianity, defines her hagiographical virtue. She marries her suitor Valerian, but on their wedding night she informs him of his fate, should he attempt to consummate their marriage:

"I have an aungel which that loveth me,
That with greet love, wher so I wake or sleepe,
Is redy ay my body for to kepe [protect].

And if that he may feelen, out of drede,
That ye me touche, or love in vileynye,
He right anon wol sle [slay] yow with the dede [deed]." (8.152–57)

Not many young men expect to be threatened with execution for consummating their marriage, but Valerian is surprisingly open-minded. If marital sexuality must be sacrificed for religious purity, Valerian will willingly cede his masculine authority in marriage in favor of his wife's spiritual governance. He does ask for confirmation of this miraculous event (8.162–68). When he receives it, he visits Pope Urban to be baptized (8.183–217), and he is blessed by an angel for his sanctity (8.218–34). Valerian asks for his brother Tiburce to "knowe the trouthe" of Christianity (8.238), and these new converts face imminent peril due to the persecutions of the prefect Almachius. The subsequent martyrdoms of Valerian and Tiburce inspire others to convert as well (8.393–404). The plot of the Second Nun's Tale moves quickly, with one conversion soon following another, and thus the Second Nun builds her theme of defeating idleness through prayerful action. Her characters are "lyk a bisy bee" (8.195) in their proselytizing, and their successes continually mount.

The climax of the Second Nun's Tale depicts Almachius interrogating Cecilia in a scene similar to a courtroom drama, in which he aggressively questions her but she responds with humility inspired by her faith. In one exchange, Almachius claims his earthly authority, hoping to cow Cecilia into submission: "Han noght oure myghty princes to me yiven, / Ye, bothe power and auctoritee / To maken folk to dyen or to lyven?" (8.470–72). Cecilia eloquently emphasizes the limits of earthly authority, pointing out that Almachius can kill but could never bestow life:

> "Thou seyst thy princes han thee yeven [given] myght
> Bothe for to sleen [slay] and for to quyken [give life to] a wight [man];
> Thou, that ne mayst but oonly lyf bireve [deprive],
> Thou hast noon oother power ne no leve [permission, authority]."
>   (8.480–83)

Cecilia refuses to offer sacrifices to Almachius's gods and accuses him of blindness, as she then calls the idol a stone (8.499–501). For her defiance, she is doomed to a martyr's death, yet her death is her reward as well, for through her suffering she will better prove the truth of her faith.

The Second Nun unites her celebration of Cecilia to her thematic condemnation of idleness in the closing stanzas of her tale. Although Almachius orders his underlings, "Brenne [burn] hire right in a bath of flambes [flames] rede" (8.515), Cecilia does not even get warm, nor does she succumb when her neck is cut three times. Rather, she spends the days of her martyrdom actively bringing new converts to her faith: "Thre dayes lyved she in this torment, / And nevere cessed hem the feith to teche" (8.537–38). In another exquisite detail to close the story, readers see the bloody sheets that mark her martyrdom (8.536). Instead of the bloody sheets of a virgin married to an earthly man, which would mark her transition into wifehood, these bloody sheets mark Cecilia's successful martyrdom, which unites her to her God in heaven after her death, so long anticipated, is finally achieved.

CANON'S YEOMAN'S PROLOGUE AND TALE

Continuing their journey to Canterbury, the pilgrims are unexpectedly joined by a Canon and his Yeoman. Because he is an authority of the

Christian Church, and more specifically a priest living under Augustinian precepts, readers might assume that the Canon is a pious man, but like the Friar, Summoner, Monk, and Prioress, he too embodies religious hypocrisy. As the Prologue continues, the Canon's Yeoman makes a surprising declaration about the mystical powers of his traveling companion:

"That al this ground on which we been ridyng,
Til that we come to Caunterbury toun,
He koude al clene turnen up-so-doun,
And pave it al of silver and of gold." (8.623–26)

Harry Bailly, noticing the Canon's shabby clothing, voices suspicion of these claims (8.627–39); the Yeoman defends the Canon until Harry asks him a rather rude question: "Why artow so discoloured of thy face?" (8.664). At this point the Yeoman confesses their con game (8.665–83); the Canon then flees (8.684–702), but the Yeoman remains to tell his tale: "Syn that my lord is goon, I wol nat spare; / Swich thyng as that I knowe, I wol declare" (8.718–19). It is now well established that the prologues to the tales allow deeper insights into the characters of the taletellers, and the Canon's Yeoman likewise exemplifies this confessional tendency.

The Yeoman begins his tale with an introductory lesson on alchemy, which creates some challenges for modern readers, who are unlikely to be familiar with the arcane terminology of this medieval pseudoscience. The primary objective of alchemy is to transform cheap materials into gold or other precious metals, and practitioners sought the "philosophres stoon" (8.862) to accomplish this feat. (The Philosopher's Stone appears most famously in modern popular culture in the British title of J. K. Rowling's first Harry Potter novel, *Harry Potter and the Philosopher's Stone*, published as *Harry Potter and the Sorcerer's Stone* in the United States.) The Yeoman then describes in detail how alchemists convince unsuspecting dupes of their honesty before luring them into their scheme (8.1022–64). Despite the complexity of the alchemical terms, the illusion of transmuting quicksilver into real silver involves mere sleight of hand (8.1176–1203). Throughout his tale, the Yeoman criticizes the Canon with whom he traveled, but he is careful to excuse the vast majority of canons who devoutly fulfill their religious duties (8.992–1011). Since his transgressions are apparent on his face through his many experiences with the metallic vapors of alchemical practices (8.1097–1100), he is inspired to speak out so that others may escape his fate.

Because it is not assigned to one of the pilgrims and therefore disrupts the symmetry of Chaucers's plan for four tales to be told by each of them, the Canon's Yeoman's contribution is anomalous in the overarching structure of the *Canterbury Tales*. Chaucer offers a link to the Second Nun's Tale in the opening line of its Prologue (8.554), but the tale does not spark any rival taletelling among the other pilgrims, and no response to it is recorded. In its confessional aspects, as well as in its condemnation of religious duplicity as incarnated in the Canon, it is reminiscent of the Pardoner and his cunning strategies for extorting money from parishioners. The Canon's Yeoman's Prologue and Tale play with themes of religious hypocrisy and confession that readers have seen throughout the *Canterbury Tales*, with the exception that this Yeoman, if not the Canon, repents his actions. At the close of his Tale, the Yeoman encourages the pilgrims to leave aside the search for the magical philosopher's stone:

> "Thanne conclude I thus, sith that God of hevene
> Ne wil nat that the philosophres nevene [name]
> How that a man shal come unto this stoon,
> I rede [advise], as for the beste, lete it goon." (8.1472–75)

This sincere advice to the pilgrims ends the Canon's Yeoman's Tale, a unique narrative in the *Canterbury Tales* in its subject matter and genre. Indeed, it is difficult to determine a particular genre for the tale: one could see it as a medieval version of a how-to manual—in this case, how to deceive the gullible through the false science of alchemy—with this information embedded in a confessional narrative of repentance. Also, despite the anachronism of the term, some readers describe the tale as an early example of journalistic writing in its straightforward reporting of the Canon and his con. A challenging narrative with its pseudoscientific lexicon, the Canon's Yeoman's Tale engages readers with its candid assessment of religious hypocrisy and the lengths to which these swindlers have gone for financial gain, such that the Canon's Yeoman's transgressions are marked on his face.

MANCIPLE'S PROLOGUE AND TALE

A minor skirmish erupts in the Prologue to the Manciple's Tale, with the Manciple and the Cook verbally sparring. The Manciple appears mildly offended by the Cook's drunkenness (9.25–45), but violence is averted because the Cook is so inebriated that he falls off his horse (9.46–55). The Manciple then cleverly resolves the potential fractiousness by encouraging the Cook to drink even more:

> "I wol not ̦wratthen [anger] hym, also moot I thryve!
> That that I spak, I seyde it in my bourde [joke, jest].
> And wite [know] ye what? I have heer in a gourde
> A draghte [drink] of wyn, ye, of a ripe grape,
> And right anon ye shul seen a good jape.
> This Cook shal drynke therof, if I may." (9.80–85)

Good fellowship replaces tension as the Cook gulps down drink after drink (9.87–93). Harry Bailly appreciates the Manciple's handling of this situation and reiterates his belief in humor and play, thus stressing again one of Chaucer's key themes throughout the *Canterbury Tales*:

> Thanne gan oure Hoost to laughen wonder loude,
> And seyde, "I se wel it is necessarie,
> Where that we goon, good drynke with us carie;
> For that wol turne rancour and disese
> T'acord and love, and many a wrong apese." (9.94–98)

The pilgrims celebrate wine's ability to turn "ernest into game" (9.100) as the proper curative to antisocial sensibilities. The irony, of course, is that wine, which first sparked the animosity between the Manciple and the Cook, now assuages it.

The Manciple then tells his story, which combines elements of beast fables and etiological tales. The Manciple's Tale relates to previous Canterbury narratives focusing on marriages and marital relations, and in this story the Greek god Phoebus Apollo learns of his wife's adultery. After he leaves home, his wife invites her lover to join her there, an event witnessed by Phoebus's white crow (9.196–241). When Phoebus returns, his crow greets him with an unwelcome message: "Cokkow! Cokkow! Cokkow!" (9.243), which Phoebus recognizes as a pun on "cuckold." The crow then explains in explicit detail the circumstances of the affair—"For on thy bed thy wyf I saugh hym swyve" (9.256)—and in a fit of anger, the god slays his wife (9.262–65). He immediately regrets his rash action and punishes the crow, saying:

"Thou songe whilom [formerly] lyk a nyghtyngale;
Now shaltow, false theef, thy song forgon [lose],
And eek thy white fetheres everichon,
Ne nevere in al thy lif ne shaltou speke.
Thus shal men on a traytour been awreke [avenged];
Thou and thyn ofspryng evere shul be blake [black],
Ne nevere sweete noyse shul ye make,
But evere crie agayn tempest and rayn,
In tokenynge [as a sign] that thurgh thee my wyf is slayn."
    (9.294–302)

The tale thus explains how the crow changed from white to black and lost its voice. The Manciple then shares with the pilgrims the moral, "Ne telleth nevere no man in youre lyf / How that another man hath dight [screwed] his wyf" (9.311–12), and reinforces this lesson with one that his mother taught him, "My sone, thenk on the crowe, a Goddes name! / My sone, keep wel thy tonge, and keep thy freend" (9.318–19), to conclude his fable. One could also see in the Manciple's Tale elements of the exemplum tradition, as the reader should learn how not to act by remembering the crow's sad fate. In either light, the tale ends with a peculiar paradox as the Manciple urges his audience to consider the value of holding one's tongue, yet does so with a long-winded denunciation of speech; that is to say, he verbosely advocates silence (9.309–62).

PARSON'S PROLOGUE AND TALE

As the sun descends, Harry Bailly observes that the game has nearly come to its conclusion: "Now lakketh us no tales mo [more] than oon" (10.16). It is the Parson's turn to tell his tale, but the tension apparent between the two men, which was evident at the close of the Man of Law's Tale, reemerges. Harry asks the Parson to conclude the game, urging him to "knytte up wel a greet mateere" with a fable (10.28–29). In requesting a fable, Harry acknowledges that he finds it acceptable for tales to teach a moral, but he also implicitly demands that the moral be couched within an entertaining narrative form. The Parson, however, rejects fables as an inappropriate genre for his spiritual mission (10.31–34) and then rejects poetry altogether, declaring that he will "telle a myrie tale in prose" (10.46). Apparently sensing the potential for the Parson to sermonize, Harry exhorts him, "Beth fructuous [fruitful], and that in litel space"

(10.71), but the Parson embarks upon a very long tale in the form of a penitential manual, one that exposes Harry's moral failings at several points. In effect, the Parson's Tale creates a hybrid form, encoding a manual on sin within the spoken and performed form of a sermon, thus uniting these disparate, but related, structures of religious discourse.

The Parson addresses the theme of penitence in his tale, which is structured in an impressively orderly manner. First he defines penitence (10.75–94), and then he explains the three effects of penitence (10.95–101) and the three types of penitence (10.102–6). Each time the Parson moves to a new topic related to penitence, he explains to his audience how this subject relates to his theme. He promises to explain "what is bihovely [appropriate to] and necessarie to verray parfit Penitence. And this stant [depends] on three thynges: / Contricioun of Herte, Confessioun of Mouth, and Satisfaccioun" (10.107–8). As part of his sermon, the Parson includes explications of the Seven Deadly Sins (Pride, Envy, Anger, Sloth, Avarice, Gluttony, and Lust), along with the spiritual remedies necessary to conquer these vices (Humility, Love of God and Neighbor, Meekness, Strength, Pity, Abstinence, and Chastity).

Continuing his squabbling with Harry Bailly, the Parson pointedly includes some of Harry's sins in his tale, prodding the Host to reform his errant ways. For example, Harry swears throughout the prologues of the other pilgrims, even tossing in a "for cokkes bones" (10.29) when requesting the Parson's tale, and the Parson finds an opportunity to upbraid swearers in his discourse on the deadly sin of Anger: "What seye we eek of hem [them, people] that deliten hem in sweryng, and holden it a gentrie or a manly dede to swere grete othes? And what of hem that of verray usage ne cesse nat [do not stop] to swere grete othes, al be the cause nat worth a straw? Certes, this is horrible synne" (10.601). By linking cursing to the gentry, the Parson concomitantly upbraids Harry for his social climbing, as evident in the Host's sycophantic kowtowing to the aristocracy. Furthermore, the Parson attacks Harry's sensibility of game and play when he criticizes people who "maken semblant as though they speeke of good entencioun, or elles in game and pley, and yet they speke of wikked entente" (10.644). It is difficult to construe Harry's motivations in the taletelling game as wicked, yet he certainly exploits the tension between play and game throughout the pilgrimage, using the sometimes thin line between the two to bolster his governance of his fellow pilgrims. Harry, though, is not the only target of the sermon, and the Parson criticizes the moral failings of other pilgrims throughout his narrative, such as when he refers to the "horrible sweryng of adjuracioun [exorcism] and conjuracioun" as practiced sometimes "in a shulder-boon of a sheep" (10.603), which plainly alludes to the Pardoner's false relic of the "sholder-boon . . . of an hooly Jewes sheep" (6.350–51).

Because the *Canterbury Tales* remained unfinished, no pilgrim could be judged to have won the taletelling contest that was announced in the General Prologue. Harry Bailly promised a free meal to the traveler who "telleth . . . / Tales of best sentence and moost solaas" (1.797–98), but Chaucer does not depict him awarding anyone "a soper [supper] at oure aller cost" (1.799). Nonetheless, in the narrative arc of the *Canterbury Tales*, from the ironies of the General Prologue to the moral exhortations of the Parson's Tale, this final contribution represents a decided move to prioritize spiritual matters over fabliau fun. This is not to say that Harry Bailly, given what readers see of his character throughout the narrative, would most approve of the Parson's Tale, but that its moral seriousness accords well with the spiritual purpose of the pilgrimage, even if some of the pilgrims evinced little concern for their moral edification throughout the many tales of their journey.

CHAUCER'S RETRACTION

In regard to Chaucer's Retraction, the primary question most readers ask is, does he mean it? Chaucer beseeches readers to pray for Jesus's mercy for him because some of the *Canterbury Tales* might "sownen into [lead to, encourage] synne" (10.1086): "Wherfore I biseke you mekely, for the mercy of God, that ye preye for me that Crist have mercy on me and foryeve me my giltes; / and namely of my translacions and enditynges of worldly vanitees, the whiche I revoke in my retracciouns" (10.1084–85). The plural *s* of "retracciouns" tacitly indicates that, as much as Chaucer may repent his bawdy works, he has repeatedly indulged in this transgression. Also, he declares that his literary intentions reveal spiritual purposes, paraphrasing Romans 15.4 as he petitions his readers' goodwill: "For oure book [Bible] seith, 'Al that is writen is writen for oure doctrine,' and that is myn entente" (10.1083). It is rather difficult to see any spiritual values being endorsed in such tales as the Miller's, Reeve's, Summoner's, Merchant's, or Shipman's fabliaux, and Chaucer would not need to apologize for such tales that "sownen into synne" had he destroyed the manuscripts or never written them. The closing prayer puts a Christian veneer on a diverse group of stories, many of which appear decidedly divorced from religious values. But as Harry Bailly would remind the pilgrims, one should not make earnest out of game, and this axiom represents Chaucer's stance regarding his own work. Certainly, one can enjoy the play of the Canterbury game without losing sight of spiritual matters, and Chaucer's attention to the requirements of atonement in his prayer for "grace of verray penitence, confessioun and satisfaccioun to doon in this present lyf" (10.1090) matches point for point the Parson's argument in his sermon (10.107–8). Thus the *Canterbury Tales* ends with Chaucer's apology for his masterpiece, but it is difficult to determine its sincerity.

In passing, the Retraction mentions a narrative that has not survived, titled *Book of the Lion* (10.1086)—likely a retelling of a narrative by either Guillaume de Machaut or Eustache Deschamps, Chaucer's French contemporaries—and its loss is be sorely lamented by all of Chaucer's fans, as is the absence of the many *Canterbury Tales* that Chaucer never wrote before his death. What remains of the Canterbury journey nonetheless has proved endlessly entertaining for readers for well over six hundred years, and Chaucer's triumph stands in his polyphonic mixture of the sacred and the profane, the visionary and the vulgar, as he captures a cross-section of English society while all the while maintaining his sense of humor about life's deepest and most philosophically vexing questions.

Miscellaneous Verse and a Treatise

ANELIDA AND ARCITE

An unfinished work that could be termed an epic complaint, *Anelida and Arcite* mixes the epic and the amatory in its depiction of Anelida, the queen of Armenia, and "fals Arcite" (11), her rakish and inconstant lover. The poem begins in the epic tradition with an invocation (1–21), in which Chaucer calls upon Mars (1) and Bellona (5), the god and goddess of war, to "contynue and guye [guide]" his song (6), as well as upon the Muse Polyhymnia, patron of sacred song. War provides an epic backdrop to a somewhat familiar story of the true woman and the false man—material that Chaucer so fruitfully mines in his *Legend of Good Women* and, with the genders of the true and false lovers reversed, in *Troilus and Criseyde*. In this poem Anelida pitifully complains of fickle Arcite's faithlessness in love.

After concluding his epic invocation, Chaucer proceeds to the story of the lovers (22–210), which begins in the same manner as his Knight's Tale, with Theseus returning from war with his wife Hippolyta and her sister Emily (22–42). The reader soon meets Anelida, but, somewhat strangely, the narrative then founders because Chaucer does not develop his plot but instead reiterates Anelida's truthfulness in contrast to Arcite's deception:

> What shuld I seyn? She loved Arcite so
> That when that he was absent any throwe [space of time],
> Anon her thoghte her herte brast a-two;
> For in her sight to her he bar hym lowe,
> So that she wende [thought] have al his hert yknowe;
> But he was fals; hit nas but feyned chere—
> As nedeth not to men such craft to lere [learn]. (92–98)

As much as Arcite is an amatory scoundrel, one notoriously inconstant in his affections, his "newe lady" controls his every action (183–96), and Anelida is left to languish in her unrequited love for him. Anelida models female suffering for readers of the poem (197–200), whereas Arcite is simply presented as the epitome of male duplicity: "he was double in love and no thing pleyn" (87).

Realizing her lover's treachery, Anelida writes Arcite a highly structured letter detailing her complaint (211–350), which consists of four sections: the proem (one stanza), the strophe (six stanzas), the antistrophe (six stanzas), and the conclusion (one stanza). Most of the stanzas contain nine lines of a complex rhyming scheme, although the fifth stanzas of the strophe and the antistrophe each contain sixteen lines. These parts effectively detail Anelida's suffering, in which her questions testify to her conflicted emotional state. "Alas! Wher is become your gentilesse?" (247), she wonders, as she also attempts to inspire herself not to despair, declaring, "And shal I preye, and weyve [waive, relinquish] womanhede?—/ Nay! Rather deth then do so foul a dede!" (299–300). Anelida also regrets not having foreseen Arcite's fickleness in love, realizing that "Ful longe agoon I oghte have taken hede [heed]" (307). Her complaint concludes on a melancholy note, as she suggests her imminent death: "But as the swan, I have herd seyd ful yore, / Ayeins his deth shal singen his penaunce, / So singe I here my destinee or chaunce" (346–48).

Following the conclusion of Anelida's complaint, one stanza remains in this unfinished poem, in which Anelida travels to Mars's temple to prepare a sacrifice (351–57). The story breaks off at this point, and so readers never learn of Anelida's fate, or perhaps of Arcite's amatory comeuppance. Desiring narrative closure, many readers cannot help but find Chaucer's unfinished works somewhat disappointing, but Anelida's complaint, if stripped of the encumbrance of its incomplete apparatus, emerges as a powerful poetic achievement in the complaint tradition, and thus an impressive display of Chaucer's poetic virtuosity.

"AN ABC"

A translation of a passage from Guillaume de Deguilleville's *Pelerinaige de la vie humaine* (Pilgrimage of Human Life), Chaucer's "An ABC" is a devotional poem to the Virgin Mary in which each stanza begins with a different letter of the alphabet. Such a strategy suggests the completeness and totality of the poet's praise, as the letters of the alphabet unite to honor their subject. Mary is extolled in particular for her role as an intermediary between sinners and God. Of the letters of the alphabet, D ("Dowte [Doubt] is ther noon" [25]), G ("Glorious mayde and mooder" [49]), H ("He vouched sauf" [57]), I ("I wot it wel" [65]), N ("Noble princesse" [97]), and X ("Xristus, thi sone" [161]) specifically address Mary's role as mediatrix, as is also evident in stanza S:

> Soth [Truth] is that God ne granteth no pitee
> Withoute thee; for God of his goodnesse
> Foryiveth noon, but it like unto thee.
> He hath thee maked vicaire [vicar, regent] and maistresse
> Of al this world, and eek governouresse
> Of hevene, and he represseth his justise
> After thi wil; and therfore in witnesse
> He hath thee corowned [crowned] in so rial wise [royal a fashion].
> (137–44)

This passage also highlights the legalistic language often found in "An ABC," which complements the poem's depiction of God as a judge listening to Mary's petitions on behalf of sinners. Beyond "An ABC," Marian devotion appears most prominently in the prologues to the tales of the Prioress and Second Nun, which corresponds well to these characters' religious vocations, if not, in the case of the Prioress, with her spiritual integrity.

"THE COMPLAINT UNTO PITY"

In many poems of the courtly love tradition, a male lover hopes that his beloved will pity him and then deign to grant him her love. Within such poems, the female beloved wields ultimate power over her lover, and many times she is depicted as arbitrary, if not cruel, when she responds to the man who suffers in his unrequited love. Unfortunately for the narrator of "The Complaint unto Pity," his lady's Pity has died while her allegorical opposite, Cruelty, remains fully capable of crushing his romantic aspirations:

> And when that I, be lengthe of certeyne yeres,
> Had evere in oon a tyme sought to speke,
> To Pitee ran I al bespreynt [sprinkled] with teres
> To prayen hir on Cruelte me awreke [to avenge].
> But er I myghte with any word outbreke
> Or tellen any of my peynes smerte,
> I fond hir ded, and buried in an herte. (8–14)

The irony of Pity's death, in that she is now buried in his beloved's heart, bespeaks the paradoxical potential of love: only his beloved could allow Pity to compel her to love him, and so she controls the emotional register that should guide her into love. With Pity dead, the narrator predicts his own death (22), since he sees no hope of winning his beloved.

The first half of "The Complaint unto Pity" sets the poem's narrative scene (1–56), and the second half consists of the narrator's "Bill of Complaint," the petition he desired to present to Pity (57–119). Standard rhetorical ploys abound in this passage, including the lover's request for mercy (92), the lover's pain (99), and the lover's reluctance to complain—even though the poem itself is a complaint (108). The poem ends in despair, with the narrator contemplating his death at the hands of Cruelty:

> This is to seyne I wol be youres evere,
> Though ye me slee by Crueltee your foo,
> Algate my spirit shal never dissevere
> Fro youre servise for any peyne or woo. (113–16)

Infusing allegorical significance into a love complaint, Chaucer creates a poem of surprising depth, despite the highly artificial and stylized requirements of the complaint genre. This lyric speaker resembles many woeful complainers of medieval literature, yet his voice manages to rise above the maudlin tenor of his musings through the complex and contradictory relationship between Pity and Cruelty, opposites embodied in his fair beloved.

"A COMPLAINT TO HIS LADY"

"A Complaint to His Lady" consists of four parts, each of which addresses the speaker's distress in love, and the poem features many generic components of a love complaint: the speaker's sleeplessness (1–2, 50); his endless weeping (12–14); his unrequited love (15–16); the allegorical qualities of his beloved, including Bountee, Sadnesse [Constancy], and Beautee (24–29); his beloved as his sweet enemy (37–39, 58); and his eagerness for death to escape his suffering (112–16). The primary theme of this love complaint is the speaker's unworthiness in contrast to his beloved's greatness: "For ye be oon the worthiest on-lyve / And I the most unlykly for to thryve" (88–89). In its close adherence to these patterns, "A Complaint to His Lady" does not innovate while treating the standard themes of complaint poetry, yet the four sections of the poem each play with a different rhyme scheme, which suggests Chaucer's attention to the various acoustic effects that rhyme offers in this lover's mournful plea to his beloved.

"THE COMPLAINT OF MARS"

Birds and planets: an unlikely alliance of characters unites to tell the story of Mars's amatory disappointments in this poetic complaint. "The Complaint of Mars" is divided into three parts: the proem, in which the avianly inspired narrator announces his poetic subject matter (1–28); the story, in which readers learn of Mars's relationship with Venus, as well as its unhappy ending (29–154); and Mars's complaint, in which the disappointed suitor laments the vagaries of love (155–298). The beginning of "The Complaint of Mars" resembles Chaucer's *Parliament of Fowls* in its setting of birds celebrating Valentine's Day as the narrator muses over how one should choose a mate. The speaker celebrates privacy in love within the context of the aubade tradition (1–7), a body of poetry that scolds the rising sun because it signals that, as the new day approaches, lovers must depart from each other and resume their everyday lives.

The love affair of Mars and Venus begins well, with the two gods blissfully enjoying each other's company:

Who regneth now in blysse but Venus,
That hath thys worthy knyght in governaunce?
Who syngeth now but Mars, that serveth thus
The faire Venus, causer of plesaunce? (43–46)

In accordance with Chaucer's Boethian sensibility, such mutable happiness is virtually predestined to fall, and despite the erotic joys of their night of passion (71–74), the approaching sun vanquishes their pleasure (78–84). Venus flees (113), and Mars follows (131), but Venus finds a new love in Mercury: "And Venus he [Mercury] salueth and doth chere, / And her receyveth as his frend ful dere" (146–47). The story of "The Complaint of Mars" concludes as the narrator prepares to recount Mars's complaint, with an odd closing suggestion for readers to take pleasure in their partners: "As I best can, I wol hit seyn and synge; / And after that I wol my leve take, / And God yeve every wyght joy of his make [mate]!" (152–54). Given the poem's theme of infidelity, it is certainly incongruous for the poet to suggest that readers find amatory pleasure while witnessing Mars's lachrymose musings about love.

Thematically a miniature version of *Troilus and Criseyde*, "The Complaint of Mars" depicts women's falseness in love in comparison to the true-hearted male protagonist, and like Troilus, who frequently muses about love's power over him, Mars now ponders love's effects in an extended complaint with many of the standard tropes of these laments. His complaint consists of five sections, with the first addressing his true service in love and Venus's worthiness of his affections (164–90), the second lamenting that no one will hear his pleas for love's mercy or relieve his suffering (191–217), the third questioning God's purpose in allowing lovers to suffer (218–44), the fourth considering how love and desire drive lovers nearly to madness (245–71), and the fifth concluding by asking for compassion from the knights and ladies who hear of his sorrow (272–98). Five lines of the concluding stanza begin with the word "compleyneth," a fitting end to a poem in which love's sorrows leave even a deity forlorn and bereft of happiness.

"THE COMPLAINT OF VENUS"

"The Complaint of Venus" appears to respond to "The Complaint of Mars," and one can read the poem as Venus's defense against charges of infidelity. At the same time, "The Complaint of Venus" does not respond specifically to the narrative situation introduced in "The Complaint of Mars," and thus, although their titles connect these poems thematically, little internal dialogue links them beyond their surface similarities. "The Complaint of Venus" is divided into three parts: a consideration of the gentility of Venus's departed lover (1–24), in which she wistfully recalls his "bounte, wysdom, governaunce, / Wel more then any mannes wit can gesse" (9–10); a complaint regarding the deceptions of Jealousy (25–48) because this allegorical force "[f]ul often tyme causeth desturbyng" (44); and a promise of Venus's constancy to her lover (49–72), in which she affirms her dedication to "love hym best ne shal I never repente" (72). This complaint ironically ends with a promise of constancy, yet had the lovers truly shared such fidelity, the complaint itself would be unnecessary.

"TO ROSEMOUNDE"

In this three-stanza complaint in ballade form, Chaucer laments his unluckiness in love. The name Rosemounde means "rose of the world," and Chaucer develops his theme of the universal praise accorded to Rosamond's beauty in his opening lines: "Madame, ye ben of al beaute shryne / As fer as cercled is the mapamounde [map of the world]" (1–2). Against this universal backdrop, Chaucer assumes the position of a woebegone and overlooked lover, ending each stanza with the same lament: "Thogh ye to me ne do no daliaunce" (8, 16, 24). Still, in his comparison of himself to a fish cooked and steeped in sauce (17–18), Chaucer maintains an ironic stance on his amatory travails, leavening a fairly standard praise of a beloved's beauty with an impish sense of humor.

"WOMANLY NOBLESSE"

A ballade composed of three stanzas and an envoi, "Womanly Noblesse" tackles the typical courtly love topos of the lover beseeching his beloved for her attentions. The speaker sounds a bit desperate in his blatant sexual attraction to the woman—"So wel me liketh your womanly contenaunce" (5)—and so he abases himself before her, hoping for her mercy: "My wil I cónforme to your ordynaunce [command], / As you best list, my peynes for to redresse" (16–17). Chaucer limits himself in the poem's three stanzas to two rhymes, on "-aunce" and "-esse," a poetic strategy that testifies to his poetic daring and innovation. Ultimately, however, this tactic results in a somewhat singsong and repetitive tone. In the envoi, the speaker bestows numerous compliments on his beloved, beseeching this "Soveraigne of beautee" to appreciate his poetic celebration of her excellence.

"CHAUCERS WORDES UNTO ADAM, HIS OWNE SCRIVEYN"

In this scrappy little epigram comprising a mere seven lines, Chaucer chastises his scribe Adam Pinkhurst, who he fears will miscopy his works.[5] Medieval poets often relied on scribes to copy their writings, but as Chaucer reveals, such work might be undertaken without the necessary diligence and attention to detail. Chaucer laments the tedious necessity of correcting Adam's mistakes and, in a fit of pique, condemns him to a scalp inflammation, should his errors continue: "Under thy long lokkes [locks of hair] thou most have the scalle [skin disease], / But [unless] after my makyng thow wryte more trewe" (3–4). *Troilus and Criseyde* also records Chaucer's exasperation with his scribes, as he prays to God "that non [no one] myswrite" his masterpiece, nor that they "mysmetre" it through "defaute of tonge" (5.1795–96). These lines, like "Chaucers Wordes unto Adam," trenchantly capture his frustration with the ways in which his art was too frequently corrupted by inattentive copyists.

"THE FORMER AGE"

"The Former Age" laments a lost golden era during which humanity lived in peace and harmony because greed did not disrupt the social fabric. "A blisful lyf, a paisible [peaceable] and a swete, / Ledden the peples in the former age" (1–2), the poem begins, and it then describes how the earth provided sustenance without the necessity of human labor: "Yit nas the ground nat wounded with the plough [plow], / But corn up-sprong, unsowe of mannes hond" (9–10). These opening stanzas reflect Chaucer's poetic reformulation of ideas expressed by such classical authors as Ovid and Boethius, as in the following passage from the latter's *Consolation of Philosophy*: "Blisful was the firste age of men. They heelden hem apayed [satisfied] with the metes that the trewe feeldes broughten forth. They ne destroyeden ne desseyvede [deceived] nat hemself with outrage. They weren wont lyghtly to slaken hir hungir at even [in the evening] with accornes of ookes [oaks]" (book 2, metrum 5.1–6). This Boethian lyric concludes by identifying the scourges of contemporary times: "For in oure dayes nis but covetyse, / Doublenesse, and tresoun, and envye, / Poyson, manslawhtre, and mordre in sondry wyse" (61–63). "The Former Age" treats its theme of the glories of the past and the decay of contemporary times with a mournful sense of humanity's potential, imbuing a standard lamentation with a powerful sense of loss.

"FORTUNE"

In Tony Kushner's play *Angels in America*, the protagonist Prior Walter advises the angels to sue God for abandonment: "And if He returns, take Him to Court. He walked out on us. He ought to pay."[6] Chaucer, approximately six hundred years earlier, plays with a similar theme in his ballade "Fortune," in which the narrator represents a plaintiff in a lawsuit against Fortune. The poem begins with the narrator's complaint that Fortune deceives, as well as his newly determined resolution to fight fate:

> Thou knewe wel the deceit of hir colour,
> And that hir moste worshipe is to lye.
> I knowe hir eek a fals dissimulour,
> For fynally, Fortune, I thee defye! (21–24)

Accusing Fortune of falsehood, however, is the equivalent of accusing Satan of evil, or Helen of Troy of being beautiful. These are simply integral parts of their characters, ones that should not be lamented so much as accepted as necessary conditions of their existence, and Fortune defends herself by pointing out to the narrator that he is "born . . . in my regne of variaunce" (45).

As in "The Former Age," many of the ideas expressed in "Fortune" are derived from Boethius's *Consolation of Philosophy*, and the legalistic framework of this poem reflects Fortune's words in Boethius's text: "Stryf or pleet [reason, dispute] with me byforn what juge that thow wolt of the possessioun of rychesses or of dignytees" (book 2, prosa 2.7–9). The narrator and Fortune exchange another round of accusations and rebuttals (49–72), and the poem concludes with an envoi to a group of unnamed princes, presumably the Dukes of York, Lancaster, and Gloucester. This stanza encourages the princes to act justly in the matter before them, in contrast to the unjust vagaries of Fortune.

"TRUTH"

The antidote to Fortune's mutability can be found in the virtue of truth, and in this ballade of three stanzas and an envoi, Chaucer exhorts his reader to embrace a Boethian conception of honor. Each stanza's concluding line reiterates a plea for honesty and uprightness: "And trouthe thee shal delivere, it is no drede" (7, 14, 21, 28). For Boethius, truth is an internal virtue, one that must be sought through meditation: "Whoso that seketh sooth [truth] by a deep thought, and coveyteth not to ben disseyvid [deceived] by no mysweyes ["misways," false paths], lat hym rollen and trenden [turn] withynne hymself the lyght of his ynwarde sighte" (book 3, metrum 11.1–4). The classical influence of Boethius here merges with Chaucer's sense of Christian truth, as the line concluding each stanza also echoes the words of the Gospel of John: "and you will know the truth, and the truth will make you free" (8.32). The fusion creates a poetic harmony from the dire circumstances surrounding humanity, in which the "wrastling for this world axeth a fal" (16).

"GENTILESSE"

When the old woman of the Wife of Bath's Tale chastises the rapist knight, she reminds him that gentility of spirit does not directly correspond with gentility of lineage: "Crist wole we clayme of hym oure gentillesse / Nat of oure eldres for hire old richesse" (3.1117–18). In "Gentilesse," Chaucer couples this moral observation with a Boethian theme to create a three-stanza ballade, in which he proclaims that "Vyce may wel be heir to old richesse" (15), a pithy yet poetic encapsulation of Boethius's condemnation of the tendency of aristocratic people to act without gentility of spirit. As Boethius argues, gentility is often a mercurial virtue, one unrelated to a person's social class: "But now of this name of gentilesse, what man is it that ne may wele seen how veyn and how flyttynge [variable] a thyng it es? For yif the name of gentilesse be referred to renoun and cleernesse of lynage [lineage], thanne is gentil name but a foreyne thyng (*that is to seyn, to hem that gloryfien hem of hir lynage*)" (book 3, prosa 6.32–38). The poem shares with "The Former Age" a melancholic regret for the lost noble spirit residing in people of the past, as it observes, "This firste stok was ful of rightwisnesse" (8), and thus subtly points to the degeneration of the "first stock" in descending generations. No end of examples of spoiled rich children growing into pampered, cosseted, and odious adults testifies that wealthy forebears do not instill an aristocracy of the spirit in the descendants of a line, and Chaucer, working in the upper circles of English society, would have ample opportunity to observe the failings of the elite in this regard.

"LAK OF STEDFASTNESSE"

The ballade "Lak of Stedfastnesse" bemoans a world turned topsy-turvy, one that is "up-so-doun" because "word and deed" are "nothing lyk" (4–5). Similar in structure to the ballades "Truth" and "Gentilesse," with seven-line stanzas concluding with a repeated sentiment, "Lak of Stedfastnesse" criticizes the transitory nature of English society, in which "Fro right to wrong, fro trouthe to fikelnesse, / That al is lost for lak of stedfastnesse" (20–21). The poem's envoi to King Richard II asks him to ameliorate the situation, as he, through his role as the people's ruler, is the only one who can "wed thy folk agein to stedfastnesse" (28).

"LENVOY DE CHAUCER A SCOGAN"

Chaucer's ironic humor shines throughout his "Lenvoy de Chaucer a Scogan," cast as an epistolary verse to a friend. The poem begins with all of heaven in an uproar—"Tobroken been the statutz hye [exalted] in hevene" (1)—resulting from Scogan's trivial offense in courtly love: "That, for thy lady sawgh nat thy distresse, / Therfore thow yave [gave] hir up at Michelmesse [the Feast of St. Michael]?" (18–19). The disproportion between cause and effect—a man giving up his pursuit of a woman and the ensuing distress of the heavens—shapes the humor of the poem, in a manner similar to the mock-epic uproar surrounding a fox running off with a rooster in the Nun's Priest's Tale.

Mocking himself as well as his friend, Chaucer then refers to the unfortunate amatory circumstances of older men:

> Now certes, frend, I dreed of thyn unhap [bad luck],
> Lest for thy gilt the wreche [vengeance] of Love procede
> On all hem that ben hoor [white-haired] and rounde of shap
>   [pudgy],
> That ben so lykly folk in love to spede [prosper, flourish]. (29–32)

His self-deprecating stance on his body—as also evident in the Prologue to Sir Thopas, when Harry Bailly makes fun of his fatness (7.700)—leads to his ironic accounting of the prospects of old men in love, which is a point he pursues for great comic payoffs in the sexual fate of John in the Miller's Tale and of January in the Merchant's Tale. The poem concludes with an envoi in which Chaucer urges Scogan to repent—"loke thow never eft [again] Love dyffye" (49)—but coupled with this exhortation to continue playing the game of love is Chaucer's depiction of himself as poetically impotent: "Ne thynke I never of slep to wake my muse, / That rusteth in my shethe stille in pees" (38–39). The phallic metaphor of a sword qua pen rusting in its sheath here deepens the poem's ironic stance on the amatory games of old men, even when these games are purely poetic.

"LENVOY DE CHAUCER A BUKTON"

In "Lenvoy de Chaucer a Bukton," another of Chaucer's epistolary verses, the poet warns his friend against his impending marriage, but his words are not to be taken seriously. Similar to the jovial tone of "Lenvoy de Chaucer a Scogan," a lighthearted and ironic approach to his subject matter suggests Chaucer wittily satirizes marriage without sincerely castigating it. When he writes, "I wol nat seyn how that yt [marriage] is the cheyne / Of Sathanas, on which he gnaweth evere" (9–10), Chaucer declares what he proclaims he will not declare, which highlights his self-aware positioning as narrator. The poem echoes the discussions of marriage in the Wife of Bath's Prologue and the Merchant's Tale, and in the envoi to this verse letter (25–32), Chaucer alludes directly to his Wife of Bath: "The Wyf of Bathe I pray yow that ye rede / On this matere that we have on honde" (29–30). This line indicates that Chaucer's friends would recognize allusions to his literature, but not necessarily that they would benefit from Alison of Bath's lessons in love.

"THE COMPLAINT OF CHAUCER TO HIS PURSE"

In this ironic complaint written in the form of a ballade, Chaucer speaks to his purse as if he were a lover pursuing his beloved: "To yow, my purse, and to noon other wight / Complayne I, for ye be my lady dere" (1–2). The humor of the poem arises in the allegorical play of his purse as the imperious lady of the romance tradition, since he will die if she does not respond to his plea: "Beth hevy ageyn, or elles mo[o]t I dye" (7, 14, 21). "She" also represents his "[q]uene of comfort and of good companye" (13), and he relies on her sense of gentility and courtesy (20) to increase herself into more ample funds. The ballade concludes with a short envoi to King Henry IV, as the king would certainly be able to assist Chaucer in assuaging his financial difficulties.

"PROVERBS"

The first four lines of this eight-line poem play on the theme of "waste not, want not," and the second four lines expand this theme to warn the reader to avoid greediness. Although the authorship of this poem has been questioned, its concluding lines, "Who so mochel wol embrace, / Litel therof he shal distreyne [keep, retain]" (7–8), echo sentiments expressed in the Tale of Melibee: "For the proverbe seith, 'He that to muche embraceth, distreyneth litel'" (7.1214). This idea is not original with Chaucer, yet the similarity of phrasing points to, even if it cannot conclusively prove, their shared status as Chaucerian works.

CHAUCERIAN POEMS

Four poems—"Against Women Unconstant," "Complaynt D'Amours," "Merciles Beaute," and "A Balade of Complaint"—appear in manuscripts with Chaucer's literature, but they are not specifically assigned to him as the author. Many medieval manuscripts contain a wide variety of materials, and often it is difficult to ascertain the connections among the various entries. Even if these poems cannot be conclusively identified as Chaucer's, they are nonetheless Chaucerian, as they reflect his themes and style.

"AGAINST WOMEN UNCONSTANT"

In the three-stanza ballade "Against Women Unconstant," the narrator laments the "newefangelnesse" (1) of his beloved. Each stanza ends with the refrain "In stede [stead] of blew [blue], thus may ye were [wear] al grene" (7, 14, 21), which refers to medieval color symbolism, in which blue represents a lover's fidelity but green represents inconstancy. (Chaucer also employs the color symbolism of blue and green in the Squire's Tale, 641–47.) The poem includes commonplace lover's laments with a sense of personal pique, such as when the narrator compares his beloved to a weathervane: "But as a wedercok, that turneth his face / With every wind, ye fare, and that is sene" (12–13). This complaint mixes standard invectives against the fickleness of lovers with sly humor, resulting in a poem that refuses to wallow in melancholia even if such sadness may indeed be warranted.

"COMPLAYNT D'AMOURS"

The speaker of this complaint, the "sorwefulleste" (1) and "unworthiest" (19) man, one who suffers love's agonies and holds no hope of solace from his beloved, faces imminent, albeit metaphorical, death. The familiar trope of the imperious courtly lady, one who delights in her suitors' failed efforts to win her affections, is repeatedly connected to themes of mortality. "My deeth, I see, is my conclusioun" (23), the speaker predicts, but he cannot hold a grudge against such a beauty: "But shal I thus yow my deeth foryive / That causeles doth me this sorwe drye? / Ye, certes, I!" (31–33). This courtly lady excels in all virtues except pity, and the narrator reports this deficiency in her character: "Why that she lefte Pite so behinde? / It was, ywis, a greet defaute in Kinde" (55–56). Opposed to Pity is this beloved's sense of play. She delights in the torments she inflicts, and the narrator masochistically accepts this pain to accommodate her pleasure. "It is hir pley to laughen whan men syketh [sigh], / And I assente al that hir list [pleased] and lyketh!" (62–63), he declares in acknowledging her power and his submissiveness. Such self-sacrifice may be lauded as a romantic ideal in this poem, but since the ideal promises to end in death, it celebrates and undermines this tradition simultaneously. For this Valentine's Day poem (85), Chaucer sets a mordant tone for commemorating the occasion, one notably lacking in exaggerated sentimentality.

"MERCILES BEAUTE"

In "Complaynt D'Amours," the lover's eyes, espying his beloved's beauty, threaten to wound him fatally (40–41), but in "Merciles Beaute," the trope is reversed, and it is the lady's eyes that harm the lover: "Your yen [eyes] two wol slee me sodenly; / I may the beautee of hem not sustene, / So woundeth hit thourghout my herte kene" (1–3). The lyric speaker's self-deprecating wit is also readily evident in this poem, as he mentions his obesity as a cause behind his troubles in love: "Sin I fro Love escaped am so fat, / I never thenk to ben in his prison lene [lean, skinny]" (27–28). Chaucer implies that he is fat numerous times, including in the Prologue to Sir Thopas (7.700), House of Fame (574), and "Lenvoy de Chaucer a Scogan" (31). Unlike many love complaints, "Merciles Beaute" concludes by rejecting love: "Sin I am free, I counte him [Love] not a bene [bean]" (39). This line captures a similar sentiment expressed by May in the Merchant's Tale, who cares little for January's lovemaking abilities:

"She preyseth nat his pleyyng worth a bene" (4.1854). (May's thoughts ironically contrast with January's assessment of love and marriage with an inverse leguminous metaphor when he declares, "Noon oother lyf . . . is worth a bene, / For wedlok is so esy and so clene" [4.1263–64]). The game of love inspires yet tires, and the lyric speaker of "Merciles Beaute" rejoices in his emancipation from such romantic play.

"A BALADE OF COMPLAINT"

For the narrator of this Chaucerian ballade, complaints provide little solace for love's pains: "Compleyne ne koude, ne might myn herte never, / My peynes halve, ne what torment I have" (1–2). They are thus useless to the speaker, and so he rejects the genre that builds his poem. However, what else can a lover do but complain when facing such troubles? The narrator concludes this brief three-stanza ballade with a plea to his beloved: "Beseching yow in my most humble wyse / T'accepte in worth this litel pore dyte [poem, ditty]" (15–16). Little in the poem suggests that this complaint will be met with succour, but the lover nonetheless offers his constancy to prove his affections: "Sith I yow serve, and so wil yeer by yere" (21). Constancy in love is an admirable quality within courtly romances, but unrewarded constancy ironically renders the virtue of little use in pursuing an imperious beloved.

A TREATISE ON THE ASTROLABE

In addition to his many poetic fictions, Chaucer wrote a scientific tract, *A Treatise on the Astrolabe*, an achievement that testifies to the breadth of his intellectual interests. Astrolabes measure the position of the sun, moon, planets, and stars in the heavens, and in the Middle Ages they were used for both scientific (astronomical) and pseudo-scientific (astrological) purposes. Chaucer dedicates his technical treatise on the astrolabe to "Lyte Lowys my sone" (1) who is at the "tendir age of ten yeer" (24), and thus *A Treatise on the Astrolabe* is a rather remarkable document both scientifically and historically, as it is a technical and scientific treatise written expressly for children. Chaucer excuses himself for not writing his essay in Latin, since his son is insufficiently versed in the language to understand it: "This tretis, divided in 5 parties, wol I shewe the [you] under full light reules and naked wordes in Englissh, for Latyn canst thou yit but small, my litel sone" (25–28).

For most modern readers, even those well versed in Middle English, it is disconcerting to find that a scientific treatise written for a ten-year-old child in the Middle Ages presents daunting interpretive challenges today. Of course, since science has progressed immeasurably beyond its state in the Middle Ages, many of Chaucer's current readers have never seen an astrolabe, let alone handled or studied how to use one. Despite the arcane subject matter of *A Treatise on the Astrolabe*, the reader's effort is repaid by the text's fascinating mix of science and astrology, such as when Chaucer describes how the sun's orbit influences its "mood":

> And this forseide [aforementioned] hevenysshe zodiak is clepid [called] the cercle of the signes, or the cercle of the bestes [beasts], for "zodia" in langage of Grek sowneth "bestes" in Latyn tunge. And in the zodiak ben [are] the 12 signes that han names of bestes, or ellis for whan the sonne [sun] entrith [enters] in eny of tho signes he takith the propirte of suche bestes, or ellis for that the sterres [stars] that ben ther fixed ben disposid in signes of bestes or shape like bestes, or elles whan the planetes ben under thilke signes thei causen us by her influence operaciouns and effectes like to the operaciouns of bestes. (part 1, section 21.49–62)

The sun virtually appears to suffer from multiple personality syndrome in this passage, taking on the aspects of the twelve signs of the zodiac as it moves about the heavens. Today we know that the sun does not orbit the planets, but the proof that the planets orbit the sun was provided by Copernicus (1475–1543) and Galileo (1564–1643) only after Chaucer's death. Based on the knowledge available to him at the time, Chaucer's *A Treatise on the Astrolabe* is a remarkably detailed and comprehensive scientific study, one that showcases the dialectical relationship between astronomy and astrology in the Middle Ages. Chaucer's literature plumbs the depths of the human experience, from the glories of romance to the fabliau humor of raw sexuality and beyond, and *A Treatise on the Astrolabe* testifies that, truly, the entire universe lay within the scope of this man, the first great poet of English literature.

3

Chaucer's Sources and Influences

Literatures prior and contemporary to Chaucer—including the writings of classical Greece and Rome, of the Judeo-Christian Bible, and of the French and Italian traditions—resonate throughout his fictions, and deciphering his many allusions to previous masterpieces adds a challenging but pleasureful element to reading the *Canterbury Tales*, *Troilus and Criseyde*, and his other works. Readers unfamiliar with classical, biblical, and French and Italian literature should not feel overwhelmed by these sources so much as inspired by them: some allusions might pass unrecognized or unnoticed when first encountered, but Chaucer's literature maintains its energy and vigor irrespective of one's familiarity with these various traditions. Furthermore, many readers will likely be moved to experience some of these canonical works—such as Virgil's *Aeneid*, Ovid's *Metamorphoses*, the book of Job, Guillaume de Lorris and Jean de Meun's *Roman de la Rose*, and Boccaccio's *Teseida*—for themselves.

Classical Sources

At the conclusion of *Troilus and Criseyde*, Chaucer exhorts his narrative to rank itself respectfully in the annals of Western literature. It should, he advises, take its place among the masterworks of the classical era:

> But litel book, no makyng thow n'envie,
> But subgit be to alle poesye [rules of poetry];
> And kis the steppes where as thow seest pace
> Virgile, Ovide, Omer, Lucan, and Stace. (5.1789–92)

With this homage to great Greek and Roman authors, Chaucer counsels his book to make obeisance to the timeless texts that preceded it by submissively kissing their path. He positions his epic romance as worthy of joining this pantheon, an act of authorial chutzpah that has nonetheless proved true over the centuries. The classical sources he names, Virgil, Ovid, Homer, Lucan, and Statius, allow a wide-ranging overview into his play with the literatures of the distant past; beyond these figures, the Roman philosopher Boethius stands as a preeminent influence on Chaucer's moral philosophy, and numerous other classical authors likewise inspired various moments in his writings.

Virgil, more fully Publius Vergilius Maro (70–19 BCE), is most famous for his *Aeneid*, an epic account of Aeneas's journey to Italy from his fallen homeland of Troy that lays the groundwork for the subsequent founding of Rome. England links its legendary history to Troy's, in that Aeneas's great-grandson Brutus is credited as the founder of Britain; indeed, in fourteenth-century England some devotees of the Trojan legend advocated renaming London as "Little Troy" or "New Troy."[1] Chaucer's respect for Virgil is evident in his *Legend of Good Women*, in which he praises his literary forebear for the guidance he provides: "Glorye and honour, Virgil Mantoan, / Be to thy name! and I shal, as I can, / Folwe thy lanterne, as thow gost byforn" (924–26). Chaucer retells Virgil's *Aeneid*, in much abridged form, in book 1 of the *House of Fame*, and he begins his account of Aeneas's legend by translating Virgil's famous opening words "Arma virumque cano" [I sing of arms and a man] as "I wol now synge, yif I kan, / The armes and also the man" (143–44).

Throughout his Virgilian writings, Chaucer pays particular attention to Aeneas's courtship and jilting of Dido, the queen of Carthage, who commits suicide after her cavalier lover's departure. Chaucer tells this story in his *House of Fame* (212–382) and as the third narrative of the *Legend of Good Women* (924–1367), in which the narrator confesses his "gret . . . routhe" (1345) to recount her story. In this retelling, her dying words to absent Aeneas reveal her strength and fidelity in comparison to his fickleness: "For thilke [that same] wynd that blew youre ship awey, / The same wynd hath blowe awey youre fey [faith (fulness)]" (1364–65). Additionally, she is mentioned in passing, with sympathy and a bit of tartness, in the *Book of the Duchess*:

> Another rage
> Had Dydo, the quene eke of Cartage,
> That slough [slew] hirself for [because] Eneas
> Was fals—which a fool she was! (731–34)

By contrast, Lavinia, King Latinus's daughter and Aeneas's eventual bride, warrants little of Chaucer's attention, and he mentions her only in passing (*BD* 331, *HF* 458, and *LGW* 257, 1331). Chaucer's interest in the Trojan legend is most apparent in *Troilus and Criseyde*, and his frequent allusions to Virgil's *Aeneid*, a trove of legendary material of critical interest to English identity, also allow him to consider the complex issues facing women in love.

Beyond his identity as one of Western literature's greatest authors, Virgil is also recognized as one of this tradition's most famous fictional characters. In the *Divine Comedy*, Dante casts the Roman writer as his guide through hell, and Chaucer often alludes to this depiction of Virgil as an infernal educator. The yeoman in the Friar's Tale (who is actually a devil) explains to his new friend the summoner that, through their acquaintanceship, he will learn more about hell than he could from both Virgil and Dante:

> "For thou shalt, by thyn owene experience,
> Konne in a chayer [professorial chair] rede [lecture, teach] of this
>   sentence
> Bet than Virgile, while he was on lyve,
> Or Dant also." (3.1517–20)

In this passage, the devil qua yeoman cites Virgil more for his authority on the social structure of hell than for his literary achievements. Likewise, in the *House of Fame*, Chaucer directs his reader to Virgil (as well as to Claudian and Dante) to learn about the eternal sufferings inflicted on the damned:

> And every turment eke in helle
> Saugh he, which is longe to telle;
> Which whoso willeth for to knowe,
> He moste rede many a rowe
> On Virgile or on Claudian,
> Or Daunte, that hit telle kan. (445–50)

Here Chaucer primarily plays with the depiction of Virgil in Dante's *Inferno* as a guide through hell, as is evident in the accompanying reference to Dante. Virgil's own poetry also addresses the question of an afterlife, most notably in book 6 of the *Aeneid* in which Aeneas travels to the underworld and Elysium to visit Dido and his father Anchises. As the greatest of Roman epic writers, Virgil embodies a grandeur and majesty for Chaucer as the definitive voice of this literary tradition, yet Chaucer also alludes to this material in an idiosyncratic fashion, with his attention most obviously claimed by Dido's love pains and Virgil's literary incarnation as an infernal escort.

Ovid's influence on Chaucer is widespread, especially the Roman's witty depictions of love and his deployment of Greek and Roman mythology to structure his narratives. Publius Ovidius Naso (43 BCE–17 CE) is best remembered for his *Ars amatoria* (*The Art of Love*) and *Metamorphoses*. *Ars amatoria* satirically details the strategies of seduction in the game of love, as the narrator mock-seriously explains how members of the Roman aristocracy flirt, and *Metamorphoses* retells numerous mythological and legendary narratives, primarily from Greek sources, including such tales as Apollo's crow (cf. Manciple's Tale), Pyramus and Thisbe (cf. *LGW* 706–923), Ariadne (cf. *HF* 405–26 and *LGW* 1886–2227), and Tereus, Procne, and Philomela (cf. *LGW* 2228–2393). In the Introduction to the Man of Law's Tale, the Man of Law agrees to tell his story, but before he commences, he compares Chaucer to Ovid: "For he hath toold of loveris up and doun / Mo than Ovide made of mencioun / In his Episteles, that been ful olde" (2.53–55). Through this comparison as spoken by one of his fictional characters, Chaucer acknowledges his reliance on Ovid as a source of inspiration. For Chaucer, Ovid is "Venus['s] clerk" who "hath ysowen [spread] wonder wide / The grete god of Loves name" (*HF* 1487–89), and much of Chaucer's literature echoes Ovidian themes in its slyly ironic and satiric treatment of love.

In many ways, Alison of Bath incarnates the female figures of Ovidian satire. Although she complains that Jankyn's "book of wikked wyves" (3.685) includes Ovid's *Ars amatoria* (3.680), she embodies numerous points of his satire. For example, Ovid describes a woman flirting with men while attending her husband's funeral: "Funere saepe viri vir quaeritur; ire solutis / Crinibus et fletus non tenuisse decet" [Yet we know that when a man / Dies and the widow's plan / Is to find a new one, a parade of funeral feeling—/ Dishevelled hair, abandoned sobs—is quite appealing].[2] Such a scene presages Alison's flirtatious behavior with Jankyn while burying her fourth husband (3.587–99). Alison cites Ovid's *Metamorphoses* in her tale's digression concerning Midas and his wife, and she exhorts her audience to consult her source material: "Redeth Ovyde, and ther ye may it leere [learn]" (3.982). Should readers follow her advice, they will find that she misquotes her source: Ovid's account of the legend depicts Midas's barber, not his wife, revealing the ruler's secret of his donkey ears, and so readers observe yet another instance of Alison twisting her sources to fit her fancy.

In contrast to Alison's sly reliance on Ovidian verse to complement her subversive message, Melibee's wife Prudence in the Tale of Melibee employs Ovid as a respected authority to build her argument for patience in the face of adversity. When Melibee mourns his bad fortune, his wife recalls Ovid's words as she formulates her comforting advice: "This noble wyf Prudence remembred hire upon the sentence of Ovide, in his book that cleped is the Remedie of Love, where as he seith, 'He is a fool that destourbeth the mooder [mother] to wepen in the deeth of hire child til she have wept hir fille as for a certein tyme'" (7.976–77). Later she admonishes Melibee to heed another of Ovid's moral lessons: "Thou ne hast nat doon to hym swich honour and reverence as thee oughte, / ne thou ne hast nat wel ytaken kep to the wordes of Ovide, that seith, 'Under the hony of the goodes of the body is hyd the venym that sleeth the soule'" (7.1413–14). It is certainly a testimony to Ovid's rich and varied writings that characters as diverse as Alison of Bath and Prudence both cite him in their arguments.

Of the five classical authors whom Chaucer cites at the close of *Troilus and Criseyde*, Homer (ninth c. BCE) is perhaps the most famous. Today his *Iliad* and *Odyssey* stand as definitive and defining epics of Western literature. Chaucer alludes frequently to Homer's epics in his literature, but, unlike his knowledge of Latin writers such as Virgil and Ovid, whose works he read in their original tongue, his knowledge of Homer was filtered through various other writers and translators. For example, the sixth-century philosopher Boethius mentions Homer in his *Consolation of Philosophy*; Chaucer's translation reads: "Homer with the hony mouth (that is to seyn, Homer with the swete ditees [poems, songs]) singeth that the sonne is cler by pure light; natheles yit ne mai it nat, by the infirme light of his bemes, breken or percen the inward entrayles of the erthe or elles of the see" (*Boece*, book 5, metrum 2.1–5). From Boethius and others writing many centuries after Homer's death, Chaucer learned of the author and his epics, as well as his pivotal role in literary history.

Despite English society's unfamiliarity with Homer's epics in their original Greek, knowledge of his literature was an expected frame of reference for Chaucer's readers. In the Franklin's Tale, Dorigen compares herself to loyal wives and cites Homer's Penelope as an ideal for her to emulate: "What seith Omer of goode Penalopee? / Al Grece knoweth of hire chastitee" (5.1443–44). In the *House of Fame*, Chaucer sees a statue of Homer standing on a pillar of iron, and he credits him as bearing up the legend of Troy:

> And by him stood, withouten les [without lies, truly],
> Ful wonder hy on a piler [pillar]
> Of yren [iron], he, the gret Omer;
> And with him Dares and Tytus
> Before, and eke he Lollius,
> And Guydo eke de Columpnis,
> And Englyssh Gaufride eke, ywis;
> And ech of these, as have I joye,
> Was besy for to bere up Troye. (1464–72)

Citing Homer as the preeminent authority on the Trojan War, Chaucer then alludes to additional famous authors to bolster his account of the Trojan legend's lineage. In these lines, which are virtually a medieval bibliography of the Trojan legend, Chaucer includes authors who are obscure to many readers today but were widely recognized throughout the Middle Ages. The accounts of the Trojan War by Dares Phrygius and Dictys Cretensis (Tytus) were more accessible in the Middle Ages than Homer's, and Lollius appears to have been Chaucer's fictional creation, perhaps based on an error of Latin translation. Guido delle Colonne's prose history of Troy, the *Historia destructionis Troiae* [History of the Destruction of Troy], was completed in 1287, and Geoffrey of Monmouth's *Historia regum Britanniae* (*History of the Kings of Britain*) was written between 1135 and 1139. It is somewhat ironic that Chaucer celebrates the author whose writings he did not read more than the authors whose works he did read, but this literary homage in the *House of Fame* testifies to the authorial celebrity attached to Homer's name, even when his literature in its original tongue was lost to the medieval West.

Lucan, more formally Marcus Annaeus Lucanus (39–65 CE), was famous for his *Pharsalia*, an incomplete account of the war between Julius Caesar and Pompey the Great that abruptly concludes with assassination attempts on Caesar after his arrival in Egypt. In the Man of Law's Tale, the narrator uses Lucan's description of Julius Caesar's victories to mark the epitome of celebration:

.

Noght trowe I the triumphe of Julius,
Of which that Lucan maketh swich a boost,
Was roialler ne moore curius
Than was th'assemblee of this blisful hoost. (2.400–403)

In this scene inspired by Lucan's writings, the sultan's mother slaughters
her son and the Christians in his court, thus cementing her characterization as evil to the core. In recounting his tragedy of Julius Caesar, the
Monk cites Lucan as one of his sources, and he attributes to his Roman
predecessor a Boethian sensibility, one congruent with his tragedies inspired by Fortune's fickleness:

Lucan, to thee this storie I recomende,
. . . .
That of this storie writen word and ende,
How that to thise grete conqueroures two
Fortune was first freend, and sitthe [since, afterward] foo.
No man ne truste upon hire favour longe,
But have hire in awayt for everemoo. (7.2719, 2721–25)

Despite the contrasting thematic interests of Lucan and Boethius, Chaucer's Monk unites Lucan's account of Caesar with his Boethian anthology
of Fortune's vagaries, in which the tragedy of Caesar's murder elicits a
response of Boethian equipoise.

Similar to the image of Homer in the *House of Fame*, Lucan is depicted
as responsible for upholding Caesar's fame:

Thoo saugh I on a piler by,
Of yren wroght ful sternely,
The grete poete daun Lucan,
And on hys shuldres bar up than,
As high as that y myghte see,
The fame of Julius and Pompe. (1497–1502)

Throughout *House of Fame*, Chaucer praises the accomplishments of his
literary forebears, thereby acknowledging his sources and identifying
himself as worthy to join their pantheon. Scholars are unsure whether
Chaucer knew Lucan's *Pharsalia* directly or learned of it through other
writers. As Chaucer learned of Homer in part from Boethius's references
to him in *The Consolation of Philosophy*, so too would he have become

acquainted with Lucan (cf. *Boece*, book 4, prosa 6.230–33). Regardless of his personal knowledge of the *Pharsalia*, Chaucer celebrates Lucan's literary accomplishments and commemorates his role in preserving the legend of Julius Caesar.

Publius Papinius Statius (45–96 CE), the fifth name mentioned in Chaucer's valedictory to *Troilus and Criseyde*, was a Roman author chiefly remembered for his narratives concerning military, political, and fraternal strife in Thebes. In the *House of Fame*, Chaucer praises him for his role in preserving this legendary material:

> The Tholosan that highte [was named] Stace,
> That bar of Thebes up the fame
> Upon his shuldres, and the name
> Also of cruel Achilles. (1460–63)

Statius's *Thebaid* addresses the conflicts over the throne of Thebes, and Chaucer quotes this text in lines celebrating Theseus's triumphant return to his homeland for the epigraph to his Knight's Tale: "Iamque domos patrias, Scithice post aspera gentis Prelia, laurigero, etc." [And now (Theseus, drawing nigh his) native land in laurelled car after fierce battling with the Scythian folk].[3] Within the fictions of his epic romance of Palamon and Arcite's battle-to-the-death for Emily's hand in marriage, Chaucer cites the *Thebaid* as his authority in describing Emily's sacrifices to Diana: "Two fyres on the auter [altar] gan she beete [spark, kindle], / And dide hir thynges, as men may biholde / In Stace of Thebes and thise bookes olde" (1.2292–94). Statius's legend of Thebes also inspired Chaucer's *Anelida and Arcite*, and Chaucer reports that he adheres strictly to Statius's text: "First folowe I Stace" (21). He quotes the same line from the *Thebaid* as he does in the epigraph to the Knight's Tale, but, somewhat oddly, *Anelida and Arcite* does not parallel any narrative account found in Statius's narrative. In *Troilus and Criseyde*, Troilus's sister Cassandra summarizes the Theban epic when she foretells his imminent disappointment in his love affair and links the lineage of his amatory rival Diomede to the protagonists of this legend (5.1485–1519), thus joining the epic subjects of Troy and Thebes.

Virgil, Ovid, Homer, Lucan, and Statius represent especially significant debts that Chaucer owes to the Greek and Roman literary traditions, but of all classical authors, none influenced Chaucer's philosophical sense of justice more than Boethius and his *Consolation of Philosophy*.

As a genre, prison literature typically recounts an author's physical and spiritual experiences during incarceration, as these texts also ponder the justice (or injustice) of such a trying experience. Perhaps surprisingly, numerous literary masterpieces were inspired and/or penned during their authors' jail time, including works by Thomas Malory, Cervantes, Sir Thomas More, John Bunyan, Dostoevsky, and Jean Genet. *The Consolation of Philosophy*, written by Anicius Manlius Severinus Boethius (ca. 480–524 CE), illustrates a dialogue between the author as narrator and Lady Philosophy as he grapples with the moral and emotional issues raised by his imprisonment and imminent execution. Chaucer meticulously rendered this Latin work into Middle English, and his detailed knowledge of it suffuses much of his literature. His translation is typically referred to as *Boece*, as in the passage from the *Legend of Good Women* in which Alceste defends Chaucer by mentioning some of his virtuous deeds: "And, for to speke of other holynesse, / He hath in prose translated Boece" (F.424–25).

In the beginning of *Boece*, Boethius laments his sad fortune: "Allas! I wepynge, am constreyned to bygynnen vers of sorwful matere, that whilom [once, formerly] in florysschyng studie made delitable ditees [verses, songs]" (book 1, metrum 1.1–3). Sentenced to death by Theodoric for allegedly plotting against him, Boethius regrets the vagaries of fortune and the uncertainties of human life. Rather than wallowing in misery, he seeks to understand the vicissitudes of human experience by engaging in an intellectually challenging dialogue with Lady Philosophy, who teaches him her wisdom as he questions her intensely. As the word "consolation" implies, the narrative thrust of the ensuing dialogue addresses whether Boethius derives comfort from Lady Philosophy's advice.

Boethius describes Lady Philosophy as a "womman of ful greet reverence by semblaunt, hir eien brennynge [eyes burning] and cleer-seynge over the comune myghte of men" (book 1, prosa 1.5–7), whose supernatural perception of humanity's condition enables her to understand clearly Boethius's troubles. In its complex consideration of human suffering and philosophical revelation, *The Consolation of Philosophy* is a demanding work, but Boethius maintains its readability through the engaging back-and-forth of his dialogue. As much as Lady Philosophy coaxes Boethius into a deeper awareness of life's spiritual complexities, she occasionally drops a barb into her speeches, such as when she asks Boethius, "Artow like an asse to the harpe?" (book 1, prosa 4.2–3). Although the title of this work suggests that Lady Philosophy seeks to console Boethius through their discussion, she does not refrain from spirited rejoinders dissuading him from self-pity. Lady Philosophy often employs allegorical narratives to clarify her points. To illustrate the transience of earthly matters, she retells the story of Orpheus and Eurydice. Orpheus travels to the underworld to bring back his lost love Eurydice, but after saving her and escaping, he violates the condition that he not look back upon her; thus she is lost to him once again. Lady Philosophy interprets the story:

> This fable apertenith [pertains] to yow alle, whosoevere desireth or seketh to lede his thought into the sovereyn day, that is to seyn, to cleernesse of sovereyn good. For whoso that evere be so overcomen that he ficche [fixes] his eien [eyes] into the put [pit] of helle, that is to seyn, whoso sette his thoughtes in erthly thinges, al that evere he hath drawen of the noble good celestial he lesith [loses] it, whanne he looketh the helles, that is to seyn, into lowe thinges of the erthe. (book 3, metrum 12.60–69)

Such allegorical interpretations frame Lady Philosophy's view of the human condition, but *Boece* does not shy away from vexing philosophical issues, such as why evil exists if God is good: "But this same is namely a ryght gret cause of my sorwe: that so as the governour of thinges is good, yif that eveles mowen ben by any weyes, or elles yif that evelis passen withouten punysschynge" (book 4, prosa 1.17–21). Why evil exists, why bad things happen to good people—these questions have tantalized and tormented humanity for centuries, and Boethius's measured consideration of them models for Chaucer a sense of patience with life's perplexities.

If one is to find consolation in *Boece*, it emerges in the theme of living righteously before eternal justice, even if that justice is not apparent to human perception:

> Withstond thanne and eschue thou vices; worschipe and love thou vertues; areise thi corage to ryghtful hopes; yilde thou humble preieres an heyhe. Gret necessite of prowesse and vertu is encharged and comaunded to yow, yif ye nil nat dissimulen; syn that ye worken and don (*that is to seyn, your dedes or your werkes*) byforn the eyen of the juge that seeth and demeth alle thinges. (book 5, prosa 6.302–10)

In Chaucer's literature, this is the advice that Troilus needs to hear before embarking on his doomed love affair with Criseyde, and these lines capture his increased awareness of the vanity of human affairs when he observes his funeral from the sanctity of the eighth sphere. With its focus on the ephemerality of earthly endeavors, Boethius's *Consolation of Philosophy* infuses much of Chaucer's literature with its philosophical depth as he ponders the fickleness of Lady Fortune and the eventual eternal rewards for human suffering.

Additional classical writers who influenced Chaucer include Aesop (6th c. BCE), whose Greek fables were translated into Latin and to whose work Chaucer alludes in such stories as the two dogs fighting over a bone (*CT* 1.1177–80) and the mare kicking a hungry wolf (*CT* 1.4054–46); Juvenal (ca. 55–ca. 127 CE), the famed satirist whom the narrator cites in *Troilus and Criseyde* (4.197–201); Livy (59 BCE–17 CE), a noted historian, whom the Physician cites as the source of his tale (*CT* 6.1–4); Cicero (106–43 BCE), to whom the Franklin refers as an expert on rhetoric ("I sleep nevere on the Mount of Pernaso, / Ne lerned Marcus Tullius Scithero"; *CT* 5.721–22); Claudian (ca. 370–ca. 404 CE), the author of *De raptu Proserpinae* (*The Rape of Proserpina*), to whom Chaucer alludes in reference to the legend of Pluto and Proserpina, as in the Merchant's Tale (4.2232) and *House of Fame* (1509); and Macrobius (*fl.* 400 CE), whose *Commentary on the Dream of Scipio* was respected as a foundational text of medieval dream theory, and who consequently appears in several of Chaucer's dream visions (*BD* 284, *PF* 111, *RR* 7, and Nun's Priest's Tale 3123). For Chaucer, these classical authors (and many others) formed a living literary tradition, one that flowered hundreds of years prior to his birth but that was kept alive through the medieval education system and through the writings of later authors who continually turned to the past to inspire their literature in the present.

Biblical Sources

In William Shakespeare's *The Merchant of Venice*, Antonio famously cautions that Satan adapts biblical teachings to his nefarious objectives:

> The devil can cite Scripture for his purpose.
> An evil soul producing holy witness
> Is like a villain with a smiling cheek,
> A goodly apple rotten at the heart.[4]

Although few of Chaucer's characters revel in evil (except perhaps the Pardoner), many of them bend the teachings of the Judeo-Christian Bible to their own purposes, building their arguments through biblical authority even when these arguments are far removed from any spiritual context. Regardless of the Canterbury pilgrims' piety, their biblical knowledge—as refracted through Chaucer as author and narrator—is detailed, and so they (and he) deploy it for myriad purposes, from the laudable to the vulgar. In and beyond the *Canterbury Tales,* the Judeo-Christian Bible helps Chaucer to deepen his themes through his multivalent references to this touchstone text of the medieval West.

In the *Canterbury Tales,* Chaucer's use of the Judeo-Christian Bible is intimately connected to the portrayal of his pilgrims. Foremost, many of the pilgrims, including the Prioress (who travels with the Second Nun and three priests), Monk, Friar, Parson, Summoner, and Pardoner, are officers of the medieval Christian Church, but except for the Parson, they also model the challenges of adhering to Christian ideals. These religious characters should know biblical teachings intimately, and their lives should therefore reflect their practice of Christian principles, yet Chaucer frequently relies on the comic disjunction between the expectations for these religious characters' actions and their behaviors. The Monk, for example, should be eager to study the Bible of his faith, but Chaucer, speaking in his naïve voice as narrator of the General Prologue, commends him for ignoring the theological study that should structure his life:

> What sholde he studie and make hymselven wood [crazy],
> Upon a book in cloystre alwey to poure,
> Or swynken [toil] with his handes, and laboure,
> As Austyn [St. Augustine] bit [commands, bids]? How shal the
>   world be served? (1.184–87)

A monk who rejects studying his religion's Bible and its exegetical interpretations shows little interest in his religious vocation, one that demands an intellectual intimacy with its foundational text.

In contrast to the Monk and his less spiritually minded brothers, Chaucer's Parson illustrates how the gospels can be utilized for the benefit of the laity:

> A good man was ther of religioun,
> And was a povre [poor] PERSOUN [Parson] of a TOUN,

But riche he was of hooly thoght and werk.
He was also a lerned man, a clerk,
That Cristes gospel trewely wolde preche. (1.477–81)

Through this simple portrait of a good man, Chaucer illustrates how the Judeo-Christian Bible, and in particular the gospels of Matthew, Mark, Luke, and John, should inspire Christians to live virtuously. Moreover, it is apparent that the Parson practices as he preaches, avoiding any taint of hypocrisy: "first he wroghte, and afterward he taughte" (1.497).

Because the gospels of the New Testament depict Jesus's life and miracles, Christians hold them as exemplary texts, and Chaucer frequently draws attention to his characters' flaws by the ways in which they refer to them. The unctuous friar of the Summoner's Tale encourages Thomas to share his wealth by citing the authority of the gospels:

"That specially oure sweete Lord Jhesus
Spak this by freres, whan he seyde thus:
'Blessed be they that povere in spirit been.'
And so forth al the gospel may ye seen,
Wher it be likker [more like] oure professioun,
Or hirs that swymmen in possessioun.
Fy on hire [their] pompe and on hire glotonye!" (3.1921–27)

The friar's quotation of the Beatitudes (Matthew 5.3–12; cf. Luke 6.20–23) alludes to God's protection of and concern for the poor, meek, and powerless, but the friar compromises the passage's moral purposes in his wheedling for cash. Indeed, this friar reinterprets Jesus's words as directed especially to friars, which is not just a theological stretch but, since friars' religious orders were founded more than a millennium after the Sermon on the Mount, a considerable chronological leap as well.

Other characters do not merely reinterpret the gospels to their own purposes but reject them outright or blatantly prioritize earthly concerns over spiritual ones. When Harry Bailly requests a tale from the Parson, the Shipman interrupts and rejects his preaching of the gospels: "Seyde the Shipman, 'Heer schal he nat preche; / He schal no gospel glosen here ne teche'" (2.1179–80). Through his tale of a morally dubious monk, the Shipman appears unconcerned with instructing his fellow pilgrims about their spiritual betterment, and his tale ends with a prayer for sexual satisfaction rather than sanctity (7.433–34). Troilus, a pagan character in a story set hundreds of years before the advent of Christianity, could not know the New Testament gospels, but Chaucer nonetheless highlights how the Trojan warrior mistakes earthly love for spiritual truth when he laments losing Criseyde with biblical terms: "God wot, I wende, O lady bright, Criseyde, / That every word was gospel that ye seyde!" (5.1264–65). Through Troilus's tears over Criseyde, Chaucer reveals the emptiness of his protagonist's amatory desires, as he mistakes his lady's lies for a deeper sense of Christian truth.

Realizing the blasphemous potential available through biblical allusions, Chaucer's fabliaux revel in the bawdy interplay of the sacred and profane. The Song of Songs is a highly eroticized biblical book in which the bridegroom and bride are often allegorically interpreted as representing God's relationship with his people, and its eroticism becomes ripe for parody in Chaucer's Miller's Tale. Absolon's plea to Alison echoes numerous images found therein:

> "What do ye, hony-comb, sweete Alisoun
> My faire bryd, my sweete cynamome?
> Awaketh, lemman [lover] myn, and speketh to me!
> Wel litel thynken ye upon my wo,
> That for youre love I swete [sweat] ther I go.
> No wonder is thogh that I swelte [become light-headed] and swete;
> I moorne as dooth a lamb after the tete.
> Ywis, lemman, I have swich love-longynge
> That lik a turtel [turtledove] trewe is my moornynge.
> I may nat ete na moore than a mayde." (1.3698–3707)

The images of the honeycomb, bird, and cinnamon all echo the Song of Songs, and this devolution of the sacred into the profane, while not particularly surprising within the vulgar parameters of Chaucer's fabliaux, highlights the slipperiness of biblical erotics. As a parish clerk (1.3312), Absolon knows the Judeo-Christian Bible well, yet he attempts to exploit his knowledge for sexual gain rather than spiritual growth.

Because the narratives of the Judeo-Christian Bible were well known within the overwhelmingly Christian context of medieval England, Chaucer often depicts the ignorance of his characters through their failure to recognize and understand biblical allusions. In the Miller's Tale, Nicholas tricks John into thinking that God will again flood the world: "That now a Monday next, at quarter nyght, / Shal falle a reyn, and that so wilde and wood / That half so greet was nevere Noes flood" (1.3516–18).

In his astounding ignorance, John does not remember God's promise to Noah after the flood: "I establish my covenant with you, that never again shall all flesh be cut off by the waters of a flood, and never again shall there be a flood to destroy the earth" (Genesis 9.11). Had John paid sufficient attention in church to catch Nicholas's lie, this fabliau tacitly suggests, he might have saved himself the humiliation of cuckoldry and the pain of a broken arm. In its portrait of Absolon, the Miller's Tale also alludes to the tradition of mystery plays, which were elaborate sequences of biblically inspired dramas: "Somtyme, to shewe his lightnesse and maistrye, / He pleyeth Herodes upon a scaffold hye" (1.3383–84). These lines deepen the reader's vision of Absolon through this link to the murderous villain of the gospels, and they also further hint at John's ignorance, in that such mystery plays performed in his town would have warned him of Nicholas's duplicity concerning the flood.

In other instances, it is not as readily apparent whether Chaucer uses the Judeo-Christian Bible to showcase his characters' ignorance or whether these biblical references should be taken at face value. In the Merchant's Tale, January demonstrates his extensive biblical knowledge by citing Rebecca, Judith, Abigail, and Esther as examples of good wives in his long speech praising the virtues of marriage (4.1267–1392); however, these biblical women are known more for deceiving their husbands and killing enemies of the Jewish people than for their positive wifely attributes. Rebecca instructs Jacob to trick his father Isaac into blessing him rather than his brother Esau (Genesis 27). Not a wife but a widow, Judith is celebrated more for her military cunning in decapitating Holofernes than for any uxorial virtues (Judith 8, 13). The Merchant correctly points out that Abigail "Saved hir housbonde Nabal whan that he / Sholde han be slayn" (4.1370–71); what he does not say is that she also insults him, calling him an "ill-natured fellow" and declaring to David that "folly is with him," and when Nabal dies soon after, Abigail immediately marries David (I Samuel 25.1–42). Esther may be the best of the wives cited by the Merchant, but, like Judith, she is more renowned for masterminding the execution of Haman, an enemy of the Jewish people, than for her wifely devotion (Esther 8). Is January thus wrong to describe these biblical women as good wives? If these four women are ironically cited as exemplary wives in the Merchant's Tale, it is then surprising that Prudence praises these same four women in the Tale of Melibee with little hint of irony undermining her presentation of them (7.1097–1100).

January proves his error in judgment by marrying lusty May, who soon cuckolds him, but these biblical wives, despite their possible failings, certainly do not match May in marital deviousness. In this instance, and in others similar to it, Chaucer establishes a tension between a character's presentation of biblical narratives and the ways in which these stories can be interpreted, which compels readers to judge for themselves the extent of the irony, or even if irony is implied at all.

Many of the Canterbury pilgrims rely on St. Paul (ca. 10–ca. 67 CE), whose conversion and missionary work are recounted in the Acts of the Apostles and who wrote many of the New Testament epistles, to build the thematic core of their tales, but they do so in surprisingly contradictory ways. In her argument against virginity, Alison of Bath audaciously refers to and then refutes Paul's argument against marriage: "Poul dorste nat comanden, atte leeste, / A thyng of which his maister yaf [gave] noon heeste [command]" (3.73–74). Alison is correct in her assertion that Paul does not prohibit marriage in his epistle to the Corinthians, as he admits that he offers his opinion on the subject, not divine fiat: "Now concerning the unmarried, I have no command of the Lord, but I give my opinion as one who by the Lord's mercy is trustworthy" (I Corinthians 7.25). He then proceeds to argue strongly against marriage: "Yet those who marry will have worldly troubles, and I would spare you that" (I Corinthians 7.28). For Alison to cite Paul's authority, only to subsequently ignore that authority, highlights her fearless assault on Christian values, yet also how she manages this by strictly adhering to biblical precedents.

In stark contrast to the Wife of Bath, who twists Paul's words to advance her spiritually dubious agenda, many pilgrims rely on biblical authority to defend their tales through an appeal to moral meaning. Despite the pilgrims' adherence to the teachings of the Judeo-Christian Bible, interpretive difficulties still emerge when different pilgrims rely on biblical passages to argue conflicting points, and these stalemates frustrate attempts to discern Chaucer's own understanding of Christianity. The Nun's Priest and the Parson argue about the moral appropriateness of the tales told during the pilgrimage when they address the very nature of storytelling. The Nun's Priest cites Paul's authority to defend his tale of randy and mock-epic chickens:

> But ye that holden this tale a folye,
> As of a fox, or of a cok and hen,

Taketh the moralite, goode men.
For Seint Paul seith that al that writen is,
To oure doctrine it is ywrite, ywis;
Taketh the fruyt, and lat the chaf be stille. (7.3438–43)

The Nun's Priest alludes to Paul to increase the moral valence of his mostly amoral but highly amusing story, and Paul indeed suggests that writings not explicitly addressing Christian ideals may bear spiritual value: "For whatever was written in former days was written for our instruction, that by steadfastness and by the encouragement of the scriptures we might have hope" (Romans 15.4). With Paul's words advocating the utility of secular narratives for spiritual purposes, the Nun's Priest suffuses his tale with a Christian moral that transforms the "chaff" of an entertaining yarn into the "fruit" of spiritual guidance.

The Parson subtly refutes the Nun's Priest's stance on stories when he refuses Harry Bailly's request for a fable. In contrast to the Nun's Priest, he cites Paul to argue against such frivolous entertainments:

"Thou getest fable noon ytoold for me,
For Paul, that writeth unto Thymothee,
Repreveth [scolds] hem that weyven [neglect] soothfastnesse
And tellen fables and swich wrecchednesse." (10.31–34)

Similar to the Wife of Bath and the Nun's Priest, the Parson demonstrates the depth of his biblical knowledge by citing Paul, who admonishes his followers against myths in his epistles to Timothy: "As I urged you . . . charge certain persons not to teach any different doctrine, nor to occupy themselves with myths and endless genealogies which promote speculations rather than the divine training that is in faith" (I Timothy 1.3–4; cf. 4.7 and 2 Timothy 4.4).[5] Through these references to Paul, the Parson frees his penitential manual of the trivial label of a "tale" and thus asserts his spiritual leadership over the pilgrims. In these conflicting citations of Paul by the Nun's Priest and the Parson, readers do not see either pilgrim misquoting or misinterpreting Paul, but it is nonetheless clear that his spiritual authority can be used to support opposing points of view.

For Chaucer, the usefulness of the Judeo-Christian Bible as a literary tool to develop his characters and stories arises in its manifold significations, despite the spiritual messages that should ostensibly shine through so clearly, and the story of Job well illustrates this multiplicity of interpretation. In the book of Job, Satan suggests that Job would curse God if his prosperity were taken away, and Satan and God make a wager on how Job will react under such circumstances: "Then Satan answered the Lord, ' . . . But put forth thy hand now, and touch all that he has, and he will curse thee to thy face.' And the Lord said to Satan, 'Behold, all that he has is in your power; only upon himself do not put forth your hand.' So Satan went forth from the presence of the Lord" (1.9–12). Job patiently abides great torments—including the loss of his children and the affliction of his body with boils—while refusing to curse God; his prosperity is restored after he successfully withstands Satan's tests. Chaucer's characters refer to Job as an iconic representation of strength and patience while enduring inconceivable pain. In the Tale of Melibee, Melibee's wife Prudence recasts the themes of the book of Job in its moral of acceptance and forgiveness as she urges her husband to follow Job's example:

> "Remembre yow upon the pacient Job. Whan he hadde lost his children and his temporeel substance [worldly goods], and in his body endured and receyved ful many a grevous tribulacion, yet seyde he thus: / 'Oure Lord hath yeve [given] it me; oure Lord hath biraft [deprived] it me; right as oure Lord hath wold, right so it is doon; blessed be the name of oure Lord!'" (7.998–99; cf. Job 1.21).

Prudence implies that Job's suffering eclipses Melibee's, and the narrative trajectory of the Tale of Melibee focuses on his eventual acceptance of his wife's advice.

Prudence finds spiritual comfort in the story of Job, but many readers throughout the centuries have found this biblical book troubling in its depiction of God's willing participation in Job's torment; for some readers, it appears an unnecessary display of arbitrary, if not cruel, power. In the Friar's Tale, the devil who succeeds in winning the summoner's soul aligns himself with God's purpose, and he cites Job's suffering to argue that demons often fulfill God's directives:

> "For somtyme we been Goddes instrumentz
> And meenes to doon his comandementz,
> Whan that hym list, upon his creatures.
> . . . .
> Witnesse on Job, whom that we diden wo." (3.1483–85, 1491)

This allusion to Job opens up numerous questions regarding the Friar's Tale: Is this summoner's downfall the result of divine intervention, or does he nonetheless maintain full responsibility for his damnation? Should readers see this corrupt summoner in any way as a metaphoric representation of Job? Although it strains the borders of a credible reading to link the summoner of the Friar's Tale to Job in terms of their personal traits, allusions often unleash too many connotative suggestions to be contained.

In this manner, it is apparent that Job (and other biblical narratives) are used for any number of rhetorical and strategic purposes, often ones anachronistically alien from the context of the biblical narrative at hand. Continuing with the example of Job, his story is far removed from considerations of medieval gender roles, but the Clerk refers to Job to encourage his audience to rethink the meaning of masculinity and femininity within his tale:

> Men speke of Job, and moost for his humblesse,
> As clerkes, whan hem list, konne wel endite [write],
> Namely of men, but as in soothfastnesse [truth],
> Though clerkes preise wommen but a lite,
> Ther kan no man in humblesse hym acquite
> As womman kan, ne kan been half so trewe
> As womman been, but it be falle of newe [newly fallen, recent].
> (4.932–38)

The Clerk's words point to the gendered dynamics inherent in biblical discourse and the ways in which male authorities accord certain biblical stories gendered meaning. He then shows the limits of reading gender through the Judeo-Christian Bible and patriarchal commentary by underscoring Job's inability to suffer as patiently as a woman could. The Clerk and Alison of Bath hold sharply dissimilar views on the status of women in medieval society, as evidenced by their strikingly different tales, yet they implicitly agree on the utility of citing biblical authority to examine the appropriateness of medieval gender roles.

Many readers attempt to distill Chaucer's religious values from the biblical references running throughout his literature, but such a desire to read a spiritual autobiography through his fictions is fraught with interpretive perils. It seems likely that Chaucer, in his frequent depictions of deceitful and duplicitous religious figures, chafed against the abuses of the Church in his day, but many devoutly religious people rightly condemn hypocrisies while fully adhering to the principles of their faith. The Parson's long tale underscores Chaucer's deep understanding of Christian Scripture, and its position at the end of the *Canterbury Tales* closes a raucous and vibrant collection of tales with a humble and lengthy excursus on penance and forgiveness. Likewise in *Troilus and Criseyde*, Chaucer transforms a pagan romance into a Christian prayer in the romance's final moments, which implicitly suggests the redemptive cast of his beliefs. Throughout Chaucer's oeuvre, he showcases the subversive potential of the Judeo-Christian Bible to question values of his culture and practices of his church, while reinforcing its central tenets.

Finally, it should be remembered that Chaucer's knowledge of the Judeo-Christian Bible, as deep as it is, also reflects centuries of biblical interpretation and exegesis. Church Fathers, saints, and other figures from the history of the Catholic Church, such as Jerome (ca. 342–420), Augustine (354–430), Gregory the Great (ca. 540–604), Bernard of Clairvaux (1090–1153), and Thomas à Becket (ca. 1117–1170), are referred to by Chaucer and his characters, and these authorities contribute to Chaucer's heady mixture of the sacred and the profane in his polyvalent writings.

French Sources

Following William the Conqueror's 1066 defeat of the English at the Battle of Hastings, the kings that ruled England for hundreds of years were French. The relationship between England and France was tense throughout much of the Middle Ages, and the Hundred Years War, waged between 1337 and 1453, worsened the vexed political kinship between these two countries united by blood and yet riven by conflict. Chaucer lived and worked in the multicultural courts of England, where educated persons were widely exposed to and frequently fluent in three languages—French, Latin, and English. Chaucer's choice to write his poetry in English reflects a revolutionary decision to prioritize the English vernacular over the French of the courts and the Latin of the ecclesiastical and administrative realms. Despite his role in elevating English into a literary language, Chaucer was heavily influenced by French literature, as he immersed himself in the works of many of his French predecessors and contemporaries.

The French influence on Chaucer shines through in his frequent use of two quintessentially French genres: ballade and fabliau. Many of Chaucer's shorter poems, including "The Complaint of Venus," "To Rosemounde," "Womanly Noblesse," "Fortune," "Truth," "Gentilesse," "Lak of Stedfastnesse," "The Complaint of Chaucer to His Purse," and "Against Women Unconstant" reflect his interest in ballades. Fabliaux appear more frequently than any other genre in Chaucer's *Canterbury Tales*. From the English tradition, only one extant fabliau, *Dame Sirith*, predates Chaucer's many fabliaux: the Miller's Tale, Reeve's Tale, Summoner's Tale, Merchant's Tale, and Shipman's Tale. Furthermore, the Wife of Bath's Prologue, some character descriptions in the General Prologue, and other comic moments throughout Chaucer's corpus highlight his appreciation of fabliaux, even when he writes in a less obviously comic genre.

Chaucer interjects small smatterings of French throughout his fabliau-inspired literature, often serving as quick grace notes to accentuate a theme, character, or setting. Pointing to the Continental roots of fabliau in the Reeve's Tale, the narrator completes his portrait of Symkyn's family and their nocturnal cacophany with a satiric dose of French:

This millere hath so wisely bibbed [imbibed] ale
That as an hors he fnorteth [snores] in his sleep,
Ne of his tayl bihynde he took no keep [i.e., he farts].
His wyf bar hym a burdon [musical accompaniment], a ful strong;
Men myghte hir rowtyng [snoring] heere two furlong;
The wenche rowteth eek, *par compaignye*. (1.4162–67)

With numerous harsh English words accentuating the family's snoring and farting, the closing mellifluence of French establishes an ironic contrast between their crude behavior and their aristocratic pretensions.

In a similar moment of fabliau humor, the Wife of Bath slips into French when referring to her vagina, employing a common euphemism for an indecorous word:

"Is it for ye wolde have my queynte allone?
Wy, taak it al! Lo, have it every deel!
Peter! I shrewe yow, but ye love it weel;
For if I wolde selle my *bele chose*,
I koude walke as fressh as is a rose." (3.444–48; cf. 3.510)

In this bilingual passage, Alison shifts from the harshness of her "queynte" to the Continental gentility of her "bele chose." Likewise, the chiseling friar in the Summoner's Tale drops French phrases into his conversation—"O Thomas, *je vous dy* [I tell you], Thomas! Thomas!" (3.1832)—adorning his smarmy wheedling with Gallic artifice. He also employs French while flirting with Thomas's wife (3.1838). Brief French phrases such as these allow Chaucer to break the monotony of monolingualism, as they also allow his characters to shift in their conversational styles.

These examples should not give the impression that Chaucer deploys French solely for comic purposes. As much as the contrast between the mellifluous French language and boorish behavior builds comedy in the fabliaux, Chaucer also uses French to display the education and breeding of those gifted with bilingualism. The Parson cites a French song in his tale: "wel may that man that no good werk ne dooth synge thilke newe Frenshe song, '*Jay tout perdu mon temps et mon labour*' [I have lost all my time and labor]" (10.247). Chaucer employs this same refrain in his Boethian lament "Fortune": "*Jay tout perdu mon temps et mon labour*; / For fynally, Fortune, I thee defye" (7–8). Even Chaucer's educated birds, who pay homage to Nature at the close of the *Parliament of Fowls*, sing their praises in French: "The note, I trowe, imaked was in Fraunce, / The wordes were swiche as ye may heer fynde, / The nexte vers, as I now have in mynde" (677–79). Emphasizing the Francophile sophistication of these amatory fowls, Chaucer imbues this richly humorous work with a delightful irony as these birds behave in a cosmopolitan fashion while courting their beloveds. In the *Book of the Duchess*, Chaucer reveals his familiarity with the French epic *Song of Roland* when the Man in Black rejects any hint that he would betray his love by declaring that, should he do so, he would be no better than the "false Genelloun, / He that purchased the tresoun / Of Rowland and of Olyver" (1121–23); similarly, the Nun's Priest compares the murderous fox intent on devouring Chauntecleer to Ganelon, Roland's betrayer (7.3226–29). Through his deployment of French phrases and references to French literature, Chaucer infuses much of his prototypically English verse with Continental flair and sophistication.

Because of the strong connections between England and France and his numerous administrative positions in royal households, Chaucer knew many contemporary French authors and texts. Guillaume de Machaut (ca. 1300–1377), generally regarded as the finest of fourteenth-century French poets and composers, wrote prolifically in numerous genres, including motets, lais, and ballades. In its consideration of suffering in love, Chaucer's *Book of the Duchess* resembles Machaut's *Jugement dou roy de Behaingne* (*The Judgment of the King of Bohemia*), a debate poem in which the king must determine who agonizes more: a lady whose lover has died, or a knight whose lady has conducted herself unfaithfully? (The knight "wins" the contest between these two doleful lovers.) In the prologue to the *Legend of Good Women*, Chaucer depicts himself being chastised for writing too many stories unsympathetic to women, and Machaut also treats this theme in his *Jugement dou roy de Navarre* (*The Judgment of the King of Navarre*), a sequel to *Jugement dou roy de Behaingne* in which ladies complain that Machaut's previous poem offends women and then cite numerous examples of their pain in love. The king decides that the women's complaint is valid, and Machaut must atone for his transgressions by writing new poems, as Chaucer similarly atones in writing his legends. Chaucer's lost *Book of the Lion*, which he mentions in the Retraction to his *Canterbury Tales*, may also reflect his admiration for Machaut, as the Frenchman's *Dit dou lyon* could be the source of this lost work.

It is likely that Chaucer knew Jean Froissart (ca. 1337–ca. 1404), who traveled to England between 1361 and 1369 in the service of Philippa of Hainault, Edward III's wife. Froissart penned numerous dream visions, including *Le paradys d'amours* [The Paradise of Love], *L'espinette amoureuse* [The Hawthorne Bush of Love], and *Le joli buisson de jonece* [The Fair Bush of Youth], as well as his chronicle covering French and English history roughly between 1325 and 1400. Froissart's "Dittie de la Flour de la Margherite" [Poem on the Marguerite Flower] may have inspired the homage to the daisy that commences Chaucer's *Legend of Good Women*, and Chaucer begins his *Book of the Duchess* by adapting Froissart's *Paradys d'amours* to his purposes. Froissart's narrator laments the ways in which sleeplessness and love-longing torment him:

Celle nuit avoie voillié,
Car mon cuer m'avoit travaillé
Pour plusieurs diverses pansees
Qui ne sont pas toutez passees.

[That night I had lain awake, because my heart had laboured over several troubling thoughts, which are still not all past.][6]

Chaucer's version of this passage retains its merging of insomnia, love, and melancholy: "I have gret wonder, be this lyght, / How that I lyve, for day ne nyght / I may nat slepe wel nygh noght" (1–3). Froissart's poetry taught Chaucer much about the portrayal of love through the narrator's self-representation, and this influence runs throughout his literature.

Oton de Graunson (ca. 1340–1397) participated actively in English court affairs, working in succession for John of Gaunt, Richard II, and Henry IV (although Graunson died prior to Henry's accession to the throne in 1399). Chaucer shows his admiration for Oton in the envoi of "The Complaint of Venus" when he petitions the audience of princes to alleviate his financial distress:

> Princes, receyveth this compleynt in gre [graciously],
> Unto your excelent benignite
> Direct after my litel suffisaunce.
> For elde, that in my spirit dulleth me,
> Hath of endyting al the subtilte
> Wel nygh bereft out of my remembraunce,
> And eke to me it ys a gret penaunce,
> Syth rym in Englissh hath such skarsete,
> To folowe word by word the curiosite
> Of Graunson, flour [flower] of hem that make [compose poetry] in
>   Fraunce. (73–82)

Noting the difficulty of translating from French to English because English has fewer rhyming words than French, Chaucer pays homage to Graunson while simultaneously hinting to the princes to whom he addresses the poem's envoi that they should be impressed by his own poetic craftsmanship. Chaucer's penchant for Valentine's Day poems, as evidenced in *Parliament of Fowls*, "The Complaint of Mars," and "Complaynt D'Amours," may have been inspired by, and certainly corresponds with, Graunson's own homages to this festive day in his works, such as his *Songe Sainct Valentin*.

Eustache Deschamps (ca. 1344–1404/5) held a strong affection for Chaucer, which is evident in a ballade Deschamps wrote in his friend's honor. Each stanza of this poem concludes with the compliment "Grand translateur, noble Geffroy Chaucier," and Deschamps celebrates Chaucer's literary skills both by comparing him favorably to Socrates, Seneca, and Ovid and by praising his translation of *Roman de la Rose*. In the poem's envoi, Deschamps compares himself to a thorn in the garden of Chaucer's poetry:

Poëte hault, loënge d'escuirie,
En ton jardin ne seroie qu'ortie,
Consideré ce que j'ay dit premier,
Ton noble plant, ta douce melodie;
Mais, pour sçavior, de rescripre te prie,
Grant translateur, noble Geffroy Chaucier.

[Esteemed poet, eminent among squires, I would only be a nettle in your garden, if you consider what I have described before, your noble plants, your sweet melody. Still I would like to know your opinion; please respond, great translator, noble Geoffrey Chaucer.][7]

No extant evidence documents whether Chaucer replied to Deschamps's request for a critique of his poetry, but shared literary themes suggest an authorial kinship between the two men. Deschamps wrote more than a thousand ballades, but he is perhaps best remembered for his *Miroir de mariage* (Mirror of Marriage), a work of more than 12,000 lines in which Franc Vouloir (Free Will) ponders whether he should marry; his false friends, including Desir and Folie, advocate marriage, but Repertoire de Science (Wisdom) advises against it. This scene bears strong parallels to the marriage debate between Justinus and Placebo that opens Chaucer's Merchant's Tale, and many of its antimarriage sentiments are also echoed and refuted in the Wife of Bath's Prologue.

Of all French authors, the thirteenth-century poets Guillaume de Lorris and Jean de Meun should not be underestimated in their influence on Chaucer and his literature. Little is known about these men's lives, but, with their allegorical romance *Roman de la Rose*, they created one of the foundational texts of medieval literature. Writing circa 1230, Guillaume de Lorris began the poem but left it incomplete at approximately 4,000 lines, and Jean de Meun finished it in the early 1280s by adding some 17,000 more lines. *Romaunt of the Rose*, a Middle English translation of Lorris and Meun's *Roman de la Rose*, is ascribed to Chaucer, but scholars debate whether he truly authored this text. It is divided into three fragments referred to as A, B, and C, and it is generally accepted that Chaucer wrote Fragment A (1–1705), that Chaucer did not write Fragment B (1706–5810), and that Chaucer probably did not write Fragment C (5811–7692).[8] Some scholars theorize that two translators were hired to finish Chaucer's incomplete Fragment A but that the project was later abandoned.

In the opening of the *Romaunt of the Rose*, in scenes descending from Guillaume's version, the Dreamer falls asleep (21–40) and sees a garden wall decorated with allegorical figures (132–474), enters inside when Idleness invites him in (509–644), and falls in love with a rose after the God of Love shoots him with his arrows of Beaute, Symplesse, Curtesie, Company, and Faire-Semblaunt (1649–1926). He succeeds in kissing the Rose with Venus's blessing (3627–3772), but the allegorical characters Shame and Wikkid-Tunge convince Jelousy to imprison Bialacoil (Fair Welcome) and the Rose in a castle. Guillaume's poem ends at this scene, with the lover mourning his loss. Jean de Meun's additions conclude with the Dreamer's triumph when he plucks the Rose, which metaphorically symbolizes sexual conquest. Before this climax, however, Jean moves through numerous plot points and digressions, including excursuses on philosophical issues such as old age, happiness, fortune, and justice. A love poem and an encyclopedic compendium, a romance and an allegory, *Roman de la Rose* inspired authors of the Middle Ages with its complex interweaving of courtly love and philosophy, all told through the simple narrative structure of a dreamer admiring a lovely rose.

Regardless of the precise authorship of the Middle English *Romaunt of the Rose*, the influence of the French *Roman de la Rose* on Chaucer's literature is vast, especially in his use of dream visions and his thematic treatments of courtly love. In the *Book of the Duchess*, Chaucer's dream begins as he finds himself in a chamber where the walls are illustrated with "bothe text and glose, / Of al the Romaunce of the Rose" (333–34). Much of the *Roman de la Rose* takes place in a garden, and Chaucer alludes to it as a model for January's garden in the Merchant's Tale:

So fair a gardyn woot I nowher noon.
For, out of doute, I verraily suppose
That he that wroot the Romance of the Rose
Ne koude of it the beautee wel devyse. (4.2030–33)

As this garden serves as the site of May and Damian's adulterous tryst, so too the love portrayed in the garden of Chaucer's source assumes a sexual cast when the Dreamer finally "plucks" the Rose that he loves so passionately. With its obvious sexual allegory, *Roman de la Rose* sparked much controversy throughout the Middle Ages, and in the *Legend of Good Women*, the God of Love chides Chaucer for translating it:

> "For in pleyn text, withouten need of glose,
> Thou has translated the Romaunce of the Rose,
> That is an heresye ayeins [against] my lawe,
> And makest wise folk fro me withdrawe." (F.328–31)

If *Legend of Good Women* is Chaucer's apology for translating *Roman de la Rose*, it is apparent that his source text sins against love in some fashion. Love is indeed the subject matter of *Romaunt of the Rose*, as the Dreamer records: "It is the Romance of the Rose, / In which al the art of love I close" (39–40); however, this love is both sacred and profane, both chaste and sexual, and, as Chaucer's apology in the *Legend of Good Women* indicates, many readers found it misogynist.

Italian Sources

As part of his courtly and administrative duties, Chaucer traveled to Italy, including Genoa, Florence, and Lombardy, and there he encountered Italy's vibrant literary culture. The Renaissance did not reach the shores of England until the sixteenth century, but because this period of renewed interest in the arts, humanities, and classical learning began in late-thirteenth-century Italy, Chaucer was likely quite impressed by the poets Dante, Petrarch, and Boccaccio, who were widely honored in Italy for their literary accomplishments.

Chaucer frequently alludes to Italy and its mythic history with conflicting images. In his retellings of the legend of Aeneas in the *House of Fame*, the hero's deceased wife Creusa urges him to fulfill his destiny by traveling to Italy: "And seyde he moste unto Itayle, / As was hys destinee, sauns faille [without doubt]" (187–88). In the Clerk's Tale, Chaucer employs fairly standard descriptions of Italy as a land of abundance and lush beauty:

> Ther is, at the west side of Ytaille,
> Doun at the roote of Vesulus [Monte Viso] the colde,
> A lusty playn, habundant of vitaille [victuals, food],
> Where many a tour [tower] and toun thou mayst biholde,

That founded were in tyme of fadres olde,
And many another delitable sighte,
And Saluces this noble contree highte [is called]. (4.57–63)

In describing the lineage of Walter, the Clerk notes that he is the "gen-tilleste yborn of Lumbardye" (4.72). The setting of the Clerk's Tale and the Merchant's Tale, Lombardy was reputed to be the home of tyrants, which ties in well with Walter's and January's autocratic tendencies. In the *Legend of Good Women*, Alceste berates Chaucer for his slanderous stories against women and urges him not to resemble a tyrant of Lombardy: "This shoolde a ryghtwis lord have in his thoght, / And nat be lyk tirauntz of Lumbardye, / That han no reward but at tyrannye" (F.373–75). From these brief scenes, Italy appears to be a land of beauty but also of intrigue, one that Chaucer depicts as admirable and yet alien.

Chaucer owes immense literary debts to Dante Alighieri (1265–1321), who is most famous for his *Divine Comedy*, in which he casts himself as the protagonist traveling through the trilogy's books—*Inferno, Purgatorio, Paradiso*—to a deeper spiritual understanding of humanity's journey through life and the afterlife. Dante's other works in Italian include *La vita nuova* (*The New Life*), which tells of his love for Beatrice, and *Il convivio* (*The Banquet*), a philosophical work concerning eternal wisdom and the human quest for knowledge; in Latin they include *De vulgari eloquentia* (On the Eloquence of the Vulgar Tongue), a defense of writing poetry in Italian rather than Latin, and *De monarchia* (*Monarchy*), an examination of current political structures. One of Chaucer's great poetic innovations was adopting vernacular English as a suitable medium for poetry, and Dante anticipated this artistic decision in his *De vulgari eloquentia*.

Chaucer refers to and borrows extensively from Dante in his writings, and their shared consideration of the theme of gentility highlights the Englishman's respect for the Italian's philosophical opinions. Chaucer's poem "Gentilesse" explicitly states the theme that gentility is not conferred by lineage, and his ideas echo those expressed by Dante in his *Convivio*:

ed è tanto durata
la così falso oppinïon tra nui,
che l'uom chiama colui
omo gentil che può dicere: "io fui

nepote, o figlio, di cotal valente,"
benché sia da nïente.

[And so ingrained / Has this false view become among us / That
one calls another noble / If he can say "I am the son, / Or grandson,
of such and such / A famous man," despite his lack of worth.][9]

Likewise, in the Wife of Bath's Tale, the old woman quotes Dante, calling
him "the wise poete of Florence" (3.1125), in her argument to her young
husband that gentility depends upon one's virtuous actions:

"Lo, in swich maner rym is Dantes tale:
'Ful selde up riseth by his branches smale
Prowesse of man, for God, of his goodnesse,
Wole [wants] that of hym we clayme oure gentilesse.'" (3.1127–30).

Agreeing with Dante about the spiritual component of true gentility,
Chaucer's characters describe it as reflective of God's goodness, not a
person's lineage. In so doing, they express a Dantean sensibility that,
through allusion and intertextuality, reinforces the moral force of their
arguments.

Dante's *Divine Comedy* inspires numerous scenes in Chaucer's literature. In the Monk's Tale, Chaucer recounts the tragedy of Ugolino of Pisa,
retelling his imprisonment with his children, during which, in order to
save his life, they offer their father the flesh of their bodies to sustain him.
The Monk praises Dante as his source:

Of this tragedie it oghte ynough suffise;
Whoso wol here it in a lenger wise,
Redeth the grete poete of Ytaille
That highte [is called] Dant, for he kan al devyse
Fro point to point; nat o word wol he faille. (7.2458–62)

With the charming observation that not one of the Italian's words fails,
Chaucer honors Dante for his peerless accomplishments.

In the *Parliament of Fowls*, Chaucer passes through a gate that proclaims on one side, "Thorgh me men gon into that blysful place / Of
hertes hele and dedly woundes cure" (127–28), but the gate's reverse
side proclaims an opposing sentiment, "Thorgh me men gon . . . / Unto
the mortal strokes of the spere / Of which Disdayn and Daunger is the
gyde" (134–36). Dante's gate to hell communicates a similar sentiment,

although only expressing the foreboding sense of doom with no leavening optimism: "Per me si va ne la città dolente, / per me si va ne l'etterno dolore, / . . . / Lasciate ogne speranza, voi ch'intrate" [Through me the way to the city of woe, / Through me the way to eternal pain, / . . . / Abandon all hope, you who enter here].[10]

When addressing religious themes, Chaucer often turns to Dante for inspiration. He translates Dante's praise of Mary in the *Paradiso* (33.1–51), which in this work is voiced by St. Bernard, into the Second Nun's Marian homage in her tale's prologue:

Thow Mayde and Mooder, doghter of thy Sone,
Thow welle of mercy, synful soules cure,
In whom that God for bountee chees [chose] to wone [dwell],
Thow humble, and heigh over every creature,
Thow nobledest so ferforth oure nature,
That no desdeyn the Makere hadde of kynde
His Sone in blood and flessh to clothe and wynde. (8.36–42)

Dante's canto begins "Vergine Madre, figlia del tuo figlio" [Virgin Mother, daughter of your son],[11] and Chaucer freely expands from Dante's hymn to celebrate Mary's virtue. Likewise, Chaucer commences and closes *Troilus and Criseyde* with allusions to Dante's *Divine Comedy*. His opening line refers to Troilus's "double sorwe," which echoes Jocasta's "doppia tristizia" in the *Purgatorio* (22.56), and he closes his epic romance with a valedictory prayer to the Trinity inspired by Dante's *Paradiso*:

Thow oon, and two, and thre, eterne on lyve,
That regnest ay in thre, and two, and oon,
Uncircumscript, and al maist circumscrive [encompass],
Us from visible and invisible foon
Defende, and to thy mercy, everichon,
So make us, Jesus, for thi mercy, digne,
For love of mayde and moder thyn benigne.
    Amen. (5.1863–70)

The story of Troilus's disappointments in love ends before this valedictory, and so it is likely that Chaucer writes here in his own voice, as he affixes Christian meaning to his Boethian romance of love won and love lost. It should be noted, however, that this prayer translates Dante's words in his *Paradiso*, "Quell' uno e due e tre che sempre vive / e regna sempre in tre e 'n due e 'n uno, / non circunscritto, e tutto circunscrive" (14.29–30), and so Chaucer's prayer may reflect his respect for Dante as much as any desire to pray.

Francesco Petrarca (1304–1374) was crowned poet laureate in Rome in 1341 to celebrate his magnificent body of work. Many of his sonnets in the Italian vernacular celebrate his beloved Laura as the ideal woman, and his notable works in Latin include *De viris illustribus* (On Illustrious Men), *Africa, Secretum meum* (*The Secret*), *Rerum memorandarum libri* (Books on Matters That Should Be Remembered), *Bucolicum carmen* (Bucolic Song), *De vita solitaria* (*The Life of Solitude*), and *Epistolae metricae* (Metrical Letters). Petrarch was widely recognized throughout Italy as the preeminent scholar of his time, and Chaucer acclaims him for his poetic virtuosity. In the Clerk's Prologue, the Clerk praises Petrarch as "Fraunceys Petrak, the lauriat poete," declaring that his "rethorike sweete / Enlumyned al Ytaille of poetrie" (4.31–33). In *Troilus and Criseyde*, Chaucer adapts Petrarchan poetry to his authorial purposes in the first "Canticus Troili," in which Troilus ponders the meaning of love:

"If no love is, O God, what fele I so?
And if love is, what thing and which is he?
If love be good, from whennes [whence] cometh my woo?
If it be wikke, a wonder thynketh me,
When every torment and adversite
That cometh of hym may to me savory thinke,
For ay thurst I, the more that ich it drinke." (1.400–406).

Petrarch's sonnet begins "S'amor non è," and Chaucer's translation thus captures the amatory question that spurs the Italian's lyric, but Chaucer also expands his source greatly, metamorphosing Petrarch's sonnet into a twenty-one-line exposition on Troilus's romantic confusion. Oddly, Chaucer cites Petrarch as his source for the tragedy of Zenobia in the Monk's Tale, advising those readers who desire more of her story, "Lat hym unto my maister Petrak go, / That writ ynough of this, I undertake" (7.2325–26); however, Boccaccio's account of the queen is more readily apparent as Chaucer's source. Beyond their influence on Chaucer during the Middle Ages, Petrarch's sonnets inspired many writers of the English Renaissance; indeed, Petrarch's name is memorialized in the term "Petrarchan sonnet." This form devotes an octave to describing the lover's precarious amatory situation, followed by a sestet to resolve the predicament. (In contrast, the English or Shakespearian sonnet features three quatrains and a closing couplet.)

Giovanni Boccaccio (1313–1375) wrote prolifically throughout his life, and many of his works directly influenced Chaucer's conception of literature. His canon includes *Il filocolo* (The Love-Afflicted), which retells the French romance of Floris and Blanchefleur; *Il filostrato* (The Love-Struck), which retells the tragic love story of Troilo and Criseida; *Teseida*, which retells the love story of Palemone and Arcita for Emilia; *De claris mulieribus* (*On Famous Women*); and *De casibus virorum illustrium* (*The Fates of Illustrious Men*). The subtitle of the Monk's Tale—"De Casibus Virorum Illustrium"—alludes to Boccaccio's work of the same title.

Toward the end of his life, Boccaccio offered public lectures on Dante's literature, and his literary criticism of the *Inferno* survives to this day. Dante's and Petrarch's influence on Boccaccio is evident, and like Dante with Beatrice and Petrarch with Laura, Boccaccio was inspired by his beloved Fiammetta. Boccaccio is most famous for his masterpiece *Il decameron* (*The Decameron*), which he composed between 1349 and 1353 and which bears deep structural similarities to the *Canterbury Tales*. In Boccaccio's work, ten young aristocrats flee from Florence because of an outbreak of plague; they take residence at a country villa and pass the time by telling ten stories for each of the ten days of their self-imposed quarantine. Chaucer found inspiration in several of Boccaccio's tales for his *Canterbury Tales*, including the Merchant's Tale (cf. *Decameron*, ninth tale of the seventh day), Shipman's Tale (cf. *Decameron*, first tale of the eighth day), Franklin's Tale (cf. *Decameron*, fifth tale of the tenth day), and Clerk's Tale (cf. *Decameron*, tenth tale of the tenth day).

Somewhat oddly, Chaucer never mentions Boccaccio by name throughout his voluminous writings, but the Italian's *Teseida* and *Filostrato* provided him with the raw materials for his Knight's Tale and *Troilus and Criseyde*. In Chaucer's Knight's Tale, Arcite adopts the name Philostrate when serving as Emily's page (1.1426–28). The name Philostrate means "conquered by love," which captures Arcite's love-longings, while it also alludes to Boccaccio's *Filostrato*. Providing Chaucer with the source material for his two great epic romances, Boccaccio's masterpieces exemplify how great narratives inspire subsequent authors to retread familiar ground in innovative ways. Analyzing Chaucer's literary debts to Boccaccio illuminates the ways in which medieval poets saw their artistry not as deriving from a modern sense of originality as representative of creative genius, but instead as an intertextual process of homage and adaptation. Praising the literary accomplishments of the past by retelling yet again such remarkably well-told stories redounded to the glory of the new tellers, who could never have accomplished their own feats without such strong poetic foundations upon which to build.

Chaucer's English Contemporaries through the Fifteenth Century

Chaucer's fame eclipses that of all other English writers of the fourteenth century, but numerous other poets wrote masterpieces of their own during this period. Notably, the late fourteenth century witnessed a renewed interest in alliterative rather than rhyming verse, and this technique guides the works of William Langland (ca. 1330–ca. 1400), the author of *Piers Plowman*, and of the *Gawain*-Poet, the anonymous author of the poems *Sir Gawain and the Green Knight*, *Pearl*, *Patience*, and *Cleanness*. *Piers Plowman* portrays an allegorical dream vision in which the dreamer seeks answers to his religious questions; Langland presents a vivid account of the search for truth amid innumerable distractions and pleasures illustrated against the bustling backdrop of English society. *Sir Gawain and the Green Knight* tells of Gawain's adventures while tracking down the mysterious Green Knight, and this chivalric romance effectively combines an Arthurian setting with a moral lesson regarding pride and spiritual chivalry. Some scholars suggest that Chaucer may have read these works, but the evidence for such claims is for the most part fleeting. Chaucer's Parson derides the alliterative tradition when he declares, "I kan nat geeste [write verse] 'rum, ram, ruf,' by lettre, / Ne, God woot, rym [rhyme] holde I but litel bettre" (10.43–44), and then indicates his preference to "telle a myrie tale in prose" (10.46). These lines hint at Chaucer's disdain for alliterative verse, and it is true that his poetry does not typically rely on alliteration for metrical effects; however, since the Parson also dismisses rhyme in these lines, it is again unwise to assume that the words or actions of Chaucer's characters reflect his personal attitudes as author.

Little evidence indicates Chaucer's acquaintance with William Langland or the *Gawain*-Poet, but ample documentation attests that other English authors of the fourteenth century both inspired his literature and were inspired by him. In the polyglot world of medieval England, John Gower (ca. 1330–1408) proved himself an adept poet in French, Latin, and English, as his three major works—*Mirour de l'omme* (*The Mirror of Mankind*), *Vox clamantis* (*The Voice of One Crying*), and *Confessio amantis* (The Confession of the Lover)—are written in these three tongues respectively. *Mirour de l'omme* allegorically considers humanity's virtues and vices, *Vox clamantis* tackles issues of politics and sovereignty in light of recent political events such as the Peasants' Revolt of 1381, and *Confessio amantis* compiles 140 tales on the subject of love. Possibly Gower was playing a game of literary one-upmanship with Chaucer in his *Confessio amantis*, in that its 140 tales surpass the 120 projected narratives of the *Canterbury Tales*. Nonetheless, the two men appear to have been friends. In early manuscripts of *Confessio amantis*, the goddess Venus asks Gower to thank Chaucer on her behalf:

> "And gret [greet] wel Chaucer whan ye mete,
> As mi disciple and mi poete:
> For in the floures of his youthe
> In sondri wise [various ways], as he wel couthe,
> Of Ditees and of songes glade,
> The whiche he for mi sake made,
> The lond fulfild is overal."[12]

Chaucer likewise expresses his respect for Gower by dedicating *Troilus and Criseyde* to him: "O moral Gower, this book I directe / To the" (5.1856–57).

Thomas Usk (d. 1388), who served as mayor of London from 1381 to 1383, extols Chaucer as "the noble philosophical poete in Englissh" in his *Testament of Love*. He does not refer to Chaucer by name in this work, instead speaking of the great author of "the boke of Troilus" and praising Chaucer through the voice of his title character Love:

> Wherfore, al that wyllen me good owe to do him worshyp and reverence bothe; trewly, his better ne his pere in schole of my rules coude I never fynde. . . . Certaynly his noble sayenges can I not amende; in goodnes of gentyl manlyche speche, without any maner of nycite of st[o]rieres ymagynacion, in wytte and in good reason of sentence he passeth al other makers.[13]

Usk casts his own literature as secondary to Chaucer's, and this trope of writing in the great master's shadow characterizes the praise many of Chaucer's contemporaries bestow upon him. Notable too is Usk's description of Chaucer's "gentyl manlyche" speech, in that he overlooks the ribald tales of such pilgrims as the Miller and Reeve to concentrate on Chaucer's more courtly verse.

Thomas Hoccleve (ca. 1369–1426), although approximately thirty years younger than Chaucer, likely knew him personally. His varied works include *The Letter of Cupid*, *La Male Regle* (which tells of his debauched years in London), and his *Regiment of Princes*, a guide for rulers dedicated to Henry, Prince of Wales, the future king Henry V. In *Regiment of Princes*, Hoccleve laments Chaucer's death and ponders the wisdom of any author, including himself, who might attempt to surpass his accomplishments:

> The firste fyndere of our fair langage
> Hath seid, in cas semblable, and othir mo,
> So hyly wel that it is my dotage
> For to expresse or touche any of tho.
> Allas, my fadir fro the world is go,
> My worthy maistir Chaucer—him I meene;
> Be thow advocat for him, hevenes queene.[14]

Indeed, Hoccleve felt so attached to Chaucer that he had a marginal illustration of his literary predecessor included in his poem's manuscript. He encourages his readers to ponder the drawing to better remember Chaucer:

> I have heere his liknesse
> Do make, to this ende, in soothfastnesse,
> That they that han of him lost thoght and mynde
> By this peynture may ageyn him fynde.[15]

It is generally believed that this manuscript illustration depicts Chaucer relatively faithfully, given the assumed familiarity between the two men.

John Lydgate (ca. 1370–1449/50), a Benedictine monk, greatly admired Chaucer's work, and he refers to Chaucer as "Floure of poetes thorghout al Breteyne, / Which sothly hadde most of excellence / In rethorike and in eloquence."[16] Much of Lydgate's literature echoes Chaucer's: Lydgate's *A Complaint of the Black Knight* resembles Chaucer's *Book of the Duchess*; *The Temple of Glass* descends from the *House of Fame*; *The Flower of Courtesy*, a Valentine's Day poem, takes Chaucer's *Parliament of Fowls* as its inspiration; and *The Fall of Princes* models its presentation of tragedies on the Monk's Tale. Lydgate's *Siege of Thebes* (ca. 1421–22) in many ways replies to Chaucer's Knight's Tale in that it takes as its setting and focus the Theban epic material that Chaucer's Knight places in the background to his story's conflict. Lydgate's *Siege of Thebes* also attests to the widespread popularity of Chaucer's *Canterbury Tales* in the fifteenth century, and Lydgate alludes frequently to Chaucer's work and casts his narrative as a continuation of Chaucer's incomplete collection of tales. *Siege of Thebes* thus represents a medieval incarnation of fan fiction, in which readers take up their favorite stories to express both their personal creativity and their sincere admiration for another author's literature. With the advent of the Internet, fan fiction has garnered much attention of late, especially with the fervor expressed by devotees of such pop-culture staples as *Star Wars*, *Star Trek*, and *Harry Potter*; this literary genre has long allowed admirers of particular authors to showcase their literary affections through their own creations. The popularity of the *Canterbury Tales* throughout the fifteenth century encouraged numerous authors to write additional tales, including a Ploughman's Tale, another Cook's Tale, and the Merchant's Tale of Beryn; such additions to the *Canterbury Tales* are referred to as the Chaucerian apocrypha.

Beyond these spurious additions to the *Canterbury Tales*, writers also reimagined Chaucer's *Troilus and Criseyde*, most notably the Scottish poet Robert Henryson (ca. 1430–ca. 1506). In his *Testament of Cresseid* he praises "worthy Chaucer" but believes the story to be incomplete:

> For worthie Chauceir in that samin buik [same book]
> In gudelie [goodly] termis and in ioly veirs [charming verse],
> Compylit [compiled] hes his cairis, quha [who] will luik [look]
> To brek my sleip ane vther quair [book] I tuik,
> In quhilk [which] I fand [found] the fatall destenie
> Of fair Cresseid, that endit wretchitlie.[17]

Criseyde does not prosper in Henryson's continuation of this Trojan legend: Diomede abandons her, and she dies of leprosy. Chaucer's narrator often appears sympathetic to Criseyde, such as when he hopes to excuse her for her betrayal of Troilus: "And if I myghte excuse hire any wise, / For she so sory was for hire untrouthe, / Iwis, I wolde excuse hire yet for routhe" (5.1097–99). Henryson's narrator, in contrast, punishes this fickle heroine for her transgressions in a particularly gruesome manner.

For all authors, a continued appreciation of their literature depends in large part on its accessibility, and numerous early printers and compilers helped to cement Chaucer's reputation by keeping his literature in circulation. Foremost, William Caxton (ca. 1420–1492), England's first printer, published most of Chaucer's writings in the 1470s and 1480s. Caxton's enthusiasm for Chaucer maintained the author's position as the Father of English Literature, and the printer praises him as "the worshipful fader & first foundeur & enbelissher of ornate eloquence in our englissh."[18] Following Caxton, numerous other early printers and publishers maintained Chaucer's status as England's greatest early writer, including William Thynne (d. 1546), John Stow (ca. 1525–1605), and Thomas Speght (fl. 1600). Continuing what his father William had begun, Francis Thynne in his *Animadversions upon the Annotations and Corrections to Some Imperfections of Chaucer's Works* undertook his editorial labors "to the end [that] Chawcers Woorkes by muche conference and manye judgmentes mighte at leng[t]he obteyne their true perfectione and glorye."[19]

Chaucer in the Renaissance

Although Chaucer's reputation as the Father of English Literature has withstood the passing of the centuries, critics have not unanimously voiced adulation of his work. During the Renaissance, many writers continued to praise Chaucer for his accomplishments, but others expressed their shock at his ostensible obscenity and their impatience with his antiquity. In the mid-1500s, Edmund Becke rued how the aristocracy preferred the bawdy humor of the *Canterbury Tales* to the moral instruction of the Judeo-Christian Bible: "If all magistrates & the nobilitie . . . wolde . . . spare an houre or ii in a day, from theyr worldly busines, emploing it about the reading of [the Bible], as they haue bene vsed to do in Cronicles & Canterbury tales, then should they also abandone . . . all blasphemyes, swearing, carding, dysing."[20] In his *Arte of Rhetorique* (1553), Thomas Wilson likewise expressed his exasperation with Chaucer's admirers: "The fine Courtier wil talke nothyng but Chaucer. The misticall wise menne, and Poeticall Clerkes will speake nothyng but quaint prouerbes, and blynd allegories, delityng muche in their awne darknesse, especially, when none can tell what thei dooe saie."[21] From Wilson's criticism, it appears that Renaissance courtiers cited Chaucer in the manner of an upper-crust affectation. Also, Wilson alludes to Chaucer's chief difficulty in maintaining his popularity during the Renaissance, an obstacle that persists to the present day: the Middle English of fourteenth-century London had become increasingly archaic by the sixteenth century, and thus many readers found his literature difficult to enjoy.

In his *Defense of Poesie* (1582), Sir Philip Sidney (1554–1586), the esteemed author of such works as the prose romance *Arcadia* and the sonnet sequence *Astrophel and Stella*, expresses his admiration for Chaucer while simultaneously casting aspersions on the "misty time" of the Middle Ages: "Chawcer undoubtedly did excellently in his *Troilus and Creseid*: of whome trulie I knowe not whether to mervaile more, either that hee in that mistie time could see so clearly, or that wee in this cleare age, goe so stumblingly after him. Yet had hee great wants, fit to be forgiven in so reverent an Antiquitie."[22] Roughly two hundred years separate Chaucer from Sidney, and so it is perhaps not surprising that Sidney finds his forebear's work somewhat archaic. Precisely because of his perceived archaism, however, other Renaissance writers describe Chaucer as a rustic but divinely inspired poet. Edmund Spenser (ca. 1552–1599), author of the monumental *Faerie Queene*, eulogizes Chaucer in his *Shepheardes Calendar* (1579) by allegorizing him into Tityrus, the god of shepherds:

> The God of shepheardes *Tityrus* is dead,
> Who taught me homely, as I can, to make [compose poetry].
> He, whilst he lived, was the soveraigne head
> Of shepheards all, that bene with love ytake.[23]

Playing with the pastoral tradition, in which poets imagine themselves as shepherds tending the fields with their lady loves, Spenser idolizes Chaucer as the deity of this literary genre. Although Chaucer's literature focuses more on courtly amorousness than bucolic hand-holding, Spenser views Chaucer's amatory verse as the precursor to the pastoral and casts himself as a student eager to learn from his master.

Writers of the Renaissance often desired to prove the advancement of English letters in their day over the works of the medieval past, and to this end some authors use Chaucer as a touchstone to measure the accomplishments of their contemporaries. Sir Thomas Wyatt (1503–1542) and Henry Howard, Earl of Surrey (1517–1547), imported the sonnet tradition to England, and both saw themselves as deeply indebted to Petrarch. One of Wyatt's most celebrated poems is "The long love that in my thought doth harbor," and this work faithfully recasts Poem 140 of Petrarch's *Rime sparse*. Surrey also translated this poem, calling it "Love, that doth reign and live within my thought." For both of these early innovators of the sonnet tradition in England, Petrarch established the baseline according to which subsequent sonneteers were measured. Surrey praises Wyatt's poetry in his elegy "Wyatt resteth here, that quick [alive] could never rest" by comparing him favorably to Chaucer:

> A hand that taught what might be said in rhyme;
> That reft Chaucer the glory of his wit;
> A mark the which, unparfited for time,
> Some may approach, but never none shall hit.[24]

With this slight jab at Chaucer, Surrey suggests Wyatt's verse surpasses that of his poetic forebear; at the same time, the poem tacitly acknowledges Chaucer as the most esteemed poet of the English literary tradition by employing him as a benchmark of literary greatness.

In a similar fashion, Ben Jonson (1572–1637), the playwright of such masterpieces as *Every Man in His Humor*, *Volpone*, and *The Alchemist*, eulogizes William Shakespeare (1564–1616) in his "To the Memory of My Beloved, The Author Mr William Shakespeare, and What He Hath Left Us": "My Shakespeare, rise: I will not lodge thee by / Chaucer or Spenser, or bid Beaumont lie / A little further, to make thee a room."[25] Surely Shakespeare would have appreciated Jonson's encomium, but he would also have likely conceded Chaucer's greatness as a writer. Scholars see traces of Chaucer's work throughout Shakespeare's canon, most notably because Chaucer's *Troilus and Criseyde* serves as the basis for Shakespeare's *Troilus and Cressida*, as does Chaucer's Knight's Tale for *The Two Noble Kinsmen*, cowritten with John Fletcher (1579–1625). Shakespeare and Fletcher acknowledge their debt to the fourteenth-century poet in this play's prologue:

> We pray our play may be so; for I am sure
> It has a noble breeder and a pure,
> A learned, and a poet never went
> More famous yet 'twixt Po and silver Trent.
> Chaucer (of all admir'd) the story gives;
> There constant to eternity it lives.[26]

Shakespeare also employs Chaucer's Knight's Tale, although in a more muted fashion, in *A Midsummer Night's Dream*, which similarly relies on Theseus's marriage to Hippolyta to catalyze the unfolding plot. For most modern readers, Shakespeare's accomplishments outpace those of Chaucer: the fourteenth-century poet is granted the title of Father of English Literature, but Shakespeare holds the higher place of honor in the pantheon of English writers. Reading these lines from *The Two Noble Kinsmen*, critics of today might well wonder if Shakespeare would agree with such an assessment of their relative merits.

Chaucer in the Eighteenth through Twentieth Centuries

In the eighteenth century, Chaucer's reputation as England's first great poet continued to be accepted, but critics increasingly lamented his archaic Middle English. In his poem "An Account of the Greatest English Poets," Joseph Addison (1672–1719) praises Chaucer for rousing English literature from its long slumber throughout much of the Middle Ages, but he also criticizes him for that which he cannot help: his literature is now approximately three hundred years old. For Addison, Chaucer's medieval vocabulary obfuscates his literary genius:

> Long had our dull forefathers slept supine
> Nor felt the raptures of the tunefull Nine [Muses]
> Till Chaucer first, the merry Bard, arose;
> And many a story told in rhyme and prose.
> But age has rusted what the poet writ,
> Worn out his language and obscured his wit;
> In vain he jests in his unpolished strain,
> And tries to make his readers laugh in vain.[27]

Samuel Johnson (1709–1784), another of the great men of English letters during the eighteenth century, compiled the first dictionary of the English language and wrote an impressive volume of literary criticism, *The Lives of the Poets*. He describes Chaucer in mixed terms:

> The history of our language is now brought to the point at which the history of our poetry is generally supposed to commence, the time of the illustrious *Geoffrey Chaucer*, who may perhaps, with great justice, be stiled the first of our versifiers who wrote poeti-

cally. He does not however appear to have deserved all the praise which he has received, or all the censure that he has suffered.[28]

Observing the apparent paradox that ancient Greek is more readily comprehensible to many readers than Middle English, Johnson notes, "*Homer* has fewer passages unintelligible than *Chaucer*."[29] From the perspective of Addison and Johnson, the esteem accorded to Chaucer's poetry is not entirely warranted, yet his foundational position in English literature is nonetheless preserved.

Responding to charges of Chaucer's inaccessibility, other critics and poets sought to invigorate England's appreciation of his literature. To this end, John Dryden (1631–1700) and Alexander Pope (1688–1744) translated his works to increase their readership. Dryden extols Chaucer's poetic accomplishments in the preface to his *Fables Ancient and Modern* (1700): "He must have been a Man of a most wonderful comprehensive Nature, because, as it has been truly observ'd of him, he has taken into the Compass of his *Canterbury Tales* the various Manners and Humours (as we now call them) of the whole *English* Nation, in his Age. Not a single Character has escap'd him."[30] Dryden defends his revered forebear against readers who "look on *Chaucer* as a dry, old-fashion'd Wit, not worth receiving" and calls him a "rough Diamond, [who] must first be polish'd e'er he shines."[31] In so doing, Dryden implies the necessity of his translations of Chaucer's writings, including new versions of the Knight's Tale, Wife of Bath's Tale, and Nun's Priest's Tale. Likewise, Alexander Pope's literary kinship with Chaucer appears throughout much of his witty verse, such as *The Rape of the Lock* (1712–1714) and *The Dunciad* (1728), and Pope proclaims that he reads Chaucer "with as much pleasure as almost any of our poets." In harmony with critics such as Addison and Johnson, who charge that Chaucer's language makes his poetry inaccessible, Pope fears that changes to the English language will make Chaucer's literature eventually unreadable:

> Now length of Fame (our second life) is lost,
> And bare threescore is all ev'n that can boast:
> Our Sons their Fathers' failing language see,
> And such as Chaucer is, shall Dryden be.[32]

Pope translated several of Chaucer's works, including "January and May; or, the Merchant's Tale" and "The Wife of Bath, her Prologue," and he renamed and recast Chaucer's *House of Fame* as *Temple of Fame*. As a youth, he also wrote a bawdy verse in imitation of Chaucer's comic style. In this brief poem, a young man hides a duck in his pants; while in the company of some female relations, the duck's head pops out, and one of the young women cries, "O Moder, Moder, . . . / Be thilke same thing Maids longen a'ter?"[33] From this example, it appears that Pope greatly admired Chaucer's fabliau sensibility.

Although sharp humor and suggestive wit characterize much of eighteenth-century literature, such as in the plays of William Congreve (*The Way of the World*, 1700), Oliver Goldsmith (*She Stoops to Conquer*, 1773), and Robert Brinsley Sheridan (*The School for Scandal*, 1777), some authors castigated Chaucer for the supposedly immoral and obscene aspects of his poetry. The celebrated author of *Robinson Crusoe*, Daniel Defoe (1660–1731), wrote: "Jeffry Chaucer is forgotten upon the same Account; and tho' that Author is excused, by the unpoliteness of the Age he lived in, yet his Works are diligently buried, by most Readers, on that very Principle, that they are not fit for modest Persons to read."[34] Defoe's criticism may strike some readers as hypocritical, given the salacious nature of his *Moll Flanders* (1722), in which his heroine supports herself through prostitution and numerous shocking misadventures. Carrying into the Romantic era, George Gordon, Lord Byron (1788–1824), whose contemporaries deemed his poetry and his lifestyle scandalous, condemned Chaucer with a perhaps surprising prudery: "Chaucer, notwithstanding the praises bestowed on him, I think obscene and contemptible:—he owes his celebrity merely to his antiquity."[35]

During the Romantic era, many authors turned to nature for inspiration and viewed poets as spontaneously and organically connected to the world around them. Three of the greatest Romanticists, William Blake (1757–1827), William Wordsworth (1770–1850), and Samuel Taylor Coleridge (1772–1834), championed Chaucer as an exemplary poet, lionizing him as a natural and undefiled voice of the past. An artist as well as a poet, Blake engraved an image of the *Canterbury Tales*, and in *A Descriptive Catalog* (1809) he celebrates Chaucer for his observational skills in creating such lifelike characters: "Chaucer is himself the great poetical observer of men, who in every age is born to record and eternize its acts. This he does as a master, as a father, and superior, who looks down on their little follies from the Emperor to the Miller; sometimes with severity, oftener with joke and sport."[36] For Blake, Chaucer's talent springs from within and reflects his innate genius. Wordsworth ranked Chaucer as one of the four great English poets whom he most needed to emulate if he were to succeed as an author: "When I began to give myself up to the profession of a poet for life, I was impressed with the conviction, that there were four English poets whom I must have continually before me as examples—Chaucer, Shakespeare, Spenser, and Milton. These I must study, and equal if I could; and I need not think of the rest."[37] Like Dryden and Pope, Wordsworth translated portions of Chaucer's literature, including the tales of the Prioress and Manciple and selections from *Troilus and Criseyde*, in an effort to revitalize the tales from their archaic language. Succinctly expressing his esteem, Coleridge stated, "I take unceasing delight in Chaucer."[38]

During the Victorian era, the growing industrialism of England and the social problems it generated (as famously depicted in Charles Dickens's 1854 novel *Hard Times*) dismayed many authors and artists. Some looked back to the Middle Ages as an idyllic time of innocence and, in this light, viewed Chaucer as an undefiled voice from the past. Elizabeth Barrett Browning (1806–1861) praises Chaucer for the childlike qualities of his writing:

> But it is in Chaucer we touch the true height, and look abroad into the kingdoms and glories of our poetical literature. . . . Childlike, too, his tears and smiles lie at the ledge of his eyes, and he is one proof more among the many, that the deepest pathos and the quickest gaieties hide together in the same nature.[39]

For Barrett Browning, Chaucer represents the totality of the human experience even as she infantilizes him. William Morris (1834–1896), whose interest in medieval literature is attested by his *Defence of Guenevere, and Other Poems* (1858), similarly describes the "spirit of Chaucer's poetry" as a celebration of life: "Look at all the picture, note all and live in all, and be as merry as you may, never forgetting that you are alive and that it is good to live."[40] In homage to Chaucer, Morris produced a lavishly illustrated version of his poetry with eighty-seven woodcuts designed by Edward Burne-Jones; this volume is known as the Kelmscott Chaucer.

Matthew Arnold (1822–1888), remembered for both his poetry and his literary criticism, acknowledges Chaucer's greatness as the Father of English Literature, declaring, "With him is born our real poetry," yet also judges that "he lacks the high seriousness of the great classics, and therewith an important part of their virtue."[41] When other critics derided Chaucer for the ostensibly raw poetics of his "unsophisticated" meter, Gerard Manley Hopkins (1844–1889) refuted these charges of irregular scansion. As the innovative creator of sprung rhythm, a poetic meter designed to capture the pace and sound of natural speech, Hopkins argued for the precise artistry of Chaucer's craft: "I have found that Chaucer's scanning, once understood, is extremely smooth and regular, much more so than is thought by . . . modern Chaucerists, and they think it regularity itself compared to what Dryden and older critics thought of it."[42] On the issue of his meter, Elizabeth Barrett Browning also vehemently defends Chaucer:

> We cannot help observing, because certain critics observe otherwise, that Chaucer utters as true music as ever came from poet or musician. . . . Not one of the "Queen Anne's men," measuring out tuneful breath upon their fingers, like ribbons for topknots, did know the art of versification as the old rude Chaucer knew it. Call him rude for the picturesqueness of the epithet; but his verse has, at least, as much regularity in the sense of true art, and more manifestly in proportion to our increasing acquaintance with his dialect and pronunciation, as can be discovered or dreamed in the French school.[43]

Such defenses of Chaucer's versification rescued him from charges that his poetry reflected an unsophisticated and ultimately crude talent. On the contrary, Hopkins and Barrett Browning assert, Chaucer's verse attests to his sublime verbal artistry.

In tandem with the prevailing Victorian view of Chaucer as a simple and yet sophisticated poet, American philosopher Henry David Thoreau (1817–1862), author of *Walden* (1854), describes Chaucer as "fresh and modern still," declaring firmly that "no dust settles on his true passages." He also comments on the reader's respect for Chaucer due to the author's childlike innocence: "And in return the reader has great confidence in him, that he tells no lies, and reads his story with indulgence, as if it were the circumlocution of a child, but often discovers afterwards that he has spoken with more directness and economy of words than a sage."[44] Such a view is somewhat patronizing toward medieval authors, as if Chaucer did not know he was creating literary art, yet Thoreau simultaneously concedes the philosophical depth apparent in much of Chaucer's writings. Ralph Waldo Emerson (1803–1882), Transcendental philosopher and essayist, paints Chaucer as the fountainhead from which all of English literature flows: "The influence of Chaucer is conspicuous in all our early literature: and, more recently, not only Pope and Dryden have been beholden to him, but in the whole society of English writers a large unacknowledged debt is easily traced. One is charmed with the opulence which feeds so many pensioners."[45] Although American writers of the eighteenth and nineteenth centuries often struggled to establish a distinctively American voice for literature, one free from the artistic pressures descending from the great English poets, Emerson's words also highlight the broad appreciation and respect still accorded to Chaucer by authors in the young United States of America.

With the rise of modernism in the early twentieth century, many authors broke with prevailing traditions and narrative forms of Western culture. T. S. Eliot (1888–1965), a leading poet of this movement, composed *The Wasteland* (1922) as an ode to modernist alienation and angst, and his poem famously begins by reimagining the opening lines of the *Canterbury Tales*. Eliot metamorphoses Chaucer's "Whan that Aprill with his shoures soote," a hymn to the newborn beauties of spring, into a seasonal elegy:

> April is the cruelest month, breeding
> Lilacs out of the dead land, mixing
> Memory and desire, stirring
> Dull roots with spring rain.[46]

Through this powerful allusion, Eliot upends Chaucer's springtime revelries and reimagines England's vernal rebirth in a land virtually barren. More than merely overturning the depiction of spring, Eliot also rewrites the generative force of Chaucer and his *Canterbury Tales* as the inspiring wellspring of English literature.

Other modernists, following their Victorian forebears, venerated Chaucer as the poet of nature, innocence, and tradition. Aldous Huxley (1894–1963), who penned the dystopian novel *Brave New World* (1932) and decried the dehumanizing aspects of modern culture in his writings, paints Chaucer as a poet of the natural world: "And it is in the heart of this living and material world of nature that Chaucer lives. He is the poet of earth, supremely content to walk, desiring no wings."[47] G. K. Chesterton (1874–1936), esteemed literary critic and author of the Father Brown mysteries, applauds Chaucer for being an artist not weighed down by his art: "Chaucer was, above all, an artist; and he was one of that fairly large and very happy band of artists who are not troubled with the artistic temperament."[48] In her *Common Reader* (1925), Virginia Woolf (1882–1941) praises Chaucer for his unparalleled storytelling ability: "To learn the end of the story—Chaucer can still make us wish to do that. He has preeminently that story-teller's gift, which is almost the rarest gift among writers at the present day." To Chaucer's critics who snipe at the bawdy fun of his work, Woolf defends his piquancy: "Much of Chaucer—a few lines perhaps in each of the Tales—is improper and gives us as we read it the strange sensation of being naked to the air after being muffled in old clothing."[49] Woolf's admiration for Chaucer's narratology is perhaps somewhat surprising, given her innovative use of a stream-of-consciousness narrative structure in such works as *Mrs. Dalloway* (1925) and *To the Lighthouse* (1927). Her perception of his genius in a simpler but nonetheless compelling style of narration testifies both to Chaucer's artistic skill and to the ample scope of her opinions.

From the preceding survey, it may appear that Chaucer belongs exclusively in the hands of elite authors, those who have joined him in the ranks of English literature's canonical authors. Chaucer, however, is a supple figure, and he is readily appropriated by writers of popular-culture fiction. Notably, he appears in, or otherwise inspires, several series of mystery novels, including those of P. C. Doherty, C. L. Grace, and Philippa Morgan. The world of NASCAR racing bears little in common with Chaucer's fourteenth-century England, yet Sharyn McCrumb weds her novel *St. Dale* to Chaucer's narrative structure in the *Canterbury Tales* as she details the adventures of modern-day pilgrims tracing the path of fallen racing legend Dale Earnhardt. Works spanning from Shakespeare's *The Two Noble Kinsmen* to McCrumb's *St. Dale* represent an eclectic range of Chaucerian allusion, yet one well in keeping with the polyphonous voices of Chaucer's many works.

Chaucer on Film

In comparison to Shakespeare, whose cinematic output is dauntingly impressive for a man dead approximately three hundred years prior to the invention of motion picture technologies, Chaucer's body of film work is relatively scant. This is likely due to the fact that Shakespeare's plays were written for performance and, consequently, can be adapted to the screen in myriad creative ways. In contrast, Chaucer's literature is intended for recitation and reading, and a scriptwriter would have to be skilled indeed to translate his ironies and wordplay into the visual medium of film. For example, the portrait of the Prioress in the General Prologue (1.118–62) is generally agreed to be one of the most piercing and effective character descriptions ever penned, but translating this portrait to the screen would likely turn Chaucer's deft satiric touches into broad farce, if the transition were successfully managed at all. It is amusing to envision this Prioress rudely dipping her fingers into a shared pot of sauce to the disgust of her dining companions (1.128–29), but depicting such a scene would turn Chaucer's subtle irony into an obvious slur.

Of the film versions of Chaucer's literature, *A Canterbury Tale* (1944) exemplifies how derivations can capture the heart of his pilgrimage in a loose and yet compelling fashion. Legendary filmmakers Michael Powell and Emeric Pressburger, the creative forces behind such cinematic classics as *Black Narcissus* (1947) and *The Red Shoes* (1948), tell a quirky but intriguing mystery in this film, in which a British and an American soldier assist a young woman to uncover the identity of the assailant who poured glue on her hair. The story takes place along the road to Canterbury, and the opening narration recites the first eighteen lines of the General Prologue; then the narrator ponders the change from yesteryear to the film's present: "But though so little's changed since Chaucer's day, / Another kind of pilgrim walks the way."[50] A shot of a falcon metamorphoses into a shot of an airplane, and viewers see that World War II soldiers now travel the Canterbury road. Sergeant Bob Johnson, a gosh-darn polite American, wins over most of the British, but Magistrate Colpeper is perturbed at his general ignorance regarding the past:

> Magistrate Colpeper: Pity. When you get home, and people ask you what you've seen in England, and you say: I saw a movie in Salisbury, and I made a pilgrimage to Canterbury and saw another one.
>
> Bob Johnson: You've got me all wrong. I know that in Canterbury I have to look for a cathedral.

For Colpeper, the past is alive, and the road to Canterbury assumes mystical and spiritual meaning in this film by connecting the present to the past: "And when I turn the bend in the road where they too saw the towers of Canterbury, I feel I have only to turn my head to see them on the road behind me," Colpeper rhapsodizes. The film concludes at Canterbury Cathedral, with the spiritual majesty of a successful pilgrimage eclipsing the mystery of nocturnal hair gluing.

The title of Pier Paolo Pasolini's *I racconti di Canterbury* (*The Canterbury Tales*, 1972) suggests that the film translates Chaucer's pilgrimage in its entirety onto the silver screen, but it concentrates almost solely on Chaucer's fabliaux, depicting the General Prologue, Merchant's Tale, Friar's Tale, Cook's Tale, Miller's Tale, Wife of Bath's Prologue, Reeve's Tale, Pardoner's Tale, Summoner's Tale, and Summoner's Prologue.[51] In this somewhat haphazard collection of Chaucerian episodes, the portrayal of Alison of Bath humorously captures the character's hustle-and-bustle as she seeks new sexual conquests, and the Summoner's Prologue, with its attention to the explosive dynamics of Satan's anus, comes alive in a grotesque but hilarious sequence reenvisioned through the art of Hieronymus Bosch (ca. 1450–1516). Pasolini turns the fragmentary Cook's Tale into a farce reminiscent of Charlie Chaplin's films, while simultaneously accelerating the sexual escapades of his source. To date, *I racconti di Canterbury* stands as the most successful cinematic retelling of Chaucerian works, given its obvious affection for its source material and its earthy visualizations of Chaucer's humor.

Perhaps the oddest moment in Chaucer's cinematic history occurs in *A Knight's Tale*, a 2001 jousting romp starring Heath Ledger in the lead role of William Thatcher. A poor man aspiring to knighthood despite the rigid caste system of medieval society, Thatcher assembles a crew of other misfits to assist him in his quest for glory so that he can win his lady's love. Paul Bettany plays the role of Chaucer, who joins Thatcher's company of friends, and this incarnation of Chaucer presents him as an egomaniacal scamp. Upon encountering Thatcher and his companions, Chaucer trumpets his identity to the blank stares of his new friends: "Geoffrey Chaucer's the name, writing's the game."[52] Chaucer assists Thatcher in such disparate tasks as forging patents of nobility so that he can compete in the jousts, teaching him to dance, and writing a love letter, as well as promoting Thatcher's jousts with brash proclamations of this "knight's" heroic achievements. "I get their attention. You've got to win their hearts," he advises Thatcher. Touches of Chaucer's literature are dramatized as well, including cameos of a summoner and a pardoner. But the film contributes its defining image to the body of Chaucerian cinema when he is introduced stark naked after having lost his money gambling. A naked Chaucer metaphorically captures the author's meaning for subsequent writers and filmmakers who reimagine his work: he is his own storyline stripped to its bare essentials, upon which they can recast the life and writings of the Father of English Literature to their unique purposes. The film ends with Chaucer declaring, "I think I'm going to have to write some of this story down," which incorrectly suggests that the film *A Knight's Tale* reflects the events of Chaucer's Knight's Tale. Little in the film derives from Chaucer's romance, but within its loose fictions, the homage expresses respect for Chaucer's accomplishments, even if its Chaucerian roots do not run very deep. Chaucer proclaims at the film's conclusion, "All human activity lies within the artist's scope," which captures humanity's kaleidoscopic variety in the historical author's *Canterbury Tales* and other works.

Through this overview of Chaucer's sources and his influence on subsequent authors, it is apparent that literature in some ways resembles a transtemporal conversation among authors in which they jockey over the relative merits of one another's writings through their own contributions to the literary tradition. It is also apparent that many authors and critics reveal more about themselves and their time period through their comments than they do about Chaucer. Caroline Spurgeon (1869–1942), an early-twentieth-century Chaucerian who collected scores of literary and historical references to Chaucer in her *Chaucer Criticism and Allusion, 1357–1900*, suggested as much: "As we watch this vast company of writers passing before Chaucer, and leaving on record their opinion of him, it is curious to reflect that the criticism Chaucer has received throughout these five centuries in reality forms a measure of judgment—not of him—but of his critics."[53] Criticism and commentary are perhaps more self-revealing endeavors than many scholars would care to admit, but they nonetheless afford a fascinating view of the ways in which Chaucer influenced the development of English literature. The interplay of Chaucer's sources and his influences showcases how authors build upon the works of other authors, as others then build upon theirs. Through allusion, allegory, irony, homage, and a host of additional literary techniques, Chaucer and other authors consider their place in the artistic tradition. Some critics see this dynamic as partially paralyzing, labeling it the "anxiety of influence," in which the pressures of the great art of the past exert a chokehold on authors seeking to create something new.[54] But the glories of the past can be liberating as well, as authors devise new ways to install themselves within the pantheon of the world's greatest authors. Chaucer managed to do so, as did many of the authors he influenced, and it is a tribute to his own poetic genius, as well as to the geniuses that followed him, that their works still sparkle with life today.

Glossary of Literary Terms
and Chaucerian Themes

This glossary concentrates primarily on the genres and themes that Chaucer uses in his literature. Excellent generalist dictionaries of literary terms include M. H. Abrams and Geoffrey Harpham's *A Glossary of Literary Terms* and William Harmon and Hugh Holman's *A Handbook to Literature*.

allegory: an extended metaphoric and symbolic narrative, which tells a story on both its surface and metatextual levels. Allegories require the reader to follow two stories simultaneously as the literal actions of the narrative take on broader, often metaphysical, meanings. Medieval allegorical masterpieces include Dante's *Divine Comedy*, the *Roman de la Rose* (and Chaucer's translation of it), and William Langland's *Piers Plowman*, each of which details a protagonist's literal journey seeking truth but also resonates with layers of spiritual meaning.

ballade: a lyric form popular in France in the fourteenth and fifteenth centuries, typically composed of seven- or eight-line stanzas with each stanza concluding with an identical line. Chaucer uses the ballade form in many of his short verses, often to contemplate the vagaries of love.

blazon: (from Fr. *blason*, a coat of arms) in the courtly love tradition, the poetic device of cataloging a female beloved's admired characteristics—her ivory skin, her red lips, her golden hair—as in the formal language of heraldry.

Breton lay: a short rhymed romance combining folkloric, chivalric, and fairy-tale motifs, associated with the ancient Bretons, a Celtic people who lived in the French region of Brittany. Writing in the twelfth century in Anglo-Norman French, Marie de France developed the *lai* into a miniature work of narrative art. Chaucer uses the genre of the Breton lay in his Franklin's Tale.

carnivalesque: (humor) based on inversions of social structure. In carnival ritual and carnivalesque literature, topsy-turviness rules, and the expected registers of society are inverted: the king is a commoner, and the commoner assumes the role of the king. In Chaucer's *Canterbury Tales*, the pilgrimage often displays carnivalesque tensions when some pilgrims imbue the experience with mirthful inversions of medieval social customs while others are invested in maintaining the status quo.

Chaucerian apocrypha or **Chauceriana:** a body of writings that built upon or were directly inspired by Chaucer's literature. These works, many of which were penned during the fifteenth century, were sometimes erroneously ascribed to Chaucer, and they testify to his great popularity as an author and to the desire of subsequent authors to continue his *Canterbury Tales*. Famous works in the Chaucerian apocrypha include John Lydgate's *Siege of Thebes* and Robert Henryson's *Testament of Cresseid*. (For a selection of Chauceriana, see Kathleen Forni's *The Chaucerian Apocrypha: A Selection* and John Bowers's *The Canterbury Tales: Fifteenth-Century Continuations and Additions*.)

chivalry: the virtues that a knight should embody, including bravery, honor, mercy to his enemies, loyalty to his lord, and pure love for his lady. The term, in French *chevalerie*, which derives from *cheval*, horse, underscores the ways in which military masculinity influenced conceptions of medieval chivalry. Elaborate tournaments and rich spectacles allowed knights to display their chivalry in both its amatory and martial perspectives, as is apparent in Palamon and Arcite's combat for Emily's love in Chaucer's Knight's Tale.

comedy: in its simplest formulation, a genre in which the narrative ends happily. In Chaucer's literature, comedy is easily distinguished from tragedy, in which the story ends unhappily. Such an overarching distinction, however, does not fully take into account Chaucer's varied uses of the comic. For example, Chaucer's fabliaux typically end humorously, but not necessarily happily: the Miller's Tale concludes with great hilarity for readers, but which of the characters winds up happy? Chaucer uses the word *comedye* in the final stanzas of *Troilus and Criseyde*, although many readers might wonder about its applicability to a narrative that concludes with the protagonist's death. Chaucer's sense of the comic is often related to his treatment of irony, parody, and the carnivalesque.

complaint: either a lyric verse form in which the speaker bemoans his/her circumstances, such as Chaucer's "The Complaint unto Pity" and "The Complaint of Chaucer to His Purse," or a sorrowful speech spoken by a character in a narrative, such as the Man in Black's lamentation in the *Book of the Duchess* (475–86). Complaints offer insights into the speaker's emotions, and they typically, if tacitly, encourage readers to focus on their own emotional response to the thematic issues at hand.

courtly love: a code of conduct for medieval lovers, which encourages them to honor each other through their mutual passion. Typically, the knightly lover fights in combats and tournaments to prove his devotion to his beloved, who shows her mercy by accepting his chaste love. Their love is frequently described in religious terms, and it is often kept secret from others. Andreas Capellanus wrote the "rules" of courtly love in his twelfth-century text *De amore*, and this terse title is often loosely translated as *The Art of Courtly Love.*

cuckold: a man whose wife is unfaithful. Chaucer uses cuckoldry as a humorous plot device in many of his fabliaux. Interestingly, the English language has no corresponding word to denote a woman whose husband is unfaithful, which highlights the gendered dynamics of much sexual farce, as well as of language itself.

debate: a literary narrative in which two characters, often allegorical figures, discuss and argue the respective merits of their opposing ideals or points of view. Debate narratives are didactic, with the winner convincing the arbiter (and readers as well) of the merits of his/her case.

demande d'amour: literally, a question of love. In courtly romances, debate poems, and lyrics, speakers frequently pose rhetorical questions concerning the force and meaning of love for the audience to consider. Such moments often create a pause in the narrative action. Chaucer uses this device to engage his readers in the philosophical and thematic issues in his texts, such as at the close of part 1 of the Knight's Tale and the conclusion of the Franklin's Tale.

dream vision: a narrative in which a dream, typically recounted by the protagonist, reveals an unexpected moral that comforts the dreamer upon awakening. Chaucer's dream visions include the *Book of the Duchess, House of Fame, Parliament of Fowls, Legend of Good Women,* and Summoner's Prologue, while the prophetic accuracy of dreams is debated in the Nun's Priest's Tale. Dream visions were a popular genre in the Middle Ages, including such works as *Dream of the Rood*, Guillaume de Lorris and Jean de Meun's *Roman de la Rose*, Dante's *Divine Comedy*, William Langland's *Piers Plowman*, and the anonymously penned *Pearl*, by the same author as *Sir Gawain and the Green Knight*.

epic: a long narrative verse that depicts the heroic exploits of a quasi-divine figure on whose actions depends the fate of his people. The style is elevated, the scope is vast, and the hero's deeds surpass those of average men. Gods participate in the unfolding events, confirming the epic's subject as beyond merely terrestrial concerns. Homer's *Iliad* and *Odyssey* and Virgil's *Aeneid* epitomize the Greek and Roman epic traditions. Chaucer most emulates this venerated genre in his Knight's Tale and *Troilus and Criseyde*, while satirizing it in his Nun's Priest's Tale.

envoi: typically, the concluding stanza of a ballade, often addressing the poem's dedicatee. Many of Chaucer's short poems, including "Womanly Noblesse," "Fortune," "Truth," and "Lak of Stedfastnesse," conclude with envois. In his "Lenvoy de Chaucer a Scogan" and "Lenvoy de Chaucer a Bukton," Chaucer expands the form into poetic epistles, which nonetheless conclude with envoi stanzas.

estates satire: an analysis of society based on the intersection of social position and morality. Such medieval satires highlight the failures of the various social roles and professions to maintain their Christian standards. Estates satires are typically ordered hierarchically, beginning with the top of society and moving down. The Three Estates of medieval English society were those who fight (the aristocracy), those who pray (the religious orders and communities), and those who work (serfs and other menial workers who support the aristocracy and clergy).

etiological tales: stories that explain the origins of a natural phenomenon, such as how the leopard got its spots or how the turtle got its shell. Chaucer's Manciple's Tale explains how the crow turned from white to black. Rudyard Kipling's *Just-So Stories* (1902) is perhaps the most famous modern collection of etiological tales.

exemplum: a narrative designed to elucidate a moral. The Monk merges his telling of Samson's tragedy with the exemplum tradition when he appends a moral to the narrative: "Beth war [Be warned] by this ensample oold and playn / That no men telle hir conseil til hir [their] wyves" (7.2091–92). Despite the moral lessons embedded in exempla, Chaucer's pilgrims often use this genre for comic effect, as when the Friar tells his tale to insult his enemy the Summoner, then concludes it with a hortatory moral: "Disposeth ay youre hertes to withstonde / The feend [Satan], that yow wolde make [who would make you] thral and bonde" (3.1659–60).

fable or **beast fable:** an instructive narrative in which animals are frequently the main characters. The Greek Aesop (ca. 620–560 BCE) is the most famous author of the fable genre, although he was possibly an apocryphal persona linked to a body of such tales. Fables typically conclude with a moral: in the story of the Tortoise and the Hare, readers learn that "slow and steady wins the race." Chaucer's Nun's Priest's Tale, with its story of amorous chickens and their mock-epic escapades, relies on the fable tradition for its basic plot structure.

fabliau: a short tale in verse featuring bawdy and scatological humor, coarse sexuality, and trickery. Fabliaux flourished in thirteenth-century France, but only one extant English example—*Dame Sirith*—predates Chaucer's. In many ways, fabliaux are the generic opposite of romance. Where romances feature aristocratic men undertaking quests and fighting in tournaments to prove their love for their idealized beloveds, fabliaux frequently feature non-courtly men (clerks, priests, and tradesmen) relying on their quick wits to cuckold other men.

folk tale: a story shared orally by members of a particular culture or social grouping. In the retelling, folk tales evolve, so it is often difficult to track down the earliest forms of a given tale. Chaucer's literature uses many folk tales and motifs, such as the testing of the patient wife in the Clerk's Tale, the repercussions of a rash promise in the Franklin's Tale, and the double-dealing of thieves in the Pardoner's Tale.

fortune: in its simplest conception, luck or chance. For Chaucer, whose ideas are based on medieval commentary on the Roman goddess Fortuna, Lady Fortune is an allegorical entity who delights in imposing good and ill on humanity, but always in a haphazard fashion. The standard depiction of Fortuna features her spinning her wheel capriciously so that those at the bottom rise to the top, while those at the top fall to the bottom. Chaucer's ideas about fortune are summarized in his short poem of the same name; they derive in large part from Boethius's *Consolation of Philosophy*. Chaucer's thematic deployment of fortune frequently complements his consideration of human free will and predestination, in which characters ponder their ability to direct the course of their lives.

game, play: as in modern English, wide-ranging terms that typically connote pleasurable pastimes. A useful distinction is that games typically feature some sort of rules structure, whereas play relies more on a sense of amusement and frivolity. The tension between play and seriousness percolates throughout the *Canterbury Tales*, with the characters frequently cloaking earnest intentions under the guise of harmless play.

gentilesse: a much debated personal quality in Chaucer's *Canterbury Tales*. Gentilesse comprises such qualities as nobility of spirit, virtue, courtesy, and honesty. Some of the aristocratic pilgrims claim gentilesse as an exclusively aristocratic virtue, but other taletellers, such as the Wife of Bath and the Franklin, explore how gentility does not derive from an aristocratic lineage. Chaucer's short poem of this name summarizes many of his beliefs about gentilesse.

hagiography: a saint's life. These exemplary narratives recount such phases in a saint's biography as his/her conversion, good deeds, missionary work, and martyrdom. They often share motifs of other medieval genres, including romance, history, and folklore, as in Chaucer's Man of Law's Tale. Interest in saints was high throughout the Middle Ages, especially given the belief in their ability to act as heavenly intercessors.

invocation: a literary device, traditionally used in epic, in which the poet requests divine assistance with his artistic labors.

irony: a rhetorical disjunction in which the speaker's words do not match his/her meaning. Chaucer's positioning himself as the naive narrator of the *Canterbury Tales*—apologizing for the tales he must tell, even though as author he completely controls these tales—provides an ironic superstructure to the narrative. Discerning irony often requires sophisticated interpretive skills, as readers must gauge the likely meaning of a speaker's words in light of their tone and context.

love, marriage, "maistrye": As in modern English, concepts with both complementary and contradictory aspects. Ostensibly, love ennobles those who feel its passions, and marriage allows lovers to unite in an eternal bond. Chaucer frequently addresses the tension between the virtuous ambitions of such love and its practice in marriage. The Wife of Bath advocates a woman's *maistrye* in marriage (3.1037–40), but the Franklin proposes in his tale that husband and wife should share mastery over each other: "Love wol nat been constreyned by maistrye" (5.764). In the *Canterbury Tales*, the stories and prologues of the Wife of Bath, Clerk, Merchant, and Franklin are often referred to as the Marriage Group for their shared focus on the requirements of a successful marriage. It should be noted that marital love and courtly love, while sharing many elements, do not necessarily overlap, given courtly love's expectations of chastity.

lyric: a poem that expresses the thoughts and feelings of its speaker, who might be the poet, a character in a larger work, or a fictional persona. Often lyrics are set to music. Numerous characters in the *Canterbury Tales* sing, such as Nicholas and Absolon in the Miller's Tale and the Squire in the General Prologue, of whom it is noted: "He koude songes make and wel endite [compose]" (1.95). In larger narratives, such as the *Book of the Duchess* and *Troilus and Criseyde*, lyrics often interrupt the action so that a character can muse upon his/her situation, in a manner somewhat analogous to characters breaking into song in musical theater.

miracle: a genre recounting a miraculous event designed to demonstrate the truth and power of the Christian faith. Miracle tales often feature the intercession of the Virgin Mary. Chaucer's Prioress's Tale is an example of such a miracle, and his poem "An ABC" develops the theme of Mary as a heavenly mediatrix.

oath: a sworn promise, a matter of honor under the code of chivalry. Chaucer's characters often swear oaths to one another, and it is instructive to view how their oaths reflect their characters. Palamon and Arcite, for example, have sworn an oath of brotherhood, but they jettison this oath after falling in love with Emily. Additional brotherhood oaths can be found in the Summoner's Tale, Pardoner's Tale, Shipman's Tale, and *House of Fame*. Lovers also pledge oaths to each other, and the marriage contract represents another form of oath-taking. As Cleopatra declares in the *Legend of Good Women*, however, sometimes such oaths are not kept: "Ye men that falsly sweren many an oth / That ye wol deye if that youre love be wroth" (666–67). The word *oath* can also refer to swearing and cursing, as apparent in the Pardoner's Tale: "Hir [Their] othes been so grete and so dampnable / That it is grisly for to heere hem swere" (6.472–73).

parody: a piece of literature or art that mocks another while imitating its form and/or style. Chaucer's most sustained parody is his Tale of Sir Thopas, in which he mercilessly skewers the romance tradition by making his titular "hero" foppish and ineffectual. A fine sustained parody of medieval literature is the film *Monty Python and the Holy Grail* (1975).

proem: an introduction to a longer piece of literature; a preface.

romance: a genre that typically features a knight journeying on a quest and encountering numerous adventures, such as fighting in tournaments, slaying dragons and monsters, and rescuing the imperiled. Such valiant activities demonstrate not only the knight's honor, virtue, and chivalry but his dedication to his fair beloved. Supernatural events occur frequently in romances, and these tales are often set in faraway lands or in times long ago. Chaucer uses elements of the romance tradition in much of his literature, especially in the Knight's Tale, the Wife of Bath's Tale, and *Troilus and Criseyde*, but he also satirizes such tales of rarefied love. In the Nun's Priest's Tale, the narrator declares of his parodic story of amorous chickens, "This storie is also trewe, I undertake, / As is the book of Launcelot de Lake" (7.3211–12), and his words point to Chaucer's gentle irony in regard to the romance genre.

saint's life: *see* **hagiography**

Seven Deadly Sins: Pride, Envy, Anger, Sloth, Avarice, Gluttony, and Lust. Pride is considered the most dangerous of the Seven Deadly Sins. The Parson addresses these transgressions in detail in his tale.

tragedy: in its medieval usage, any narrative with an unhappy ending. Chaucer's Monk's Tale compiles numerous tragedies, and these stories feature protagonists who enjoyed prosperity but now suffer through death or other great misfortune. The genre becomes more complex in its consideration of philosophical themes concerning human free will and predestination, as in Boethius's *Consolation of Philosophy* and Chaucer's translation of it.

Pronouncing Chaucer's Middle English

Learning to pronounce Middle English may appear daunting at first, but a few simple rules pave the way. John Gardner, author of the novel *Grendel* and a biographer of Chaucer, cheekily advises: "Chaucer's Middle English is relatively easy to fake."[1] Apply these rules, and Chaucer's literature will spring to life in all of its daring acoustics. Listen to recordings to develop an ear for Middle English; affordable audio materials are available from the websites Chaucer Studio and Chaucer Metapage Audio Files. Once the simplified rules here are mastered, consult Helge Kökeritz, *A Guide to Chaucer's Pronunciation*, for more detailed instruction.

I. Consonants

Pronounce Middle English consonants in the same manner as modern English consonants. Also, pronounce all consonants in a word, and pronounce every syllable. Even such consonant clusters as *gn* (*gnawen*, to gnaw), *kn* (*knight*), and *wr* (*wrastlen*, to wrestle) should be pronounced as two letters. Pay special attention to these consonants:

ch sounds like the *ch* in modern English "chicken" and "church," not like the French *ch* of *champagne* and *chic*.

f sounds like the *f* in modern English "if" and "off," not like the *f* in "of." Because some common words that end in *f* (such as "elf" and "wolf") are pluralized with a *v* ("elves" and "wolves"), it is easy to slip into the *v* sound with a Middle English *f*.

gh has no modern English equivalent. Approximate it with the *ch* of the Scottish *loch* or of the German *ich*.

r is trilled like the Spanish *r*.

s is hissed like the *s* of modern English "sissy" and "plus." It should not have the *z* sound of modern English "his" and "wars" and "result."

II. Vowels and Diphthongs

A. MODERN SHORT AND LONG VOWELS

Most students have not reviewed the differences between short and long vowels since elementary school, so a brief refresher may be in order. A simple mnemonic is that the long vowels are pronounced like the vowel's name.

Vowel	Short Vowel Sound	Long Vowel Sound
a	rat	rate
e	met	mete *or* meet
i	bit	bite
o	rot	rote
u	jut	jute

B. MIDDLE ENGLISH SHORT VOWELS

Middle English short vowels are mostly pronounced like modern English short vowels.

Short *a* (Middle English *man, hath, al*) sounds like the *o* in modern English "hot."

Short *e* (Middle English *fressh, hem*) sounds like the modern short *e*.

Unstressed final *e* (Middle English *roote, sweete, tendre*) is pronounced as a schwa, like the final *a* in modern English "gala" or "sofa." Some linguists advocate not pronouncing final *e* at all.

Short *i* or *y* (Middle English *gentil, hym*) sounds like the modern short *i*.

Short *o* (Middle English *fox, hors*) sounds like modern short *o*.

Short *u* (Middle English *sunne, ful*) sounds like the *u* in modern English "bush" or "put," not like the short *u* of "fun."

C. MIDDLE ENGLISH LONG VOWELS

Most commonly, a vowel is long when doubled or when followed by a consonant and a final *e*.

Long *a* (Middle English *name, maken*) sounds like the *a* in modern English "father."

Long *e* (Middle English *he, sweete*) sounds like the *a* in modern English "fame."

Long *i* or *y* (Middle English *ride, fyve*) sounds like the *ee* in modern English "feet."

Long *o* (Middle English *ooth, soote*) sounds like the *o* in modern English "ghost."

Long *u* (Middle English *vertu, rude*) sounds like the *u* in modern English "rude."

D. DIPHTHONGS

Diphthongs are not pure vowels but rather monosyllabic combinations of vowel sounds created by the voice sounding one vowel and then gliding into another. The following Middle English diphthongs are each spelled in two ways, but they share a common pronunciation.

au/aw is the vowel sound of modern English "out."

ai/ei is the vowel sound of modern English "weigh."

eu/ew is the vowel sound of modern English "slew."

oi/oy is the vowel sound of modern English "boy."

ou/ow is the vowel sound of modern English "too." (Just remember that "How now, brown cow?" would be pronounced in Middle English as "Hoo noo, broon coo?") When *o* and *ou* precede *gh*, they are pronounced similarly to modern English.

III. A Primer: Pronouncing Common Words Correctly

In learning to pronounce Middle English, concentrate first on short words that appear repeatedly. Practicing these very common words helps immeasurably in speaking Middle English correctly. Be patient with yourself, too: after a lifetime of pronouncing *of* as if it rhymes with "love," it is difficult to immediately begin pronouncing it as "off."

Middle English Word	Pronunciation Based on Modern English
a	ah
and	*rhymes with* fond
as	*rhymes with* loss
be	bay
by	be
he	hay
how	who
I	ee
is	*rhymes with* hiss
lyk	leek

Middle English Word	Pronunciation Based on Modern English
myn	mean
now	nu
of	off
she	shay
that	*rhymes with* hot
we	way
yow	you

Word List of Chaucer's Middle English

The following words appear frequently in Chaucer's literature. Mastering them will make reading Middle English easier, and thus more enjoyable. For a more complete lexicon, see Norman Davis et al., *A Chaucer Glossary*; for extensive analysis of the etymologies and usages of Middle English words, see the *Middle English Dictionary*.

adoun: down
agayn, ageyn, ayein, ayen: against, toward, in return
anon, anoon: at once, immediately
arn: are
artow: are you
asken, axen: to ask
auctoritee: authority
aventure: chance, fortune
avys: advice
ay: always, all the time
ben, been: to be, are
benedicite: bless you (Latin)
bet: better
bidde (*past* **bad**): to command, tell, order, request
biheten, bihoten (*past* **bihighte**): to promise
bihove: to be necessary
blake: black
brennen (*past* **brende, brente**): to burn, inflame
can, connen, cunnen, kan (*past* **coude**): to know how to, be able to
cas, caas: happening, affair, chance; **per cas:** by chance
catel: goods, possessions, property
cheere: face, facial expression

clepen: to call, name

curteisye: generosity, nobility, courtly behavior (more than polite)

daunger: disdain, aloofness, reserve (toward a lover)

descryven: to describe

devysen: to describe, explain

disese: discomfort, displeasure, distress

douten: to fear, doubt, be unsure

ech, ich, ych: each (distinguish from **ich,** I)

echon, echoon: each one

eek, eke: also, moreover, furthermore (often used simply to complete the meter of a line of a poetry)

eft: afterwards, again, another time

ensample, ensaumple: example, instructive story, model

entente: intention, meaning, desire

er, or: before

everich: each, every

eye, ye (*plural* **eyen, yen**)**:** eye

faren (*past* **ferde**)**:** to go, depart, travel; to befall, happen

fay, fey: faith, honor

fayn, feyn: glad (ly), willing (ly), eager (ly)

feele, fele: many

fer: far; **ferrer:** farther; **ferreste:** farthest

fere: companion, friend

for: for; because of; in spite of

ful: very, quite

gentil: noble, aristocratic (also noble in spirit)

gentillesse: nobility (of birth or spirit)

ginnen (*past* **gan, gon**)**:** to begin

glosen: to comment, interpret

gon, goon (*past* **yede**)**:** to go

habit: dress, clothes

hap: chance, fortune

hastow: you have; have you

heigh, hey, hy, hye: high, noble (often in social rank)

hem: them

hende: courteous, noble, polite (often used ironically in Chaucer's fabliaux)

henten: to seize, grasp, attack

her(e), hir(e): her; their
hit: it
hool: whole, complete, healthy
hoten (*past* **highte**): to be called; to promise
ich: I (distinguish from **ich**, each; *see* **ech**)
if, yif: if
ilik(e), ylik(e), yliche: like, alike, equal (ly), similar (ly)
ilke, thilke: same, very
iwis, ywis: certainly, truly
kynde: nature, kind
leef, leve, lief: dear, pleasing
lesen: to lose
leten (*past* **leet**): to let, allow
letten (*past* **lette**): to hinder, prevent
lever(e): rather; **him was levere:** he would rather
lewed: ignorant, simple
list: it pleases
looth: displeasing, hateful
lust: pleasure
make: mate, spouse
maugre: despite, in spite of
mede, meede: reward; meadow
merye, murye, myrie: merry, cheerful, pleasant
meten (*past* **mette**): to meet; to dream
mo: more
moot, mot: must, may
mowen: may, might; to be able
nadde: had not
nam: am not
namo, namoore, namore: no more
neigh, ney, ny: near; **nerre:** nearer; **next(e):** nearest
nere: was not; near, nearer
niste: did not know
nolde: would not
nones, nonys: occasion, purpose
noot, not (past **niste**): does not know
nyce: ignorant, silly
nys: is not

of: of; off

on, oon: one

ones, onis: once

or: or; before

paraunter, paraventure: perhaps, possibly

pardee, pardieu: by God! (mild French oath), certainly, surely

pleynen: to complain, mourn, lament

preef: proof, test; **preven:** to prove, establish

prive(e), privy: private, secret

queynte: cunning, curious; female genitalia

quiten, quyten (*past* **quitte**): to requite, pay back

quod: said

rathe: early

recchen, rekken: to consider, reckon

reden (*past* **redde, radde**): to advise, counsel, explain

resoun: reason, argument

reven (*past* **rafte, refte**): to remove, steal, rob

routhe, reuthe, rewthe: pity, mercy

seistow: you say

sely: happy, innocent, simple, blessed

sentence: meaning, judgment

siker (ly): sure (ly), certain (ly)

sin, sith, sithen, syn: since

solas: comfort, delight

soote, sote, swote: sweet, fresh

sooth, soth: truth; true

soothly, sothly: truly

soveraynetee, soveryntee: sovereignty, authority

speden (*past* **spedde**): to prosper, succeed; to carry out

stenten, stinten: to stop, cease

stevene: voice

sweven: dream

swich: such

thilke: this, that, that very (often emphatic)

tho: those; then

trouthe: fidelity; a promise; truth

trowen: to believe, trust

unnethes: hardly, scarcely

war: aware, cautious, wary

waxen, wexen (*past* **wax, wex, wox**): to increase, grow

wenden (*past* **wente**): to go, leave, depart

wenen (*past* **wende**): to think, suppose, imagine

whilom: once, formerly

wight: person, creature

witen (*present* **wo** (**o**)**t**, *past* **wiste**): to know

wonen (*past* **woned**): to dwell, live; to be accustomed to

wood: mad; **woodnesse:** madness

ye: *see* **eye**

yede (*past tense of* **goon**): went, departed

yeven, yiven (*past* **yaf**): to give

Plot Outlines of *Troilus and Criseyde* and the *Canterbury Tales* by Line Number

Reading *Troilus and Criseyde* and the *Canterbury Tales* elicits endless pleasures, but for the first-time reader, they are challenging texts. The following breakdowns of their narrative action should help novice readers of Chaucer to navigate these complex stories without relying on online summaries.

Troilus and Criseyde

BOOK 1

1–56	Narrator speaks of love and its sorrows
57–91	Introduction of the traitorous Calkas, who foresees Troy's defeat and has gone over to the Greeks
92–133	Introduction of Criseyde, Calkas's widowed daughter
134–47	Narrator's digression on the Trojan War
148–82	Criseyde's appearance at Athena's festival
183–203	Prince Troilus's arrival; his disdain for love
204–66	Cupid's revenge on Troilus; narrator discusses love
267–322	Troilus falls in love at the temple
323–99	Troilus returns home and ponders the effects of love
400–420	Troilus's song (first "Canticus Troili")
421–34	Troilus's prayer to the God of Love
435–546	Troilus's lovesickness and lament
547–623	Pandarus enters; they discuss Troilus's lovesickness
624–721	Pandarus explains how he can help Troilus in love
722–833	Pandarus insists that Troilus address his lovesickness
834–54	Fortune discussed

855–75   Pandarus asks the name of his friend's beloved; Troilus finally confesses it is Pandarus's niece Criseyde

876–1092   Pandarus promises to help Troilus win Criseyde's heart

BOOK 2

1–49   Narrator invokes the muse Clio and disavows accountability for the story

50–154   Pandarus's own lovesickness; his visit to Criseyde

155–210   Pandarus describes the brothers Hector and Troilus to Criseyde

211–322   Pandarus builds tension, finally telling Criseyde of Troilus's love

323–85   With exaggerated rhetoric Pandarus encourages Criseyde to look favorably on Troilus; he tells her not to worry if their love is discovered

386–406   Criseyde asks for advice; Pandarus counsels her to enjoy life and to love while she is still young

407–48   Criseyde's tears; Pandarus warns that if she spurns Troilus, both men will die

449–504   Criseyde's reasoning and decision

505–95   Pandarus lies about how he learned of Troilus's love

596–665   Criseyde ponders; Troilus rides by; Criseyde reacts

666–700   Narrator's commentary

701–812   Criseyde thinks about Troilus and considers a relationship with him

813–75   Criseyde in the garden; Antigone's song

876–903   Criseyde's response to Antigone's song

904–31   Criseyde, in bed, dreams an eagle steals her heart

932–1001   Troilus and Pandarus discuss Criseyde's response

1002–64   Pandarus's plan and advice in love

1065–92   Troilus's letter to Criseyde

1093–1201   Pandarus delivers Troilus's letter

1202–46   Criseyde's letter to Troilus

1247–1302   Troilus rides by; Pandarus's and Criseyde's opinions on her loving Troilus

1303–51   Pandarus delivers Criseyde's letter; Troilus's love increases

1352–1400   Pandarus's plan for Troilus and Criseyde to meet

1401–63   Pandarus talks with Troilus's brother Deiphebus

1464–91 Pandarus falsely tells Criseyde that Poliphete plans to sue her in court, but that Deiphebus will help her

1492–1554 Pandarus instructs Troilus to feign illness at Deiphebus's house

1555–1757 The dinner at Deiphebus's house, with Criseyde in attendance

BOOK 3

1–49 Ode to Venus and invocation of Calliope

50–217 Troilus and Criseyde meet at Deiphebus's house, with Pandarus present

218–420 Troilus and Pandarus discuss honor and love

421–511 Description of Troilus and Criseyde's relationship

512–616 Pandarus's plan to unite Troilus and Criseyde at his house

617–93 Fortune intervenes; Criseyde is invited to stay the night

694–749 Pandarus encourages Troilus to continue with the plan

750–945 Pandarus and Criseyde debate whether she will see Troilus

946–80 Pandarus prepares the scene for the lovers

981–1057 Criseyde confronts Troilus about his supposed jealousy

1058–1127 Troilus's reaction to Criseyde's tears

1128–1309 Troilus and Criseyde are reconciled

1310–1414 The joy of Troilus and Criseyde's time together

1415–1547 Morning; the lovers discuss their love, then part

1548–82 Criseyde and Pandarus discuss the previous evening

1583–1666 Troilus discusses his love with Pandarus, who urges caution

1667–1743 Troilus and Criseyde's mutual delight grows

1744–71 Troilus's song (second "Canticus Troili")

1772–1820 Love for Criseyde makes Troilus a better man

BOOK 4

1–28 Narrator speaks of Fortune, Troilus, and Criseyde

29–63 The war goes badly for the Trojans

64–140 Calkas asks the Greeks to barter for Criseyde

141–75 Troilus reacts to news of the Criseyde-for-Antenor trade

176–217 Hector defends Criseyde; the Trojan parliament decides

218–343 Troilus's lovesickness returns

344–658 Troilus and Pandarus discuss Criseyde's imminent departure

659–805 Criseyde reacts to news of the trade

806–945   Criseyde and Pandarus confer
946–1085   Troilus muses on predestination, God's omniscience, and human free will
1086–1127 Pandarus and Troilus confer
1128–1246 Criseyde and Troilus meet to discuss their sad situation; she faints; he prepares to kill himself
1247–1526 Criseyde pledges to return to him from the Greeks; Troilus counters that they should run away
1527–1701 Criseyde rejects his proposal and promises again to return

BOOK 5

1–14   Narrator addresses the Fates and time
15–91   The exchange of Criseyde for Antenor
92–196   Diomede flirts with Criseyde as they ride to her father
197–280   Troilus laments Criseyde's departure
281–504   Troilus and Pandarus discuss Criseyde's departure; they decide to visit Sarpedoun's kingdom
505–637   They return; Troilus remains inconsolable
638–44   Troilus's song (third "Canticus Troili")
645–87   Troilus continues to lament Criseyde's absence
688–770   Criseyde ponders her fate and her love for Troilus
771–98   Diomede considers wooing Criseyde
799–840   Physical descriptions of Diomede, Criseyde, and Troilus
841–952   Diomede visits Criseyde
953–1085   Criseyde's response to Diomede, in which she denies her love for Troilus
1086–99   Narrator's commentary, attempting to excuse Criseyde
1100–1232 Troilus and Pandarus wait for Criseyde
1233–88   Troilus's dream of a boar embracing Criseyde; Pandarus dismisses allegorical interpretations of dreams
1289–1435 Troilus's beseeching letter and Criseyde's ambiguous response
1436–1540 Troilus asks his sister Cassandra to interpret his dream; she tells him Diomede has won Criseyde's love
1541–68   Death of Hector
1569–1631 Troilus's lovesickness and Criseyde's letter
1632–1743 Troilus reacts to Criseyde's letter and to the discovery that she has given his love token, a brooch, to Diomede

1744–1870 Narrator concludes with a brief mention of Troilus's death (1806) and his ascent to the eighth sphere

Canterbury Tales

GENERAL PROLOGUE

1–18	Celebration of springtime
19–42	Chaucer meets his fellow pilgrims at the Tabard Inn
43–78	Portrait of the Knight
79–100	Portrait of the Squire
101–17	Portrait of the Yeoman
118–64	Portrait of the Prioress (mentioning the Second Nun and three priests)
165–207	Portrait of the Monk
208–69	Portrait of the Friar
270–84	Portrait of the Merchant
285–308	Portrait of the Clerk
309–30	Portrait of the Sergeant of Law (also called the Man of Law)
331–60	Portrait of the Franklin
361–78	Portrait of the Five Guildsman (the Haberdasher, Carpenter, Weaver, Dyer, and Tapestry Weaver)
379–87	Portrait of the Cook
388–410	Portrait of the Shipman
411–44	Portrait of the Physician
445–76	Portrait of the Wife of Bath
477–528	Portrait of the Parson
529–41	Portrait of the Plowman
542–66	Portrait of the Miller
567–86	Portrait of the Manciple
587–622	Portrait of the Reeve
623–68	Portrait of the Summoner
669–714	Portrait of the Pardoner
715–46	Chaucer declares he must accurately report the pilgrims' words and behavior, or be false to his material
747–821	Harry Bailly, the Host of the Tabard Inn, proposes a taletelling game; the pilgrims consent
822–58	The pilgrims set out the next morning; they draw lots; the Knight will tell the first tale

KNIGHT'S TALE

Part 1

859–92   Theseus defeats the Amazons and marries Hippolyta
893–951   Theban widows beg Theseus to confront the tyrant Creon
952–1032   Theseus kills Creon; he takes Palamon and Arcite prisoner
1033–1186   Palamon and Arcite each fall in love with Hippolyta's sister
            Emily; they argue
1187–1274   Theseus frees and banishes Arcite; Arcite envies Palamon,
            who remains in prison where he can see Emily
1275–1354   Palamon envies Arcite, who could raise an army to win Em-
            ily's hand

Part 2

1355–1450   Arcite, his appearance altered by lovesickness, returns to Ath-
            ens and serves as Emily's page under the name Philostrate
1451–87   Palamon escapes from prison
1488–1662   Palamon and Arcite meet; they vow to fight to the death over
            Emily
1663–1880   Theseus, Hippolyta, and Emily encounter Palamon and Arcite;
            Theseus orders a tournament to decide who shall marry
            Emily

Part 3

1881–1966   Description of the Temple of Venus (to whom Palamon prays)
1967–2050   Description of the Temple of Mars (to whom Arcite prays)
2051–88   Description of the Temple of Diana (to whom Emily prays)
2089–2208   Preparations for the tournament; introduction of Palamon's
            ally Lygurge and Arcite's ally Emetreus
2209–70   Palamon's prayer to Venus (for Emily)
2271–2366   Emily's prayer to Diana (for chastity)
2367–2437   Arcite's prayer to Mars (for victory)
2438–82   Venus and Mars argue over which knight will win; Saturn
            promises that both men's prayers will be answered

Part 4

2483–2662   The tournament is fought, and Arcite wins
2663–2816   Arcite dies in a horse accident and bestows Emily on Palamon
2817–2966   Emily and Palamon mourn Arcite; his funeral is described

2967–3074 Theseus attempts to summarize the moral and philosophical lessons learned from Arcite's death
3075–3108 Palamon and Emily marry

MILLER'S PROLOGUE AND TALE

Prologue

3109–19 The pilgrims' reactions to the Knight's Tale
3120–43 The Miller's drunken clamor to be next
3144–66 The Reeve's interruption; the Miller's response
3167–86 Chaucer apologizes for the drunken Miller's churlish tale

Tale

3187–3220 Characterization of Nicholas, the clerk
3221–32 Characterization of John, Nicholas's landlord and Alison's husband
3233–70 Characterization of Alison with much animal imagery
3271–3306 Nicholas and Alison begin their affair
3307–96 Characterization of Absolon, Nicholas's rival for Alison's affections; Absolon's attempts to woo Alison
3397–3610 Nicholas sets out to convince John that a flood of biblical proportions is imminent, to divert him
3611–56 Nicholas and Alison deceive John and sneak away to copulate
3657–3743 Absolon comes to court Alison, and is tricked into kissing her anus
3744–3810 Absolon seeks revenge, and burns Nicholas's buttocks with a hot iron coulter
3811–54 John falls from the ceiling, breaking his arm

REEVE'S PROLOGUE AND TALE

Prologue

3855–66 The pilgrims' response to the Miller's Tale
3867–98 The Reeve's words on aging
3899–3920 The Host demands the Reeve tell his tale; the Reeve promises narrative revenge against the Miller

Tale

3921–68 Characterization of Symkyn, a miller, and his wife
3969–86 Description of their daughter Maline; her grandfather's aspirations for her marriage

3987–4045 Symkyn cheats a college of grain; the students Allen and John go to Symkyn's to monitor the present transaction

4046–4115 Symkyn frees Allen and John's horse; while they search for it, he steals more than before

4116–67 As it is now late, Allen and John must stay the night at Symkyn's house

4168–98 In revenge for Symkyn's thievery, Allen deflowers Maline

4199–4233 John, to match Allen's sexual exploit, tricks Symkyn's wife into joining him in bed

4234–48 Allen takes leave of Maline, who reveals the location of the students' stolen grain

4249–4324 Allen mistakenly tells Symkyn (thinking he is John) of his night with Maline; a melee ensues

COOK'S PROLOGUE AND TALE

Prologue

4325–43 Roger the Cook applauds the Reeve's Tale

4344–64 The Host and Roger spar about truth, game, and storytelling

Tale

4365–98 Introduction of Perkyn Revelour, an apprentice

4399–4422 Perkyn is fired; he goes to live with a friend, whose wife is a prostitute . . . [broken off]

MAN OF LAW'S INTRODUCTION, PROLOGUE, TALE, AND EPILOGUE

Introduction

1–32 The Host worries that time is passing too quickly

33–98 He asks for a tale from the Man of Law, who agrees and then recounts Chaucer's literary accomplishments

Prologue

99–133 Introduction of ostensible theme: poverty

Tale, Part 1

134–89 Syrian merchants encounter the Roman emperor's daughter Custance and tell their sultan about her

190–259 The sultan and his men plan to convert to Christianity so that he can marry Custance

260–322 Despite her misgivings, Custance travels to Syria

323–85   The sultan's mother falsely promises also to convert

Part 2

386–437   The mother and her allies slaughter the sultan and other Christians for forsaking their religion

438–511   Custance is put out to sea and floats to England

512–81   A constable and his wife Hermengild take Custance into their home

582–609   A knight lusts after Custance, who rejects him; he kills Hermengild and frames Custance for the murder

610–89   During Custance's trial, the knight is felled by divine retribution, proving Custance's innocence

690–93   King Alla marries Custance

694–700   His mother Donegild despises her

701–23   Custance bears Alla a son, Mauricius

724–56   A messenger to Alla bears news of Mauricius's birth, but Donegild alters the letters to say that Custance has borne a "fiendly creature"

757–819   Alla responds with equanimity, but Donegild again alters the letters so it appears that Alla orders Custance banished

820–75   Custance and Mauricius are put out to sea

Part 3

876–96   Alla kills Donegild for causing Custance's banishment

897–952   Custance lands on a new shore; a lord's steward plans to love/rape her, but divine intervention kills him

953–87   A Roman senator encounters Custance while sailing back from Syria and brings her to his home

988–1162 Alla comes to Rome to do penance for executing his mother; he reunites with Custance and Mauricius

Epilogue

1163–90   Harry Bailly asks the Parson for a tale; the Shipman objects and volunteers

WIFE OF BATH'S PROLOGUE AND TALE

Prologue

1–162   The Wife praises marriage and condemns virginity

163–92   The Pardoner interrupts; the Wife insists on continuing

193–451	The Wife tells of her first three husbands and how she controlled them
452–502	The Wife tells of her fourth husband, an adulterer
503–626	The Wife speaks of seducing and marrying young Jankyn
627–828	The Wife describes Jankyn's "book of wicked wives," which sparked a fight, and how she tamed him
829–56	The Friar and the Summoner squabble

Tale

857–88	The Wife's tale of Arthurian romance begins with a knight raping a maiden
889–912	The knight is condemned to die, but the women of Arthur's court plead for mercy; the queen sends him on a quest to discover what women most desire
913–50	The knight undertakes his quest
951–82	The Wife digresses to tell Ovid's story of Midas
983–1022	The knight encounters a mysterious old woman who offers the answer to his quest
1023–72	The quest successfully concluded, the old woman demands marriage to the knight as her reward
1073–1103	On the wedding night, the knight shrinks from bedding a wife so ugly, old, and lowborn
1104–1216	The old woman rebuts the knight's reasons for rejecting her, primarily by discussing the trait of *gentillesse*
1217–56	The old woman offers her husband the choice of having her young but faithless or old but true; he asks her to choose, and is given the best of both
1257–64	The Wife of Bath ends her tale by cursing disobedient husbands

THE FRIAR'S PROLOGUE AND TALE

Prologue

1265–77	The Friar compliments the Wife of Bath on her tale
1278–1300	The Friar insults the Summoner, who vows payback; the Host tells the Friar to begin his tale

Tale

1301–31	The Friar tells of a summoner working for an archdeacon who prosecutes sexual sinners

1332–37	The Summoner interrupts; the Host quiets him
1338–74	The Friar continues describing his summoner, who colludes with prostitutes to blackmail their clients
1375–1446	The summoner, out to extort money from an old woman, meets a yeoman; they swear an oath of brotherhood
1447–1522	The yeoman confesses that he is a fiend from hell; they discuss the forms that fiends assume on earth
1523–36	The summoner reaffirms his commitment to his new brother; they agree to share their winnings
1537–70	They come upon a cart mired in mud and the carter cursing his horses to hell; the fiend says he cannot have them, though, because the words are not meant literally
1571–1664	The summoner attempts to extort money from the old woman, who damns him to hell; the fiend promises to take him to hell that very evening

SUMMONER'S PROLOGUE AND TALE

Prologue

| 1665–74 | The Summoner shakes with anger over the Friar's tale |
| 1675–1708 | He tells a dream vision of a friar's visit to hell, where damned friars swarm from Satan's butt |

Tale

1709–60	The Summoner describes a friar who relieves the pious of their money, promising to pray for them but then failing to follow through
1761–64	The Friar interrupts, but the Summoner continues
1765–96	The greedy friar visits Thomas, a sick man, and says he has been praying for him
1797–1822	The friar greets Thomas's wife with elaborate courtesy
1823–35	Thomas's wife and the friar discuss Thomas's anger
1836–78	Thomas's wife and the friar discuss dinner, her newly dead son, and his prayers for the boy
1879–1947	The friar explains why his prayers are so effective
1948–80	Given his long illness, Thomas is skeptical, but the friar insists Thomas should continue his financial support
1981–2093	The friar preaches to Thomas about the sin of anger
2094–2155	The friar asks for money, and Thomas inflicts his flatulent revenge

| 2156–2242 | The friar goes to the lord of the village to ask how to divide a fart among his fellow friars |
| 2243–94 | The lord's squire Jankyn solves the riddle and wins his reward |

CLERK'S PROLOGUE AND TALE

Prologue

| 1–20 | The Host, demanding a tale from the Clerk, insults his masculinity and manner of speech |
| 21–56 | The Clerk agrees to tell a tale inspired by Petrarch |

Tale, Part 1

57–84	Description of Walter, a young marquis
85–140	The wisest man in Walter's land, on behalf of the people, asks him to marry
141–96	Walter agrees, provided he may choose his spouse

Part 2

197–231	Description of Griselda, a poor but honorable girl
232–87	The wedding day arrives, but no bride has been named
288–336	Walter asks Griselda's father for her hand
337–64	Walter demands obedience in marriage; Griselda consents
365–448	Walter and Griselda marry; the people love and respect her; she bears Walter a daughter

Part 3

449–511	Walter tells Griselda his people disapprove of her and the child; Griselda promises to obey his will
512–74	Walter's sergeant takes Griselda's daughter, ostensibly to kill her
575–609	Walter secretly arranges for her fostering

Part 4

610–86	Walter again tests Griselda by having the sergeant take their son in the same manner
687–721	Walter is astonished by Griselda's patient suffering
722–35	Walter's people believe he is a murderer
736–84	Walter instigates another test, this time pretending to divorce Griselda so he can marry a young girl (actually their daughter)

Part 5

785–938   Walter sends Griselda back to her father's home, with only the smock on her back

Part 6

939–1050   Walter asks Griselda to oversee preparations for his new bride, a task she agrees to undertake

1051–1176   Walter reveals to Griselda that he has merely been testing her, and the family is reunited

Lenvoy de Chaucer

1177–1212   The narrator ironically urges wives to defend themselves against their husbands

1212a–g   The Host wishes his wife had heard this tale

MERCHANT'S PROLOGUE, TALE, AND EPILOGUE

Prologue

1213–44   The Merchant complains about his shrewish wife

Tale

1245–66   January, an old man, decides to marry

1267–1392   The extended, ironic "marriage encomium"

1393–1468   January asks his friends for their advice

1469–1518   January's friend Placebo praises marriage

1519–65   His friend Justinus disparages it

1566–76   January approves Placebo's view and rejects Justinus's

1577–1610   January fantasizes about wedded bliss

1611–88   January calls his friends to tell of his deliberations; Justinus again warns him against marriage

1689–1767   January marries his young bride May

1768–94   January's squire Damian sees and falls in love with May

1795–1865   Unvarnished description of the wedding night

1866–1943   Believing that Damian is sick, January sends May to comfort him, and Damian gives her a love note

1944–2020   May falls in love with Damian

2021–56   January's garden, where he exercises his connubial rights with May

2057–96   January goes blind and becomes extremely possessive of May

2097–2131   May and Damian devise a plan to deceive January

2132–2218   January takes May to the garden, but she plans to trick him and to take her pleasures with Damian

2219–2319   The gods Pluto and Proserpina argue over May's imminent deception of January, but resolve their differences amicably

2320–2418   While May and Damian are fornicating, January's sight is restored, but she tricks him into disbelieving the evidence of his own eyes

Epilogue to the Merchant's Tale

2419–40   Harry Bailly discusses his troublesome wife

SQUIRE'S INTRODUCTION AND TALE

Introduction

1–8   Harry Bailly asks for a tale from the Squire, who agrees

Tale, Part 1

9–41   Introduction of Cambyuskan (Genghis Khan), his wife Elpheta, sons Algarsif and Cambalo, and daughter Canacee

42–109   At Cambyuskan's court, a mysterious knight enters

110–31   The knight's lord sends as a gift a magic brass horse that can travel anywhere almost instantaneously

132–55   Canacee is given a magic mirror and ring

156–73   The mysterious knight also presents a magic sword with power to harm and to heal

174–262   Cambyuskan's people marvel at the magical gifts

263–304   Description of Cambyuskan's lavish feast

305–46   The knight teaches Cambyuskan how to use the magic horse

Part 2

347–75   The revelers sleep, and Canacee has a vision

376–471   Canacee, out walking, meets a distraught falcon; with her magic ring, she asks about the falcon's distress

472–651   The falcon shares the sad story of her faithless lover

652–70   The Squire attempts to move his story from Canacee to Cambyuskan, Algarsif, and Cambalo

Part 3

671–94   The Franklin politely interrupts the Squire and, praising his gentility, ends the young man's story

695–708   Harry Bailly interrupts the Franklin, who agrees to tell his tale

FRANKLIN'S PROLOGUE AND TALE

Prologue

709–28   The Franklin prepares to tell his tale, a Breton lai, but apologizes for his poor rhetorical skills

Tale

729–60   The knight Arveragus loves Dorigen, and she consents to marry him

761–802   The narrator discusses the role of *maistrye* in marriage

803–46   After their marriage, Arveragus departs to fight in England, and Dorigen mourns his absence

847–94   Dorigen worries about rocks lining the shore, which Arveragus must successfully navigate to return

895–978   At a party, the squire Aurelius confesses his love for Dorigen

979–1005   To underscore her rejection, Dorigen tells Aurelius that only if he removes all the rocks along the shore will she grant him her love

1006–86   Lovesick, Aurelius prays to Apollo for mercy

1087–1100   Arveragus returns to Dorigen

1101–1225   Aurelius's brother takes him to a magician, who can make the rocks disappear for a thousand pounds

1226–1338   Aurelius agrees to the deal and, after the rocks apparently disappear, reminds Dorigen of her pledge

1339–1456   Faced with keeping her promise to Aurelius, Dorigen contemplates suicide

1457–98   Arveragus tells Dorigen that she should honor her pledge, despite the pain it causes him

1499–1544   Dorigen goes to Aurelius to fulfill her vow, but he releases her from her promise

1545–1624   Arveragus and Dorigen live happily together; the magician forgives Aurelius his debt

PHYSICIAN'S TALE

1–71   Description of Virginius's virtuous daughter Virginia

72–104   A digression on childraising

105–63	The corrupt judge Apius sees Virginia, desires to deflower her, and plots accordingly with the churl Claudius
164–90	Claudius claims to Apius's court that Virginia is his slave
191–257	Realizing the court case is a ruse to corrupt his daughter, Virginius beheads her to preserve her virginity
258–86	Apius kills himself; Claudius is exiled

PARDONER'S INTRODUCTION, PROLOGUE, AND TALE

Introduction

| 287–319 | The Physician's Tale moves Harry to an effusion of emotion; he asks the Pardoner for a merry tale |
| 320–28 | The Pardoner agrees, but the others demand a moral tale |

Prologue

329–40	The Pardoner discusses his preferred theme for preaching: *Radix malorum est Cupiditas* [the root of evils is greed]
341–76	He describes the "holy" relics he sells, including a sheep's shoulder bone and a mitten
377–88	He explains the rhetorical trap he uses in church to ensure that parishioners give generously
389–462	He openly describes his vicious nature to the pilgrims

Tale

463–84	The Pardoner introduces a company of revelers, who gamble, swear, eat, and drink excessively
485–588	The Pardoner cites numerous examples of those who through drunkenness and gluttony have fallen
589–628	The Pardoner moves on to the sin of gambling
629–60	The Pardoner now preaches against swearing
661–84	The exemplum begins: a young boy informs the three revelers that Death has taken a friend of theirs
685–710	The three revelers decide to kill Death
711–67	An old man tells them where they can find Death
768–75	The three revelers find gold where the old man told them they would find Death
776–894	They devise competing plans to murder one another for a larger share of the gold; all three die
895–945	The Pardoner closes by condemning various sins and offering

to sell his fake relics and absolution to the pilgrims, beginning with Harry Bailly

946–68   Harry Bailly grossly insults the Pardoner; the Knight intercedes to reconcile them

SHIPMAN'S TALE

1–19   Description of a wealthy merchant and his beautiful wife

20–52   Description of the merchant's friend, a monk named John

53–88   The merchant invites John to visit

89–213   The wife tells John of her unhappiness in marriage and her need for a hundred franks to pay her clothing debt

214–54   The merchant and his wife discuss household governance

255–98   John borrows a hundred franks from the merchant

299–306   The merchant departs on a business trip

307–24   The merchant's wife sleeps with John in exchange for one hundred franks

325–64   The merchant returns and asks John to repay the loan; John tells him he gave the money to his wife

365–434   The merchant asks his wife for the money, but she convinces him she thought the monk gave it to her for her use in thanks for their hospitality

435–52   Harry Bailly enjoys the Shipman's tale, and asks the Prioress to tell the next tale

PRIORESS'S PROLOGUE AND TALE

Prologue

453–87   The Prioress prays to Jesus and asks Mary to guide her tale

Tale

488–557   Introduction of a young boy dedicated to Christianity who frequently sings a hymn praising Mary

558–85   The Jews of this city kill the boy

586–613   The boy's mother looks for her lost child; he miraculously sings his Marian hymn in death

614–34   The Christians of the city marvel at this miracle and then slaughter the Jews

635–91   The child explains the miracle and then dies again

PROLOGUE AND TALE OF SIR THOPAS

Prologue

692–711 Abruptly noticing Chaucer, Harry Bailly asks him to tell the next tale

Tale, First Fit

712–35 Description of Sir Thopas, his beauty and fancy clothing
736–83 Thopas enjoys hunting and courtship, and so goes to the forest
784–96 Thopas prays to Mary for the love of an elf-queen
797–832 On his quest for the elf-queen, Thopas encounters the giant Oliphaunt and quickly retreats

Second Fit

833–90 Thopas asks his minstrels to tell tales as he arms himself to battle Oliphaunt

Third Fit

891–918 Thopas sets out to seek Oliphaunt
919–35 Harry Bailly interrupts, telling Chaucer to end the worthless tale
936–66 Chaucer agrees to tell a different tale, "a litel thyng in prose"

TALE OF MELIBEE

967–75 The enemies of Melibeus/Melibee attack his wife Prudence and daughter Sophie; he is distraught
976–85 Prudence, remembering the teachings of Ovid, attempts to console Melibeus
986–1001 Melibeus and Prudence discuss the necessity of grieving
1002–10 Prudence advises Melibeus to seek the counsel of friends, kin, elders and neighbors
1011–15 A surgeon promises to heal Sophie of her wounds
1016–19 Many advise Melibeus to seek vengeance
1020–34 A wise man advises caution before aggression
1035–49 The majority are for war; Melibeus accedes
1050–63 Prudence offers advice, but Melibeus does not want to take counsel from his wife
1064–1114 Prudence argues that wives give their husbands good advice; Melibeus agrees to listen

1115–71	Prudence explains how he should choose his counselors
1172–99	She explains what sort of advisors he should avoid
1200–1222	She explains how to scrutinize the advice given to him
1223–31	She explains when he can alter course from the advice given to him
1232–60	Melibeus asks Prudence's opinion of his present counselors; she suggests that they were not wisely chosen
1261–1330	Melibeus agrees; Prudence endorses the physicians' advice but explains how Melibeus has misunderstood it
1331–40	Prudence interprets the wise advice that Melibeus should defend his household to mean that he should be loved by his neighbors
1341–48	Prudence agrees with the counselors' advice that Melibeus should act with diligence and deliberation
1349–1404	Prudence argues that former enemies and the young make poor advisors, and that Melibeus should not seek vengeance
1405–26	Prudence cannot explain why God allowed men to harm Melibeus and his family
1427–43	Melibeus suggests that good can come from vengeance, for it enforces justice; Prudence says judges must enforce justice
1444–60	Melibeus hopes that Fortune will help him obtain vengeance; Prudence admonishes that Fortune is fickle
1461–1517	Melibeus worries that, unless he takes vengeance, nothing will deter future harmdoing; Prudence advises him to embody patience
1518–39	Melibeus agrees that patience is a virtue, but doubts he can endure suffering with perfect patience; Prudence again counsels against vengeance
1540–1671	Melibeus believes his wealth will help him gain vengeance; Prudence warns against the power of wealth
1672–80	Now that Prudence has advised Melibeus what not to do, he wonders what she believes he should do; she advises him to make peace with his foes
1681–1710	Melibeus accuses Prudence of not caring about his honor; she responds to the contrary
1711–68	Melibeus says he will do as Prudence counsels, and she again advises reconciliation; she then goes to Melibeus's enemies and preaches the virtues of peace

1769–1831   Prudence brings Melibeus's enemies for a parley
1832–88   Melibeus wants to exile the men, but Prudence succeeds in reconciling her husband and his enemies

MONK'S PROLOGUE AND TALE

Prologue

1889–1923   Harry Bailly comments again on his shrewish wife
1924–90   Harry Bailly asks the Monk to tell the next tale; the Monk agrees to speak of tragedies

Tale

1991–98   The Monk declares his theme of tragedy and falling from Fortune's favor
1999–2006   The tragedy of Lucifer, who falls to hell
2007–14   The tragedy of Adam, expelled from paradise
2015–94   The tragedy of Samson, betrayed by Delilah
2095–2142   The tragedy of Hercules, accidentally killed by his lover Dianira
2143–82   The tragedy of Nebuchadnezzar, who goes mad but then recovers
2183–2246   The tragedy of Nebuchadnezzar's son Belshazzar, divinely punished for defiling sacred vessels
2247–2374   The tragedy of the warrior queen Zenobia of Palmyra and her two sons, captured by Aurelianus
2375–90   The tragedy of Pedro of Castile, killed by his brother
2391–98   The tragedy of Pierre de Lusignan, killed by his lieutenants
2399–2406   The tragedy of Bernabò Visconti, imprisoned and killed by his nephew
2407–62   The tragedy of Ugolino of Pisa, starved to death in prison with his children
2463–2550   The tragedy of Nero, who commits suicide when his people rebel
2551–74   The tragedy of Holofernes, slain by Judith
2575–2630   The tragedy of Antiochus, king of Syria, who is incapacitated and then dies while reeking horribly
2631–70   The tragedy of Alexander the Great, conqueror of the world, poisoned by his own people

2671–2726 The tragedy of Julius Caesar, assassinated by "Brutus Cassius" (Chaucer's mistaken combination of the two men)

2727–66 The tragedy of Croesus, hanged after escaping execution by fire

NUN'S PRIEST'S PROLOGUE, TALE, AND EPILOGUE

Prologue

2767–2805 The Knight stops the Monk's Tale; Harry Bailly asks the Monk to tell a tale about hunting

2806–20 The Monk refuses; the Nun's Priest agrees to go next

Tale

2821–46 The setting of the story, a poor widow's farm

2847–81 Courtly descriptions of the rooster Chauntecleer and his wife Pertelote

2882–3156 Chauntecleer shares his nightmare with Pertelote; the two disagree on whether dreams are prophetic

3157–3214 The debate ends; Chauntecleer and Pertelote enjoy conjugal passion, but Chauntecleer still believes disaster impends

3215–3401 A fox captures Chauntecleer and runs away with him

3402–46 Chauntecleer deceives the fox and escapes; the Nun's Priest draws a moral

3447–62 Harry Bailly extols the Nun's Priest's masculinity

SECOND NUN'S PROLOGUE AND TALE

Prologue

1–28 The Second Nun condemns idleness and praises St. Cecilia, the subject of her tale

29–84 Invocation of Mary

85–119 The etymology of Cecilia's name

Tale

120–61 The virgin bride Cecilia warns Valerian that God's angel will kill him if he consummates their marriage

162–217 Valerian seeks confirmation, miraculously sees an angel, and converts to Christianity

218–34 The angel appears in Cecilia and Valerian's bedroom and urges them to maintain their chastity

235–357	Valerian's brother Tiburce is converted to Christianity
358–99	The judge Almachius, who persecutes Christians, executes Valerian and Tiburce
400–409	The officer Maximus, a new convert, preaches of witnessing Valerian's and Tiburce's souls ascend to heaven; Almachius flogs him to death
410–511	Cecilia argues with Almachius about the respective power of earthly and heavenly rulers
512–53	Almachius orders Cecilia's gruesome execution, but she miraculously survives for three days with her neck cut; at her wish, her house becomes a church

CANON'S YEOMAN'S PROLOGUE AND TALE

Prologue

554–92	A Canon and his Yeoman ride up and join the pilgrims
593–626	Harry Bailly asks the Yeoman whether the Canon has a merry disposition; the Yeoman says he has, and he can also turn the road to Canterbury into silver and gold
627–83	Harry Bailly inquires why the Canon is then so poorly dressed; the Yeoman confesses the Canon is a fraud
684–719	The Canon warns his Yeoman to be silent, but then rides off when the Yeoman refuses

Tale, Part 1

720–49	The Yeoman laments his participation in alchemy
750–829	He discusses the tricks and tools and names the four "spirits" (liquids) and seven "bodies" (metals) of alchemy
830–97	The Yeoman laments the "cursed craft" of alchemy and the pursuit of the philosopher's stone
898–971	He describes the reactions of alchemists when their pots explode, destroying their investments

Part 2

972–1011	The Yeoman describes a false canon and apologizes to true ones
1012–51	The false canon ingratiates himself with a priest and wins his confidence
1052–87	The alchemical con begins; the Yeoman pities the priest

1088–1101   The Yeoman denies his tale's canon is the one he was riding with; he laments his complexion's ruin by alchemy

1102–1282   The false canon convinces the priest he can transform quicksilver (mercury) into silver

1283–1340   He convinces the priest he can turn copper into silver

1341–87   The priest pays forty pounds for the secret recipes

1388–1481   The Yeoman moralizes on humanity's greed and the folly of alchemical pursuits

MANCIPLE'S PROLOGUE AND TALE

Prologue

1–24   Harry Bailly notices that the Cook is sleeping and might fall off his horse

25–45   The Manciple points out that the Cook is drunk

46–55   This angers the Cook, who does fall off his horse

56–68   With the Cook incapacitated, Harry Bailly asks the Manciple to tell a tale

69–104   The Manciple pacifies the Cook with more wine

Tale

105–29   Description of the god Phoebus Apollo

130–38   Description of his white crow, which can sing beautifully and also speak

139–95   Description of his wife, who he fears will cuckold him

196–241   Apollo's crow witnesses the wife's adultery

242–65   The crow informs Apollo, who slays her in anger

266–308   Apollo repents his rashness and punishes the crow

309–62   The Manciple's moral: people should hold their tongues

PARSON'S PROLOGUE AND TALE

Prologue

1–29   As evening approaches, Harry Bailly asks the Parson to tell the final tale

30–74   The Parson proposes a tale of "morality and virtuous matter"

Tale, Part 1

75–94   The Parson introduces his theme of penitence

95–101   The three effects of penitence

102–6   The three kinds of penitence

107–27   The three necessary parts of penitence: contrition, confession, and satisfaction

128–32   The four foundations of understanding contrition

133–291   The six causes that should move a person to contrition

292–315   The manner of people's contrition and how it benefits them

Part 2

316–21   The Parson moves to the theme of confession

322–36   The Parson discusses original sin

337–49   The Parson discusses concupiscence

350–57   The Parson discusses the temptations of sin

358–86   The Parson distinguishes between venial and mortal sin

The Seven Deadly Sins

387–89   The Parson introduces the Seven Deadly Sins, of which Pride is the common root

390–483   Pride and its remedy Humility

484–532   Envy and its remedy Love of God and Neighbor

533–676   Anger and its remedy Meekness

677–738   Sloth and its remedy Strength

739–817   Avarice and its remedy Pity

818–35   Gluttony and its remedy Abstinence

836–955   Lust and its remedy Chastity

956–57   The Ten Commandments (passing mention)

958–81   The seven conditions that worsen sin

982–1028   The four conditions of true confession

Part 3

1029–80   The Parson addresses the satisfaction, or completion, of penance

CHAUCER'S RETRACTION

1081–92   Chaucer apologizes for the profane *Canterbury Tales* and ends with a prayer

Notes

Preface: Chaucer and Genre Theory

1. Alistair Fowler, *Kinds of Literature* (Cambridge, Mass.: Harvard University Press, 1982), 31–32.

Chapter 1. Chaucer's Life and Times

1. For the derivation of the name Chaucer, see Henry Harrison, *Surnames of the United Kingdom* (1912; Baltimore: Genealogical Publishing, 1969), and P. H. Reaney, *A Dictionary of English Surnames*, 3rd ed. (Oxford: Oxford University Press, 1995).

2. Martin M. Crow and Clair C. Olson, eds., *Chaucer Life-Records* (Austin: University of Texas Press, 1966), 1. Like many of Chaucer's biographers, I rely on this reference for reconstructing events from his life. Subsequent citations of this text are noted parenthetically with the abbreviation *CLR*; translations of these materials are my own.

3. For conversions of medieval money to its contemporary purchasing power, see the "Currency Converter" at the United Kingdom's National Archives website (nationalarchives.gov.uk/currency/).

4. Thomas Speght, ed., *The Workes of Our Antient and Learned English Poet, Geffrey Chaucer, Newly Printed* (London: Adam Islip, at the charges of Bonham Norton, 1598); unnumbered page in the section titled "His Life," in the subsection titled "His Education."

5. Christopher Cannon located additional documents related to the *raptus* charge beyond those recorded in *Chaucer Life-Records*; see his "*Raptus* in the Chaumpiegne Release and a Newly Discovered Document Concerning the Life of Geoffrey Chaucer," *Speculum* 68 (1993): 79–94.

6. Colin Platt, *King Death: The Black Death and Its Aftermath in Late-Medieval England* (Toronto: University of Toronto Press, 1996), 9.

7. John Mirk, *John Mirk's Festial*, edited by Susan Powell (Oxford: Oxford

University Press for the Early English Text Society, 2009), 63; I have modernized archaic letters.

8. For a sampling of Wycliffite thought, see Anne Hudson, ed., *Selections from English Wycliffite Writings* (Cambridge: Cambridge University Press, 1978).

Chapter 2. Chaucer's Literature

1. Two related yet distinct prologues begin Chaucer's *Legend of Good Women*, the F and the G versions, and most scholars agree that the more common F Prologue precedes the revised G version.

2. Andreas Capellanus, *The Art of Courtly Love*, trans. John Jay Parry (New York: Columbia University Press, 1941), 185.

3. A critical consensus does not entail critical unanimity, and it should be noted that some readers disagree with the interpretation of the Knight, Parson, and Plowman as ideal pilgrims, pointing to passages in the Knight's portrait that paint him as a mercenary and in the Parson's tale that suggest potentially heretical views. See, respectively, the studies by Terry Jones, *Chaucer's Knight: The Portrait of a Medieval Mercenary*, rev. ed. (London: Methuen, 1994), and Frances McCormack, *Chaucer and the Culture of Dissent: The Lollard Context and Subtext of the "Parson's Tale"* (Dublin: Four Courts, 2007).

4. The Latin phrase *In principio* is translated as "In the beginning," and this phrase commences the biblical books of Genesis and John.

5. For the identity of Chaucer's scribe as Adam Pinkhurst, see Linne R. Mooney, "Chaucer's Scribe," *Speculum* 81.1 (2006): 97–138.

6. Tony Kushner, *Angels in America: A Gay Fantasia on National Themes* (New York: Theatre Communications, 1995), 267.

Chapter 3. Chaucer's Sources and Influences

1. For a discussion of London and its relationship to the Trojan legend, see Sylvia Federico, *New Troy: Fantasies of Empire in the Late Middle Ages* (Minneapolis: University of Minnesota Press, 2003), esp. 1–28.

2. Ovid, *The Art of Love*, trans. James Michie (New York: Modern Library, 2002), 3.431–32, at 140–41.

3. Statius, *Thebaid*, ed. and trans. J. H. Mozley (Cambridge: Harvard University Press, 1969), 12.519–20, at 482.

4. William Shakespeare, *The Merchant of Venice*, in *The Riverside Shakespeare*, ed. Blakemore Evans, 2nd ed. (Boston: Houghton Mifflin, 1997), 1.3.98–101.

5. Many modern biblical scholars question whether Paul truly wrote the Epistles to Timothy. Regardless of the identity of these texts' historical author, Chaucer treats the biblical epistles as if they are Paul's.

6. The text and translation are taken from James I. Wimsatt, *Chaucer and His French Contemporaries* (Toronto: University of Toronto Press, 1991), 225.

7. Ibid., 249–50.

8. For a more detailed account of the authorship of *Romaunt of the Rose*, see Geoffrey Chaucer, *The Romaunt of the Rose*, ed. Charles Dahlberg (Norman: University of Oklahoma Press, 1999), 3–24.

9. Dante Alighieri, *Il Convivio*, trans. Richard Lansing (New York: Garland, 1990), book 4, canzone 2, at 140–41.

10. Dante Alighieri, *Inferno*, trans. Robert Hollander and Jean Hollander (New York: Doubleday, 2000), canto 3, lines 1–2, 9, at 42–43.

11. Dante Alighieri, *Paradiso*, trans. Robert Hollander and Jean Hollander (New York: Doubleday, 2007), canto 33, line 1, at 818–19.

12. John Gower, *Confessio amantis*, in *The Complete Works of John Gower*, ed. G. C. Macaulay, 4 vols. (Oxford: Clarendon, 1899–1902), 3:466, lines 2941–47.

13. Thomas Usk, *Testament of Love*, ed. Gary W. Shawver (Toronto: University of Toronto Press, 2002), 3.4.232, 236–39, at 160.

14. Thomas Hoccleve, *The Regiment of Princes*, ed. Charles R. Blyth (Kalamazoo, Mich.: Medieval Institute, 1999), 185, lines 4978–84.

15. Ibid., 186, lines 4995–98.

16. John Lydgate, *The Siege of Thebes*, ed. Robert R. Edwards (Kalamazoo, Mich.: Medieval Institute, 2001), 30, lines 40–42.

17. Robert Henryson, *The Testament of Cresseid*, in *The Poems of Robert Henryson*, ed. Denton Fox (Oxford: Clarendon, 1982), 113, lines 58–63.

18. William Caxton, in his epilogue to Chaucer's translation of Boethius, qtd. in *Chaucer: The Critical Heritage*, ed. Derek Brewer (London: Routledge, 1978), 1:75. Brewer's two-volume work (*1385–1837* and *1837–1933*) proves indispensable in tracing Chaucer's reputation through the centuries, as does Caroline Spurgeon's *Five Hundred Years of Chaucer Criticism and Allusion, 1357–1900*, 3 vols. (Cambridge: Cambridge University Press, 1925).

19. Francis Thynne, *Animaduersions vppon the Annotacions and Corrections of some imperfections of impressiones of Chaucers workes* (London: N. Trübner for the Early English Text Society, 1865; reprinted London: Oxford University Press, 1965), 75.

20. Edmund Becke, qtd. in Brewer, *Chaucer: The Critical Heritage*, 1:102.

21. Thomas Wilson, *Wilson's Arte of Rhetorique*, ed. G. H. Mair (Oxford: Clarendon, 1909), 3.162.

22. Sir Philip Sidney, *The Defence of Poesie* in *The Prose Works of Sir Philip Sidney*, ed. Albert Feuillerat, vol. 3 (Cambridge: Cambridge University Press, 1963), 37.

23. Edmund Spenser, *The Shepheardes Calendar*, in *The Yale Edition of the Shorter Poems of Edmund Spenser*, ed. William A. Oram et al. (New Haven, Conn.: Yale University Press, 1989), 112, lines 81–84 of "June."

24. Henry Howard, Earl of Surrey, *Selected Poems*, ed. Dennis Keene (Manchester: Carcanet, 1985), 58, lines 13–16.

25. Ben Jonson, "To the Memory of My Beloved," in *Ben Jonson*, ed. Ian Donaldson (Oxford: Oxford University Press, 1995), 137, lines 19–21.

26. William Shakespeare and John Fletcher, *The Two Noble Kinsmen*, in *The Riverside Shakespeare*, 1692, lines 9–14.

27. Joseph Addison, *The Poetical Works of Joseph Addison; Gay's Fables, and Somerville's Chase*, ed. George Gilfillan (Edinburgh: James Nichol, 1859), 27–28, lines 9–16.

28. Samuel Johnson, qtd. in Brewer, *Chaucer: The Critical Heritage*, 1:208.

29. Ibid., 1:212.

30. John Dryden, *The Poems and Fables of John Dryden*, ed. James Kinsley (London: Oxford University Press, 1962), 531.

31. Ibid., 533.

32. Alexander Pope, *An Essay on Criticism*, in *Poetical Works*, ed. Herbert Davis (London: Oxford University Press, 1966), 77, lines 480–83.

33. Pope, "Imitations of English Poets (Done by the Author in His Youth): Chaucer," in *Poetical Works*, 229, lines 23–24.

34. Daniel Defoe, qtd. in Brewer, *Chaucer: The Critical Heritage*, 1:174.

35. George Gordon, Lord Byron, qtd. in Brewer, *Chaucer: The Critical Heritage*, 1:249.

36. William Blake, *A Descriptive Catalog* (1809; Oxford: Woodstock, 1990), 14.

37. William Wordsworth, *Translations of Chaucer and Virgil*, ed. Bruce E. Graver (Ithaca, N.Y.: Cornell University Press, 1998), 3.

38. Samuel Taylor Coleridge, *Table Talk*, ed. Carl Woodring, 2 vols. (Princeton, N.J.: Princeton University Press, 1990), 2:278.

39. Elizabeth Barrett Browning, *Last Poems, Translations, Greek Christian Poets, The Book of the Poets, Miscellanies*, vol. 6 of *The Complete Works of Elizabeth Barrett Browning*, ed. Charlotte Porter and Helen A. Clarke (New York: Crowell, 1900; reprint, New York: AMS, 1973), 243–44.

40. William Morris, *Signs of Change*, vol. 23 of *The Collected Works of William Morris* (New York: Russell & Russell, 1966), 52.

41. Matthew Arnold, qtd. in Brewer, *Chaucer: The Critical Heritage*, 2:220.

42. Claude Colleer Abbott, ed., *The Correspondence of Gerard Manley Hop-

kins and Richard Watson Dixon (London: Oxford University Press, 1955), 66–67, letter dated 3 October 1881.

43. Browning, *Last Poems, Translations*, 245. Samuel Taylor Coleridge presaged Hopkins's and Browning's defense of Chaucer's meter, suggesting that readers merely need a little editorial guidance "to feel the perfect smoothness and harmony of Chaucer's verse" (*Table Talk*, 2:279).

44. Henry David Thoreau, *A Week on the Concord and Merrimack Rivers*, ed. Carl Hovde (Princeton, N.J.: Princeton University Press, 1980), 370–71.

45. Ralph Waldo Emerson, "Shakspear, or the Poet," in *Representative Men: Seven Lectures*, ed. Wallace E. Williams and Douglas Emory Wilson, vol. 4 of *The Collected Works of Ralph Waldo Emerson* (Cambridge: Belknap, 1987), 113.

46. T. S. Eliot, *The Annotated "Waste Land" with Eliot's Contemporary Prose*, ed. Lawrence Rainey (New Haven, Conn.: Yale University Press, 2005), 57, lines 1–4.

47. Aldous Huxley, *On the Margin* (1923; London: Chatto & Windus, 1948), 205.

48. G. K. Chesterton, *All I Survey* (1933; Freeport, N.Y.: Books for Libraries, 1967), 209.

49. Virginia Woolf, *The Common Reader* (1925; New York: Harcourt Brace, 1953), 12, 15.

50. *A Canterbury Tale*, dir. Michael Powell and Emeric Pressburger, perf. Eric Portman, Sheila Sim, Dennis Price, 1949.

51. *I racconti di Canterbury*, dir. Pier Paolo Pasolini, perf. Hugh Griffith, Laura Betti, Ninetto Davoli, 1972. Of these ten episodes, five—Merchant's Tale, Cook's Tale, Miller's Tale, Reeve's Tale, and Summoner's Tale—are fabliaux, and the other five—General Prologue, Friar's Tale, Wife of Bath's Prologue, Pardoner's Tale, Summoner's Prologue—contain sufficient bawdy moments that Pasolini readily reimagines them as Chaucerian fabliaux.

52. *A Knight's Tale*, dir. Brian Helgeland, perf. Heath Ledger, Paul Bettany, Shannyn Sossamon, 2001.

53. Spurgeon, *Five Hundred Years of Chaucer Criticism and Allusion*, cxxiv–cxxv.

54. Harold Bloom, *The Anxiety of Influence: A Theory of Poetry*, 2nd ed. (New York: Oxford University Press, 1997).

Pronouncing Chaucer's Middle English

1. John Gardner, *The Life and Times of Chaucer* (New York: Knopf, 1977), 315.

Selected Readings

No brief bibliography can do justice to the vast amount of scholarship on Chaucer's life and literature. Excellent essays, in such scholarly journals as *Chaucer Review* and *Studies in the Age of Chaucer*, can be found through a research library. This books-only selection begins with editions of Chaucer's writings and Chaucerian reference works, followed, in accordance with the structure of this book, by biographies of Chaucer, studies of his literature, and studies of his sources and influences. Helpful websites are also included.

Editions and Facsimiles of Chaucer's Literature

Barney, Stephen A., ed. *Troilus and Criseyde*. New York: Norton, 2006.

Benson, Larry D., ed. *The Riverside Chaucer*. 3rd ed. Boston: Houghton Mifflin, 1987.

Boenig, Robert, and Andrew Taylor, eds. *The Canterbury Tales*. 2nd ed. Peterborough, Ont.: Broadview, 2012.

Fisher, John H., ed. *The Complete Poetry and Prose of Geoffrey Chaucer*. 2nd ed. New York: Holt, Rinehart, and Winston, 1989.

Fisher, Sheila, trans. *The Selected Canterbury Tales*. New York: Norton, 2011.

Kolve, V. A., and Glending Olson, eds. *The Canterbury Tales: Fifteen Tales and the General Prologue*. 2nd ed. New York: Norton, 2005.

Lynch, Kathryn L., ed. *Dream Visions and Other Poems*. New York: Norton, 2007.

Mann, Jill, ed. *The Canterbury Tales*. London: Penguin, 2005.

Parkes, M. B., and Elizabeth Salter, eds. *Troilus and Criseyde: A Facsimile of Corpus Christi College Cambridge MS 61*. Cambridge: Brewer, 1978.

Phillips, Helen, and Nick Havely, eds. *Chaucer's Dream Poetry*. London: Longman, 1997.

Ruggiers, Paul, ed. *The Canterbury Tales: A Facsimile and Transcription of the Hengwrt Manuscript, with Variants from the Ellesmere Manuscript*. Norman: University of Oklahoma Press, 1979.

Windeatt, Barry, ed. *Troilus and Criseyde*. London: Penguin, 2003.

Reference Books

Andrew, Malcolm. *The Palgrave Literary Dictionary of Chaucer*. New York: Palgrave Macmillan, 2006.

Benson, Larry D. *A Glossarial Concordance to the "Riverside Chaucer."* New York: Garland, 1993.

Boitani, Piero, and Jill Mann, eds. *The Cambridge Companion to Chaucer*. 2nd ed. Cambridge: Cambridge University Press, 2003.

Boswell, Jackson Campbell, and Sylvia Wallace Holton. *Chaucer's Fame in England: STC Chauceriana, 1475–1640*. New York: MLA, 2004.

Brewer, Derek, ed. *Chaucer: The Critical Heritage*. 2 vols. London: Routledge and Kegan Paul, 1978.

Brown, Peter, ed. *A Companion to Chaucer*. Oxford: Blackwell, 2000.

Cooper, Helen. *The Canterbury Tales*. Oxford Guides to Chaucer. Oxford: Oxford University Press, 1989.

Davis, Norman, Douglas Gray, Patricia Ingham, and Anne Wallace-Hadrill. *A Chaucer Glossary*. Oxford: Clarendon, 1979.

de Weever, Jacqueline. *A Chaucer Name Dictionary*. New York: Garland, 1987.

Ellis, Steve, ed. *Chaucer: An Oxford Guide*. Oxford: Oxford University Press, 2005.

Fein, Susanna, and David Raybin, eds. *Chaucer: Contemporary Approaches*. University Park: Pennsylvania State University Press, 2010.

Gray, Douglas, ed. *The Oxford Companion to Chaucer*. Oxford: Oxford University Press, 2003.

Kökeritz, Helge. *A Guide to Chaucer's Pronunciation*. New York: Holt, Rinehart, and Winston, 1962.

Lerer, Seth, ed. *The Yale Companion to Chaucer*. New Haven, Conn.: Yale University Press, 2006.

Minnis, A. J., with V. J. Scattergood and J. J. Smith. *The Shorter Poems*. Oxford Guides to Chaucer. Oxford: Clarendon, 1995.

Rossignol, Rosalyn. *Critical Companion to Chaucer: A Literary Reference to His Life and Work*. New York: Facts on File, 2007.

Rowland, Beryl, ed. *Companion to Chaucer Studies*. Rev. ed. Oxford: Oxford University Press, 1979.

Saunders, Corinne, ed. *Chaucer*. Blackwell Guides to Criticism. Oxford: Blackwell, 2001.

Spurgeon, Caroline F. E. *Five Hundred Years of Chaucer Criticism and Allusion, 1357–1900.* 3 vols. Cambridge: Cambridge University Press, 1925.

Windeatt, Barry. *Troilus and Criseyde.* Oxford Guides to Chaucer. Oxford: Clarendon, 1992.

Biographical Studies and Sources on Chaucer's Life and Times

Bisson, Lillian M. *Chaucer and the Late Medieval World.* New York: St. Martin's, 1998.

Brewer, Derek. *The World of Chaucer.* Cambridge: Brewer, 2000.

Carlson, David R. *Chaucer's Jobs.* New York: Palgrave Macmillan, 2004.

Crow, Martin M., and Clair C. Olson, eds. *Chaucer Life-Records.* Austin: University of Texas Press, 1966.

Gardner, John. *The Life and Times of Chaucer.* New York: Knopf, 1977.

Howard, Donald R. *Chaucer: His Life, His Works, His World.* New York: Dutton, 1987.

Jones, Terry, Robert Yeager, Terry Dolan, Alan Fletcher, and Juliette Dor. *Who Murdered Chaucer? A Medieval Mystery.* New York: St. Martin's, 2003.

Pearsall, Derek. *The Life of Geoffrey Chaucer: A Critical Biography.* Oxford: Blackwell, 1992.

Singman, Jeffrey L., and Will McLean. *Daily Life in Chaucer's England.* Westport, Conn.: Greenwood, 1995.

West, Richard. *Chaucer: 1340–1400.* New York: Carroll & Graf, 2000.

Studies of Chaucer's Literature

Aers, David. *Chaucer.* Brighton, Sussex: Harvester, 1986.

Beidler, Peter G., ed. *Masculinities in Chaucer: Approaches to Maleness in the "Canterbury Tales" and "Troilus and Criseyde."* Cambridge: Brewer, 1998.

Benson, C. David. *Chaucer's Drama of Style: Poetic Variety and Contrast in the "Canterbury Tales."* Chapel Hill: University of North Carolina Press, 1986.

Blamires, Alcuin. *Chaucer, Ethics, and Gender.* Oxford: Oxford University Press, 2006.

Bowden, Betsy. *Chaucer Aloud.* Philadelphia: University of Pennsylvania Press, 1987.

Burger, Glenn. *Chaucer's Queer Nation.* Minneapolis: University of Minnesota Press, 2003.

Cannon, Christopher. *The Making of Chaucer's English.* Cambridge: Cambridge University Press, 1998.

Collette, Carolyn P. *Species, Phantasms, and Images: Vision and Medieval Psychology in the "Canterbury Tales."* Ann Arbor: University of Michigan Press, 2001.

Condren, Edward I. *Chaucer and the Energy of Creation: The Design and the Organization of the "Canterbury Tales."* Gainesville: University Press of Florida, 1999.

———. *Chaucer from Prentice to Poet: The Metaphor of Love in Dream Visions and "Troilus and Criseyde."* Gainesville: University Press of Florida, 2008.

Cox, Catherine S. *Gender and Language in Chaucer.* Gainesville: University Press of Florida, 1997.

Crane, Susan. *Gender and Romance in Chaucer's "Canterbury Tales."* Princeton, N.J.: Princeton University Press, 1994.

Crocker, Holly A. *Chaucer's Visions of Manhood.* New York: Palgrave Macmillan, 2007.

David, Alfred. *The Strumpet Muse: Art and Morals in Chaucer's Poetry.* Bloomington: Indiana University Press, 1976.

Delany, Sheila, ed. *Chaucer and the Jews.* New York: Routledge, 2002.

Dinshaw, Carolyn. *Chaucer's Sexual Poetics.* Madison: University of Wisconsin Press, 1989.

Donaldson, E. Talbot. *Speaking of Chaucer.* New York: Norton, 1970.

Ferster, Judith. *Chaucer on Interpretation.* Cambridge: Cambridge University Press, 1985.

Fradenburg, L. O. Aranye. *Sacrifice Your Love: Psychoanalysis, Historicism, Chaucer.* Minneapolis: University of Minnesota Press, 2002.

Ganim, John M. *Chaucerian Theatricality.* Princeton, N.J.: Princeton University Press, 1990.

Hallissy, Margaret. *Clean Maids, True Wives, Steadfast Widows: Chaucer's Women and Medieval Codes of Conduct.* Westport, Conn.: Greenwood, 1993.

Hansen, Elaine Tuttle. *Chaucer and the Fictions of Gender.* Berkeley: University of California Press, 1992.

Horobin, Simon. *Chaucer's Language.* New York: Palgrave Macmillan, 2007.

Howard, Donald R. *The Idea of the "Canterbury Tales."* Berkeley: University of California Press, 1976.

Kendrick, Laura. *Chaucerian Play: Comedy and Control in the "Canterbury Tales."* Berkeley: University of California Press, 1988.

Knapp, Peggy. *Chaucer and the Social Contest.* New York: Routledge, 1990.

———. *Chaucerian Aesthetics.* New York: Palgrave Macmillan, 2008.

Kolve, V. A. *Chaucer and the Imagery of Narrative.* Stanford, Calif.: Stanford University Press, 1984.

———. *Telling Images: Chaucer and the Imagery of Narrative II.* Stanford, Calif.: Stanford University Press, 2009.

Lambdin, Laura C., and Robert T. Lambdin, eds. *Chaucer's Pilgrims: An His-*

torical Guide to the Pilgrims in the "Canterbury Tales." Westport, Conn.: Greenwood, 1996.

Laskaya, Anne. *Chaucer's Approach to Gender in the "Canterbury Tales."* Cambridge: Brewer, 1995.

Leicester, H. Marshall, Jr. *The Disenchanted Self: Representing the Subject in the "Canterbury Tales."* Berkeley: University of California Press, 1990.

Lerer, Seth. *Chaucer and His Readers.* Princeton, N.J.: Princeton University Press, 1993.

Lindahl, Carl. *Earnest Games: Folkloric Patterns in the "Canterbury Tales."* Bloomington: Indiana University Press, 1987.

Lynch, Kathryn L. *Chaucer's Philosophical Visions.* Cambridge: Brewer, 2000.

Mann, Jill. *Chaucer and Medieval Estates Satire: The Literature of Social Classes and the "General Prologue" to the "Canterbury Tales."* Cambridge: Cambridge University Press, 1973.

———. *Feminizing Chaucer.* New ed. Cambridge: Brewer, 2002.

McGerr, Rosemarie P. *Chaucer's Open Books: Resistance to Closure in Medieval Discourse.* Gainesville: University Press of Florida, 1998.

Miller, Mark. *Philosophical Chaucer: Love, Sex, and Agency in the "Canterbury Tales."* Cambridge: Cambridge University Press, 2004.

Myles, Robert. *Chaucerian Realism.* Cambridge: Brewer, 1994.

Olson, Paul A. *The "Canterbury Tales" and the Good Society.* Princeton, N.J.: Princeton University Press, 1986.

Patterson, Lee. *Chaucer and the Subject of History.* Madison: University of Wisconsin Press, 1991.

———. *Temporal Circumstances: Form and History in the "Canterbury Tales."* New York: Palgrave Macmillan, 2006.

Percival, Florence. *Chaucer's Legendary Good Women.* Cambridge: Cambridge University Press, 1998.

Pugh, Tison, and Marcia Smith Marzec, eds. *Men and Masculinities in Chaucer's "Troilus and Criseyde."* Cambridge: Brewer, 2008.

Robertson, D. W. *A Preface to Chaucer.* Princeton, N.J.: Princeton University Press, 1963.

Schibanoff, Susan. *Chaucer's Queer Poetics: Rereading the Dream Trio.* Toronto: University of Toronto Press, 2006.

Schildgen, Brenda Deen. *Pagans, Tartars, Moslems, and Jews in Chaucer's "Canterbury Tales."* Gainesville: University Press of Florida, 2001.

Shoaf, R. Allen. *Chaucer's Body: The Anxiety of Circulation in the "Canterbury Tales."* Gainesville: University Press of Florida, 2001.

Strohm, Paul. *Social Chaucer.* Cambridge, Mass.: Harvard University Press, 1989.

Sturges, Robert S. *Chaucer's Pardoner and Gender Theory.* New York: St. Martin's, 2000.

Van Dyke, Carolynn. *Chaucer's Agents: Cause and Representation in Chaucerian Narrative.* Cranbury, N.J.: Associated University Presses, 2005.

Wallace, David. *Chaucerian Polity: Absolutist Lineages and Associational Forms in England and Italy.* Stanford, Calif.: Stanford University Press, 1997.

Weisl, Angela Jane. *Conquering the Reign of Femeny: Gender and Genre in Chaucer's Romance.* Cambridge: Brewer, 1995.

Wood, Chauncey. *Chaucer and the Country of the Stars: Poetic Uses of Astrological Imagery.* Princeton, N.J.: Princeton University Press, 1970.

Sources and Influences of Chaucer's Literature

Barrington, Candace. *American Chaucers.* New York: Palgrave Macmillan, 2007.

Besserman, Lawrence. *Chaucer's Biblical Poetics.* Norman: University of Oklahoma Press, 1998.

Bowers, John M., ed. *The Canterbury Tales: Fifteenth-Century Continuations and Additions.* Kalamazoo, Mich.: Medieval Institute Publications, 1992.

Bryan, W. F., and Germaine Dempster, eds. *Sources and Analogues of Chaucer's "Canterbury Tales."* Chicago: University of Chicago Press, 1941.

Bryant, Brantley L., ed. *Geoffrey Chaucer Hath a Blog: Medieval Studies and New Media.* New York: Palgrave Macmillan, 2010.

Calabrese, Michael A. *Chaucer's Ovidian Arts of Love.* Gainesville: University Press of Florida, 1994.

Chance, Jane. *The Mythographic Chaucer: The Fabulation of Sexual Politics.* Minneapolis: University of Minnesota Press, 1995.

Clarke, K. P. *Chaucer and Italian Textuality.* Oxford: Oxford University Press, 2011.

Correale, Robert M., and Mary Hamel, eds. *Sources and Analogues of the "Canterbury Tales."* 2 vols. Cambridge: Brewer, 2002–5.

Edwards, Robert R. *Chaucer and Boccaccio: Antiquity and Modernity.* New York: Palgrave Macmillan, 2002.

Ellis, Steve. *Chaucer at Large: The Poet in the Modern Imagination.* Minneapolis: University of Minnesota Press, 2000.

Finley, William K., and Joseph Rosenblum, eds. *Chaucer Illustrated: Five Hundred Years of the "Canterbury Tales" in Pictures.* New Castle, Del.: Oak Knoll, 2003.

Forni, Kathleen. *The Chaucerian Apocrypha: A Counterfeit Canon.* Gainesville: University Press of Florida, 2001.

———, ed. *The Chaucerian Apocrypha: A Selection.* Kalamazoo, Mich.: Medieval Institute Publications, 2005.

Fyler, John M. *Chaucer and Ovid.* New Haven, Conn.: Yale University Press, 1979.

Ginsberg, Warren. *Chaucer's Italian Tradition.* Ann Arbor: University of Michigan Press, 2002.

Gust, Geoffrey W. *Constructing Chaucer: Author and Autofiction in the Critical Tradition.* New York: Palgrave Macmillan, 2009.

Havely, N. R., ed. and trans. *Chaucer's Boccaccio: Sources for "Troilus" and the "Knight's" and "Franklin's Tales."* Cambridge: Brewer, 1980.

Kelly, Henry Ansgar. *Chaucerian Tragedy.* Cambridge: Brewer, 1997.

Koff, Leonard Michael, and Brenda Deen Schildgen. *The "Decameron" and the "Canterbury Tales."* Cranbury, N.J.: Associated University Presses, 2000.

Miller, Robert P., ed. *Chaucer: Sources and Backgrounds.* New York: Oxford University Press, 1977.

Miskimin, Alice S. *The Renaissance Chaucer.* New Haven, Conn.: Yale University Press, 1975.

Muscatine, Charles. *Chaucer and the French Tradition.* Berkeley: University of California Press, 1957.

Neuse, Richard. *Chaucer's Dante: Allegory and Epic Theater in the "Canterbury Tales."* Berkeley: University of California Press, 1991.

Nolan, Barbara. *Chaucer and the Tradition of the Roman Antique.* Cambridge: Cambridge University Press, 1992.

Payne, F. Anne. *Chaucer and Menippean Satire.* Madison: University of Wisconsin Press, 1981.

Prendergast, Thomas A. *Chaucer's Dead Body: From Corpse to Corpus.* New York: Routledge, 2004.

Richmond, Velma Bourgeois. *Chaucer as Children's Literature.* Jefferson, N.C.: McFarland, 2004.

Schless, Howard H. *Chaucer and Dante: A Revaluation.* Norman, Okla.: Pilgrim Books, 1984.

Taylor, Karla. *Chaucer Reads "The Divine Comedy."* Stanford, Calif.: Stanford University Press, 1989.

Trigg, Stephanie. *Congenial Souls: Reading Chaucer from Medieval to Postmodern.* Minneapolis: University of Minnesota Press, 2002.

Wallace, David. *Chaucer and the Early Writings of Boccaccio.* Cambridge: Brewer, 1985.

Wimsatt, James I. *Chaucer and His French Contemporaries: Natural Music in the Fourteenth Century.* Toronto: University of Toronto Press, 1991.

Windeatt, B. A., ed. *Chaucer's Dream Poetry: Sources and Analogues.* Cambridge: Brewer, 1982.

Websites

Chaucer Metapage: englishcomplit.unc.edu/chaucer
The Chaucer Studio: creativeworks.byu.edu/chaucer
Corpus of Middle English Prose and Verse: quod.lib.umich.edu/c/cme/
Geoffrey Chaucer: courses.fas.harvard.edu/~chaucer/
Geoffrey Chaucer (c.1343–1400): www.luminarium.org/medlit/chaucer.htm
The Labyrinth: Resources for Medieval Studies: labyrinth.georgetown.edu/
Middle English Compendium: quod.lib.umich.edu/m/mec/
Middle English Dictionary: quod.lib.umich.edu/m/med/
The New Chaucer Society: artsci.wustl.edu/~chaucer/
The ORB: On-line Reference Book for Medieval Studies: the-orb.net

Index

"ABC, An," 127–29, 197

Achilles, 10, 19, 37, 50, 148

"Adam Scriveyn." *See* "Chaucers Words unto Adam, His Owne Scriveyn"; Pinkhurst, Adam

Addison, Joseph, 180–81

Aeneas, 16, 19, 29, 37, 142–43, 167

Aeneid, 15–17, 29, 37, 142–43, 194

Aesop, 151, 195

"Against Women Unconstant," 137, 161

Alceste, 27, 33, 149, 168

Allegory, 15, 24, 27, 88, 99, 108, 150, 166, 167, 189, 191

Alliterative verse, 173

Andreas Capellanus, 45, 193

"Anelida and Arcite," 125–27, 148

Apollo, 18, 121–22, 144

Ariadne, 30–31, 144

Aristotle, 111

Arnold, Matthew, 183–84

Aubade, 129

Augustine, 152, 160

Bacchus, 24

Bailly, Harry. *See* Harry Bailly

"Balade of Complaint, A," 139

Ball, John, 7

Ballade, 27, 131, 133–37, 139, 161, 163–65, 191, 194

Beauchamp, Sir William, 4, 5

Becke, Edmund, 177

Becket, St. Thomas à, 52, 160

Bernard of Clairvaux, 160, 170

Bettany, Paul, 188

Bible. *See* Judeo-Christian Bible

Black Death. *See* Plague

Blake, William, 182–83

Blanche, Duchess of Lancaster, 15

Blazon, 12, 15, 42, 106–7, 113, 191

Boccaccio, Giovanni, 56, 167, 171, 172–73

Boethius, 6, 111, 132, 133, 134, 142, 145, 147, 148–51, 195, 198

Book of the Duchess, 6, 9–16, 27, 162, 163, 166, 175, 193, 197

Book of the Lion, 125, 163

Bosch, Hieronymous, 188

Breton lai, 93, 95, 191–92

Brotherhood oaths. *See* Oaths and brotherhood oaths

Browning, Elizabeth Barrett, 183, 184

Byron, George Gordon, Lord, 192

Caesar, Julius, 19, 28, 111, 146–48

Canon's Yeoman and Canon's Yeoman's Prologue and Tale, 118–20, 230–31

Canterbury Tale, A (1944 film), 187–88

Canterbury Tales, The, 6, 51, 62, 73, 79, 97, 120, 124, 172, 176, 192. *See also specific pilgrims, prologues, and tales*

Carnivalesque, 52, 62, 104, 193

Cassandra, 49, 148

Caxton, William, 177

Ceres, 24

Ceyx and Alcion, 10

Chaucer, Agnes, 3

Chaucer, Agnes Copton, 1

Chaucer, Elizabeth, 3
Chaucer, Geoffrey: birth and birth year, 1;
    career in court and administration, 2–6,
    15; as character and narrator, 9, 13, 32,
    52–56, 62, 106, 152, 196; death, 8; family
    life, 1–4; influence on subsequent au-
    thors, 173–86; literature on film, 186–89;
    multilingualism, 2, 160; religious beliefs,
    159–60; use of classical tradition and
    mythology, 10, 15–16, 19, 141–51
Chaucer, John, 1
Chaucer, Lewis, 3
Chaucer, Philippa de Roet, 2–3, 33
Chaucer, Thomas, 3
Chauceriana and Chaucerian apocrypha,
    192. See also Fan fiction
"Chaucers Words unto Adam, His Owne
    Scriveyn," 132
Chaumpaigne, Cecily, 4
Chesterton, G. K., 185–86
Chivalry, 173, 192, 197, 198
Chrétien de Troyes, 91, 94
Cicero, 151
Claudian, 19, 143, 151
Cleopatra, 28, 197
Clerk and Clerk's Prologue and Tale, 53,
    83–87, 159, 167–68, 171, 172, 195, 197,
    220–21
Coleridge, Samuel Taylor, 182–83
Comedy, 34, 39, 47, 51, 162, 192–93
Complaint, 11, 126, 127–31, 136–39, 161, 164,
    193
"Complaint of Chaucer to His Purse, The,"
    5, 136, 161
"Complaint of Mars, The," 129–30
"Complaint of Venus, The," 130–31, 161
"Complaint to His Lady, A," 129
"Complaint unto Pity, The," 128
"Complaynt D'Amours," 138
Confessio amantis, 174
Consolation of Philosophy / Boece, 6, 111, 132,
    133, 145, 147–51, 195, 198
Cook and Cook's Prologue and Tale, 53,
    68–70, 120–21, 188, 216
Courtly lady, 35, 41, 42, 47, 138

Courtly love, 26, 42, 45, 113, 128, 131, 135, 166,
    191, 193, 197
Cuckoldry, 64, 70, 87, 88, 90, 95, 102, 104,
    121, 155, 156, 193, 195
Cupid, 24, 27, 33

Dame Sirith, 161, 195
Daniel, 9, 114
Dante, 143, 167, 168–71, 172, 191, 194
Debate, 59, 88, 89, 90, 93, 108, 114, 163, 165,
    193
Decameron, 56, 172
Defoe, Daniel, 182
Deguilleville, Guillaume de, 127
Demande d'amour, 40, 59, 95, 193
Deschampes, Eustache, 125, 164–65
Diana, 24, 60, 148
Dido, 13, 16, 29, 142, 143–44
Doherty, P. C., 186
Dream vision, 9, 13, 16, 82, 193–94. See also
    Book of the Duchess; House of Fame; Par-
    liament of Fowls; Legend of Good Women;
    Summoner and Summoner's Prologue
    and Tale
Dryden, John, 191

Edward III, 2, 4, 7
Elijah, 17
Eliot, T. S., 185
Emerson, Ralph Waldo, 195
Enoch, 17
Epic, 17, 34, 37–38, 40, 45, 47, 49, 57, 60–61,
    115, 125, 194
Estates satire, 7, 53, 194
Etiological tale, 32, 121, 194
Exemplum, 79–80, 81, 82, 96, 99–100, 122,
    194–95

Fable, 76, 112–13, 115, 116, 121, 122, 151, 157,
    181, 195
Fabliau, 62–68, 70, 73–76, 78, 82–83, 87–90,
    101, 102–4, 124, 154, 161, 162, 182, 188, 192,
    193, 195
Fame / fame, 15–21
Fan fiction, 176

Five Guildsmen. *See* Guildsmen

Fletcher, John, 179–80

Folklore and folktale, 70, 72, 94, 191, 195, 196

"Former Age, The," 132–33

"Fortune" (poem), 133, 161, 162, 194

Fortune and Lady Fortune, 11–12, 34, 42, 44, 51, 61, 89, 111, 133, 147, 149, 151, 162, 195

Franklin and Franklin's Prologue and Tale, 53, 92–95, 96, 97, 145–46, 151, 172, 192, 193, 195, 196, 197, 223

Friar and Friar's Prologue and Tale, 53, 73, 78, 79–81, 83, 143, 152, 158–59, 188, 195, 218–19

Froissart, Jean, 163–64

Game, play, and earnest, 43, 62, 69, 121, 125, 196

Ganymede, 17

Gardner, John, 199

Gawain-Poet, 173, 194

Gender: Chaucer's literary misogyny, 27; female constancy, 12, 16, 29; female holiness, 117; female passivity, 28; female sexuality, 64; female submissiveness, 74, 87; female suffering, 28, 32–33, 84–85, 126; female virtue, 26, 30, 109; male duplicity, 126; male fickleness in love, 28; male governance, 73; male passivity, 37–34; in marriage, 87; of myth, 33

General Prologue, 2, 51–57, 66, 68, 81, 84, 92, 95, 104, 110, 124, 152, 161, 187, 188, 197

Genre, x–xii, 68. *See also* Allegory; Ballade; Breton lai; Comedy; Complaint; Debate; Dream vision; Epic; Estates satire; Etiological tale; Exemplum; Fable; Fabliau; Folklore and folktale; Hagiography; Lyric, lyric speaker, and lyric interlude; Miracle; Parody; Romance; Sermon; Tragedy

"Gentilesse" (poem), 134, 161, 168, 196

Gentility and gentilesse, 92, 113, 134, 168, 169, 196

Geoffrey of Monmouth, 19

Gospels, 134, 152–54

Gower, John, 173–74

Grace, C. L., 186

Graunson, Oton de, 164

Gregory the Great, 160

Grove, John, 4

Guildsmen, 53, 55

Guillaume de Lorris, 141, 165–66

Hagiography, 38, 59, 70, 71–72, 84–86, 116–17, 196

Harry Bailly, 8, 56, 69, 70, 72, 84–87, 92–93, 97–98, 104, 106, 107, 110, 112, 116, 119, 122, 124, 153

Helen of Troy, 33

Henry IV, 3, 5–6, 164

Henryson, Robert, 176, 192

Hercules, 29, 111

Hoccleve, Thomas, 175

Homer, 19, 21, 37, 142, 145–46, 148, 181, 194

Hopkins, Gerard Manley, 184

House of Fame, 6, 9, 15–21, 27, 138, 142, 144, 146–48, 167, 175, 182, 193, 197

Hundred Years War, 2, 7–8, 160

Huxley, Aldous, 185

Hypermnestra, 33

Hypsipyle, 29, 30

Iliad, 37, 145, 194

Invocation, 16, 18, 116, 125, 196

Irony, 23, 78, 80, 83, 102, 103, 112, 121, 128, 155, 156, 162, 187, 189, 193, 196, 198

Jason, 29–30

Jean de Meun, 141, 165–66, 194

Jerome, 160

Jesus, 16, 74, 75, 115, 124, 153

Joan of Arc, 7–8

Job, Book of, 109, 157–58

John of Gaunt, 3, 7, 15

Johnson, Samuel, 180–81

Jonson, Ben, 179

Josephus, 19

Judeo-Christian Bible, 8, 99, 111, 124, 151–60, 177. *See also* Gospels; Jesus; Job, Book of; Song of Songs

Jupiter, 17, 111

Juvenal, 151

Knight and Knight's Tale, 17, 25, 27, 30, 52, 54, 56, 57–61, 65, 101, 113, 126, 148, 172, 176, 179–80, 181, 189, 192–94, 198, 214–15

Knight's Tale, A (2001 film), 188–89

Kushner, Tony, 133

Lady Fortune. *See* Fortune and Lady Fortune

"Lak of Stedfastnesse," 135, 161, 194

Langland, William, 173, 191, 194

Ledger, Heath, 188

Legend. *See* Hagiography

Legend of Good Women, 6, 9, 17, 26–34, 46, 95, 96, 125, 142, 144, 149, 163, 167, 168, 193, 197

"Lenvoy de Chaucer a Bukton," 136, 194

"Lenvoy de Chaucer a Scogan," 135–36, 194

Livy, 151

Lucan, 19, 141, 146–48

Lucrece, 30, 31, 97

Lydgate, John, 175–76, 192

Lyric, lyric speaker, and lyric interlude, 13, 15, 128, 132, 138, 139, 171, 191, 193, 197

Machaut, Guillaume de, 10, 125, 162–63

Macrobius, 114, 151

Manciple and Manciple's Prologue and Tale, 2, 120–22, 144, 183, 194, 231

Man of Law and Man of Law's Introduction, Prologue, Tale, and Epilogue, 2, 33, 43, 70–73, 85, 122, 144, 146–47, 196, 216–17

Marie de France, 191–92

Marriage, 43, 61, 73–74, 77, 85, 87–88, 90, 93, 108, 117, 121, 136, 156, 165, 180, 196–97

Mars, 22, 59, 60–61, 125, 127, 129–31, 164

McCrumb, Sharyn, 196

Medea, 10, 13, 29–30, 31–32

Melibee, Tale of, 107–9, 145, 155–56, 158, 226–28

Merchant and Merchant's Prologue, Tale, and Epilogue, 53, 87–91, 94, 104, 135, 138–39, 155–56, 165, 166, 168, 172, 181, 188, 197, 221–22

"Merciles Beaute," 138–39

Mercury, 50–51, 130

Middle English glossary, 203–7

Middle English pronunciation, 199–202

Miller and Miller's Prologue and Tale, 53, 55, 57, 61–65, 83, 88, 90, 94, 135, 154–55, 188, 197, 215

Miracle, 75, 105, 106, 197

Mirk, John, 7

Monk and Monk's Prologue and Tale, 53, 110–12, 147–52, 169, 171, 172, 176, 194–95, 198, 228–29

Monty Python and the Holy Grail, 198

Morgan, Philippa, 186

Morpheus, 10, 16

Morris, William, 183

Nature, 24, 26, 52, 162

Nun's Priest and Nun's Priest's Prologue, Tale, and Epilogue, 7, 17, 112–16, 156–57, 181, 194, 195, 198, 229

Oaths and brotherhood oaths, 57, 79, 80, 100, 102, 103, 197

Odyssey, 145, 194

Orpheus, 150

Ovid, 10, 19, 108, 141–42, 144–45, 148, 164

Pardoner and Pardoner's Introduction, Prologue, and Tale, 53, 97–101, 116, 152, 188, 195, 197, 224–25

Parliament of Fowls, 6, 9, 22–26, 27, 129, 162, 169, 175, 192, 193

Parody, 65, 107, 112, 115, 154, 198

Parson and Parson's Prologue and Tale, 8, 53, 54, 72, 122–24, 125, 152–53, 157, 160, 162, 198, 231–32

Pasolini, Pier Paolo, 188

Pastoral, 178

Paul, St., 156–57, 235n5

Peasants' Revolt of 1381, 6–7, 174

Penelope, 33, 146

Petrarch, Franceso, 167, 171–72, 178, 179

Philomela, 31–32, 144

Phyllis, 13, 32

Physician and Physician's Tale, 30, 53, 95–97, 223–24

Piers Plowman, 173, 191, 194

Pilgrimage, 52, 62, 101, 187, 188

Pinkhurst, Adam, 132, 234n5
Plague, 6, 56, 78, 172
Plowman, 53, 54
Pluto, 19, 89–90, 151
Pope, Alexander, 181–82
Powell, Michael, and Emeric Pressburger, 187–88
Prioress and Prioress's Prologue and Tale, 53–54, 104–6, 127, 152, 183, 187, 197, 225
Proem, 16, 17, 126, 129, 198
Proserpina, 19, 89–90, 151
"Proverbs," 137

Racconti di Canterbury, I (1972 film), 188
Rape and raptus, 4, 30, 31, 76–77, 151
Reeve and Reeve's Prologue and Tale, 53, 66–68, 90, 161, 188, 215–16
"Retraction," 33, 90, 124–25, 163, 232
Richard II, 4, 5, 135, 164
Romance, 17, 24, 34–39, 41, 45–46, 47, 49, 57, 60–63, 70, 77–78, 95, 106–14, 198
Romaunt of the Rose / Roman de la Rose, 6, 10, 27, 164, 165–67, 191, 194
Romulus, 17

Saturn, 61
Second Nun and Second Nun's Prologue and Tale, 116–18, 127, 152, 170, 229–30
Seneca, 82, 99, 164
Senex amans, 63
Sermon, 72, 79, 98–99, 100, 122–23, 125, 153
Seven Deadly Sins, 123, 198
Shakespeare, William, 5, 28, 111, 151, 179–80, 183
Shipman and Shipman's Tale, 53, 72–73, 101–4, 153
Sidney, Sir Philip, 178
Sir Thopas, Prologue of and Tale of, 106–8, 135, 138
Social class, 53–55, 61–62
Song of Songs, 154
Speght, Thomas, 2, 177
Spenser, Edmund, 178
Spurgeon, Caroline, 189

Squire and Squire's Introduction and Tale, 52, 91–93, 137, 197, 222–23
Statius, 10, 19, 21, 142, 148
Stow, John, 177
Straw, Jack, 7
Summoner and Summoner's Prologue and Tale, 2, 53, 73, 79, 81–83, 152, 153, 162, 188, 194, 197, 219–20
Surrey, Henry Howard, Earl of, 178–79
Swynford, Katherine, 3

Theseus, 30–31, 32, 58, 60, 126, 148, 180
Thisbe, 28, 46, 144
Thopas, Sir, 106–8, 135, 138
"To Rosemounde," 131, 161
Tragedy, 34, 38, 39, 41, 44, 46–47, 49–51, 110–12, 147, 169, 171, 192, 198
Treatise on the Astrolabe, A, 3, 139–40
Troilus and Criseyde, 6, 17, 27, 32, 34–51, 125, 130, 132, 141, 143, 148, 151, 153–54, 160, 170, 171, 172, 176, 179, 183, 192, 194, 197, 198, 209–13
"Truth," 133–34, 161, 194
Tyler, Wat, 7

Usk, Thomas, 174–75

Valentine's Day, 22, 24, 26, 129, 138, 164, 175
Venus, 16, 17, 24, 59, 60–61, 129–31, 144, 166
Virgil, 15–17, 19, 21, 29, 37, 142–44, 194

Wife of Bath and Wife of Bath's Prologue and Tale, 26, 53, 55, 73–78, 87, 83, 102, 108, 134, 136, 144–45, 156, 161, 165, 169, 181, 188, 196–97, 198, 217–18
William the Conqueror, 160
Wilson, Thomas, 177
"Womanly Noblesse," 131–32, 161, 194
Woolf, Virginia, 186
Wordsworth, William, 182–83
Wyatt, Sir Thomas, 178–79
Wycliffe, John, 8

Yeoman (in General Prologue), 52

Tison Pugh is professor of English at the University of Central Florida. He is the author of *Queering Medieval Genres* and of *Sexuality and Its Queer Discontents in Middle English Literature* and coeditor of *Approaches to Teaching Chaucer's "Troilus and Criseyde" and the Shorter Poems* and of *Men and Masculinities in Chaucer's "Troilus and Criseyde."* He was awarded the UCF College of Arts and Humanities Distinguished Researcher Award in 2007 and the UCF College of Arts and Humanities Excellence in Undergraduate Teaching Award in 2004 and 2009.

New Perspectives on Medieval Literature: Authors and Traditions

EDITED BY R. BARTON PALMER AND TISON PUGH

This series offers compact, comprehensive, and up-to-date studies of important medieval authors and traditions written by leading scholars. These volumes will appeal to undergraduate and graduate students, academics, and general readers interested in the vibrant world of medieval literature. Our philosophy in New Perspectives on Medieval Literature is that good scholarship should excite both interest in and accessibility to a field of study, and this principle of combining the scholarship of teaching with student learning informs our editorial decisions.

An Introduction to Christine de Pizan, by Nadia Margolis (2011; first paperback edition, 2012)

An Introduction to the "Gawain" Poet, by John M. Bowers (2012)

An Introduction to British Arthurian Narrative, by Susan Aronstein (2012)

An Introduction to Geoffrey Chaucer, by Tison Pugh (2013)